Germany through Jewish Eyes

What can Jewish history tell us about German history? How can we understand the history of modern Germany from a Jewish perspective? And how do we bring the voices of German Jews to the fore? *Germany through Jewish Eyes* explores the dramatic course of German history, from the Enlightenment, through wars and revolutions, unification and reunification, Nazi dictatorship, Holocaust, and the rebuilding of a prosperous, modern democracy – all from a Jewish perspective. Through a series of chronologically ordered life-stories, Shulamit Volkov examines how the lived experience of German Jewry can provide new insights into familiar events and long-term developments. Her study explores the plurality of the Jewish gaze, considering how German Jews sought full equality and integration while attempting to preserve a unique identity, and how they experienced security and integration as well as pronounced hatred. Volkov's innovative study offers readers the opportunity to look again at the pivotal moments of German history with a fresh understanding.

Shulamit Volkov is Professor Emerita of History at Tel Aviv University. She holds research interests in German social history, the history of antisemitism and the history of the German Jews. Previous publications include *Germans, Jews, and Antisemites: Trials in Emancipation* (Cambridge, 2006) and *Walther Rathenau: Weimar's Fallen Statesman* (Yale, 2012).

Germany through Jewish Eyes
A History from the Eighteenth Century to the Present

Shulamit Volkov
Tel Aviv University

Shaftesbury Road, Cambridge CB2 8EA, United Kingdom

One Liberty Plaza, 20th Floor, New York, NY 10006, USA

477 Williamstown Road, Port Melbourne, VIC 3207, Australia

314–321, 3rd Floor, Plot 3, Splendor Forum, Jasola District Centre, New Delhi – 110025, India

103 Penang Road, #05–06/07, Visioncrest Commercial, Singapore 238467

Cambridge University Press is part of Cambridge University Press & Assessment, a department of the University of Cambridge.

We share the University's mission to contribute to society through the pursuit of education, learning and research at the highest international levels of excellence.

www.cambridge.org
Information on this title: www.cambridge.org/9781009506496

DOI: 10.1017/9781009506465

© Shulamit Volkov 2024

This publication is in copyright. Subject to statutory exception and to the provisions of relevant collective licensing agreements, no reproduction of any part may take place without the written permission of Cambridge University Press & Assessment.

When citing this work, please include a reference to the DOI 10.1017/9781009506465

Originally published in German by C. H. Beck as *Deutschland aus jüdischer Sicht*, 2022

First published in English by Cambridge University Press, 2024

A catalogue record for this publication is available from the British Library.

A Cataloging-in-Publication data record for this book is available from the Library of Congress

ISBN 978-1-009-50649-6 Hardback
ISBN 978-1-009-50648-9 Paperback

Cambridge University Press & Assessment has no responsibility for the persistence or accuracy of URLs for external or third-party internet websites referred to in this publication and does not guarantee that any content on such websites is, or will remain, accurate or appropriate.

Contents

Acknowledgments	*page* vi
Introduction: A Jewish Gaze – Plural and Unique	1
Part I: Learning to Know Germany: 1780–1840	11
1 Enlightenment without Toleration	13
2 Benevolent Autocracy	28
3 The Half-Open Society	44
Part II: Liberty, Unity, Equality: 1840–1870	61
4 Pogroms and Revolution	63
5 Germany's Entangled Modernities	78
6 Unification as Rupture	93
Part III: Living in Germany: 1870–1930	109
7 Achievements and Unacknowledged Dangers	111
8 Joined and Disjoint in War	131
9 Hopes Shattered	147
Part IV: A Lost Homeland: 1930–2000	163
10 The Abyss	165
11 Victims, Witnesses, Plaintiffs	183
12 Strangers at Home	203
Epilogue: Berlin is not Weimar	221
Index	227

Acknowledgments

My first, rather unsure steps in the direction of this book were made in a series of lectures held at the Ludwig Maximilian University of Munich at the invitation of Professor Michael Brenner, head of the Chair for Jewish History and Culture at that university. He is therefore first on my list of thanks upon the publication of this book. My stay in Munich was generously financed by a fellowship of the Allianz Insurance Company, and my later expenses by the Meitner–Humboldt Research Award for 2016. This is an opportunity for me to wholeheartedly thank both of these funding institutions. The manuscript has been read with the greatest care by two colleagues, who, in addition to their knowledge and expertise, also represented for me – unknowingly – two generations of German scholars: Professor Dr. Jürgen Kocka and Dr. Philipp Lenhard. The first has been my trusted colleague and friend for many years. We have met and discussed both historical and contemporary themes innumerable times for more than four decades. Still, his readiness to go through this manuscript and comment upon it so thoroughly has been a touching gesture of friendship. I met Philipp Lenhard during my long stay in Munich during the Winter Semester 2014–2015 and quickly learned to appreciate his historical knowledge and sophistication. He too has sometimes had to put aside more important work in order to go through the chapters that were sent to him periodically during the last couple of years. I am deeply thankful for his precise and professional commentary. Liz Friend-Smith and the team at Cambridge University Press, especially Ruth Boyes and Steven Holt, were of immense help in finally producing this book and my heart-felt thanks are due to them, too.

Finally, I wish to thank my life companion, Celino Bleiweiss, who has had to hear my ruminations on German history at breakfasts and as we were driving along some of the most beautiful landscapes at the foothills of the Alps or along the shores of the Mediterranean, north and south of Tel Aviv. I have greatly benefited from his long acquaintance with Germany, his overall life experience living in that country, and his many insights. Most importantly, his warm and quiet love was simply indispensable. This book is dedicated to him.

Introduction: A Jewish Gaze – Plural and Unique

The tale of the Jews living in Germany could be told as a chapter of Jewish history as well as a chapter of German history. This last option, however, has only rarely been seriously taken up. Despite the fact that history writing concerning the Jews in the German-speaking world of Central Europe has developed from its inception in parallel with the general historiography of that region, attempts to bring the two together were few and far between. In fact, those two branches of history took their professional, academic shape in parallel, according to the teachings of Leopold von Ranke and under a strong Hegelian influence during the early decades of the nineteenth century. Soon, however, Jewish history became a branch of the *Wissenschaft des Judentums* and long remained a more or less exclusive Jewish domain. While German history developed as part of a new, internationally practiced discipline, concerned with power politics, diplomacy, statecraft in general, and the nation-state in particular, Jewish history, lacking such a powerful political sphere, failed to develop the same interests and was gradually marginalized.

Moreover, German history, not unlike other European historiographies, usually left out most lower-class elements and all minority groups – rich or poor, central or peripheral. To be sure, methodological links between all European historiographies, including the Jewish history writing, continued to exist. Historians – regardless of nationality or denomination – were by the middle of the nineteenth century all dedicated to the effort of reconstructing the past on the basis of authentic documents, and Jewish historians were, naturally, doing the same. But, in the meantime, working on Jewish history alone seemed appealing enough for Jewish scholars, and writing German history focused on themes that seemed both more pressing and more important.

In any case, as academic history began to be written, the majority of Jews whose lives evolved outside the scholarly sphere were probably just as uninterested in it as their non-Jewish counterparts. History was not yet seen as a tool of self-definition and self-presentation. The *Jewish* main source of identity, like that of most non-Jews, had for generations been one or another religion. Among Christians, even the Reformation, splitting their faith deeper than ever before, at first only strengthened the centrality of religiously based identities in Europe, and it was only later that this same Reformation began to allow the development of some new, fully or partly secularized forms of identity. Thus, in a process that proved to be far from linear, Europeans learned to conceive of themselves not only as men – and women – belonging to a certain religious congregation, but as members of one or another ethnicity, *Volk*, or nationality. In Germany, where, for a variety of reasons, men were becoming ever more strongly attached to relatively small, or so-called particular political units, they soon learned to see themselves as Prussians, Bavarians, or Hanoverians, for instance; not necessarily – and usually not mainly – as Germans. For them, the process of becoming members of a nation or citizens of a single nation-state was even more protracted and more complex than elsewhere on the European continent.

Just as Goethe and Schiller, late in the eighteenth century, could ask "where Deutschland actually was" and claim they "could not find it,"[1] most German-speaking inhabitants of that part of the world were for a long time unsure as to where that Germany lay and whether their loyalty could ever belong to it. Still, even among them, the process of nationalization was gradually fortified and eventually completed. At the same time, questions of Jewish identity, seemingly rather straightforward in the past, became ever more perplexing.

In fact, even during the Middle Ages, as all group definitions were saturated with religious imagery, Jews were also seen as an ethnographically definable group, possessing social and cultural characteristics that went far beyond their religion and its unique moral and behavioral rules. After all, the biblical view of the Hebrews as a folk lay deep in the consciousness of Christian Europe, and, although there was no general agreement as to the actual link between those ancient Hebrews and contemporary Jews, some such link had always been assumed. Then, during the early modern period, German theologians – sometimes called Orientalists or even, more specifically, Hebraists – showed increasing interest in the precise habitus of contemporary Jews, their daily life, and in particular their languages.[2] By the middle of the eighteenth century, the biblical narrative itself was no longer seen as a purely religious text and began to be treated as a secular, historical source material. One began to

---

[1] Johann Wolfgang von Goethe and Friedrich Schiller, *Xenien: Literaturpolitische Distichen*, number 95, "Das Deutsche Reich."
[2] For this, see especially Aya Elyada, *A Goy Who Speaks Yiddish: Christians and the Jewish Languages in Early Modern Europe*, Stanford, CA, 2012.

apply to it the new, proto-scientific tools of the day: linguistic scrutiny, early archeology, and the basic anthropological concepts of that time. Thus, Jewish life in contemporary Europe was observed for information concerning the ancient Hebrews and the other way around. An implicit link between the two allowed the drawing of both positive and negative implications for deciding about the status of contemporary Jews, for instance, as this in itself became an ever more fiercely debated topic.

The most influential interpreter of the not-only-religious past of the ancient Hebrews was the philosopher and theologian Johann Gottfried Herder. He never doubted the existence of a profound literary corpus produced by them as a folk, though he too, like Voltaire on the other side of the Rhine, despised the Jews of his days, their group characteristics, and their communal life-style. Using the past as part of his arguments, Johann David Michaelis, a much respected Orientalist at the University of Göttingen, insisted that these characteristics, shaped under the burning sun of the vast Middle Eastern deserts, as he claimed, could never be altered, nor could they ever fit life in enlightened Europe or suit the by then quickly evolving German national culture. Parallel to this anti-Jewish trend ran yet another, showing respect for the ancient Hebrews, even using them as an additional prototype in the forming of a budding German nationalism. To be sure, it was the Greeks that served as the main model for Germany, but that was by no means the only one. Jews played a role in the story of Christian salvation, and they could also play a role in the pre-Enlightenment and post-Enlightenment narrative of the independent, German folk, the seed of a new nation.[3]

Interestingly, Jews themselves often believed that they really possessed unique features outside of and beyond their religion. After all, they all shared a joint halachic hierarchy, strict intra-group marriage rules and an extensive system of social solidarity. Since they had always constituted a widely spread diaspora, they clearly saw themselves – and were seen by others – as more than a religion though less than a nationality. By the early nineteenth century, we find Jews in Germany busily writing their history, trying to come to terms with their own complex identity as well as with the various images of themselves, including the many prejudices put forward by others and widespread among their neighbors. In the age of emancipation, with creeping secularization and the upheavals brought about by revolution and industrialization, they too searched for new sources of identity, a new definition of themselves – as a group and as individuals.

---

[3] On this, see Ofri Ilani, *In Search of the Hebrew People: Bible and Nation in the German Enlightenment*, Bloomington, IN, 2018, and the by now classic studies of E. M. Butler, *The Tyranny of Greece over Germany*, Cambridge, 1935 and see also Anthony Smith, *The Cultural Foundations of Nations: Hierarchy, Covenant and Republic*, Oxford, 2008.

4   Introduction

They – like the non-Jews among whom they lived – needed a new overall view of their past that could help in shaping their future. Each group sought its own unique history, while an ever deeper gap was widening between them. In both cases, mere remembrance, transmitted from generation to generation by prescribed ceremonies and holy texts, was no longer sufficient. Memory of past events now had to be replaced or at least supported by a critical narrative.[4] Both Christians and Jews were now seeking a presumably scientific narrative, suited to their needs, anchored in original documents, and fitting the climate of a new age. As the nineteenth century proceeded, Jews, just like Germans, sought to establish learned institutions for these purposes, collected documents, published scholarly journals, and tried their hand in writing local as well as overall national histories – each running its own course.

Before this gap between the two historiographies could close, it first became far wider, in fact deeper than could be imagined. In the aftermath of the Holocaust, Germans and Jews were separated as never before, and this could not but be reflected in their history writings. Despite some remarkable efforts, the reemerging post-1945 historiography concerning the Jews, especially in West Germany, could not breach this gap. The early volumes of the *Leo Baeck Institute Yearbook*, published in London since 1956 by émigré Jewish scholars, stressed local perspectives and the inspiring tales of outstanding individuals. It expressed the pain of losing the bond with Germany, but did not really reach out in order to restore it.[5] And non-Jewish historians, who now felt called upon to engage in German Jewish history, concentrated on similar topics, added regional studies of somewhat wider proportions, and only rarely ventured to treat more inclusive, general themes. Even when the focus was on antisemitism, surely a *German* rather than *Jewish* phenomenon, historians tended to target local developments, writing on specific German regions or states, only slowly mapping the whole area.[6]

---

[4] On this, see especially Ismar Schorsch, *From Text to Context: The Turn to History in Modern Judaism*, Hanover, NH, 1994. Also compare Josef Hayim Yerushalmi, *Zakhor: Jewish History and Jewish Memory*, Philadelphia, PA and Seattle, WA, 1982.

[5] On the history of the Leo Baeck Institute, see Christhard Hoffmann (ed.), *Preserving the Legacy of German Jewry: History of the Leo Baeck Institute 1955–2005*, Tübingen, 2005.

[6] See Reinhard Rürup, "Die Emanzipation der Juden in Baden," *Zeitschrift für die Geschichte des Oberrheins*, 114 (1966), 241–300; Arno Herzig, *Judentum und Emanzipation in Westfalen*, Münster, 1973; Steffi Jersch-Wenzel *Juden und "Franzosen" in der Wirtschaft des Raumes Berlin-Brandenburg zur Zeit des Merkantilismus*, Berlin, 1975. For a reevaluation, see Till van Rahden, "History in the House of the Hangman: How Postwar Germany Became a Key Site for the Study of Jewish History," in Steven E. Aschheim and Vivian Liska (eds.), *The German-Jewish Experience Revisited*, Berlin, 2015, 171–192.

It could have been assumed that in post-war Germany even the non-specialists would no longer be able to bypass Jewish topics in writing German history. The enormity of the catastrophe, brought upon the European Jews by the Nazis, their helpers and helpers' helpers, could not allow such matters to be set aside any longer. In the past, after all, lack of interest in German-Jewish history could be explained by the small, insignificant size of the Jewish minority. Events that were directly related to them, such as mob attacks, public debates on matters of religious dogma, intra-communal strife, or the repeated waves of inner migration and both immigration into Germany and emigration away from it – all were crucial for the tale of Jewish history, but in more general historical texts were for a long time considered negligible. In grand-style German histories of the day, Jews appeared in subsections entitled "demography," "religion," or "minorities," sometimes curiously even under "culture" or "education." But all these were addenda to the main text, somewhat like extensive footnotes.

This was true even for early treatments of the history of National Socialism. Karl Dietrich Bracher famously wrote the first such scholarly account, but only a small section of his book, *The German Dictatorship*, published in 1969, dealt with the six years of the Second World War and still less – some 12 of 550 pages – with the Holocaust. Significantly, this was not only a German phenomenon. One of the most useful and widely read textbooks on modern Europe, for instance, *Europe since Napoleon*, written by the English historian David Thomson and published in 1961, does not mention more than the mere elementary facts of what was by him still called the Final Solution. In books that were published during the first post-war generation, Jewish experience during the Nazi era remained – at the very best – a separate matter, hardly ever an integral part of the relevant period. Only later, together with other historiographical changes, did a measure of rapprochement between Jewish and non-Jewish history begin to emerge. Younger historians began working on the fate of the Jews in peace and in war, trying to integrate this tale within their own narrative.

Since the last few decades of the twentieth century, particularly important was the growth of a new Jewish historiography in North America. There, as one gradually abandoned the once-so-central concept of a melting pot, one began stressing the role of ethnic minorities, defined now by their so-called hyphenated identity. Like Irish-Americans, Italian-Americans, or Polish-Americans, one could now also write about Jewish-Americans, and soon about Jewish-Germans or Jewish-Russians, though still not much about Jewish-Moroccans or Jewish-Iraqis – important topics only later on. The preference of historians during those years for writing monographs rather than mammoth multi-volume works likewise enhanced the tendency to specialize and thus led to concentration on Jews within a single national context and within one linguistic or cultural setting. Junior historians could now master the sources in a single language, familiarize themselves with the history of one host society, and concentrate on the past of one Jewish community. Last but not least, this approach encouraged practitioners to apply new historical tools, often borrowed from the social sciences, and to do so with facility and expertise.

More than anything, it was the growing importance of social history that finally helped change the old paradigm in the study of the Jewish diaspora. It produced a new narrative, based on a deeper interest in local contexts, eventually undermining the single, simplified line of argument which had been so dominant in past decades. In the spring of 1983, for instance, at a conference dealing with what the pioneering social historian in Israel Jacob Katz then chose to call "*the* Jewish model of modernization," the fragility of even such a rather limited model soon became apparent.[7] The study of modernization, long considered the focus of social history, could display important similarities among the various Jewish case studies, but it could not produce a single, coherent model. The affinity of Jews to non-Jews in their various domiciles often seemed now more meaningful than the affinity of Jews among themselves. Social history almost forced the Jewish into the non-Jewish narrative.

At the same time, it was the same social history that weakened the interest in Jewish history as such for almost a whole generation of politically conscious historians and renewed its isolation within the various national historiographies, that of Germany included: "In fact, it was social history, so long dominant in West Germany, that completely lost sight of German-Jewish history," wrote historian Stefanie Schüler-Springorum in summarizing this phase.[8] We could sometimes read during these years detailed and sophisticated Jewish histories, significantly in the plural to be sure, but these were neither incorporated within the various relevant histories in general, nor integrated within the German one in particular.

The turn to post-modernity has made us even more aware of such fissures. As new winds began to blow in literary and cultural studies, one was now bound to hear that all modern narratives were far too inclusive and in any case represented only tales of the "establishment," so to speak. History was always the tale of the white, male, economically

---

[7] See Jakob Katz (ed.), *Towards Modernity: The European Jewish Model*, New Brunswick, NJ, 1987.
[8] See Stefanie Schüler-Springorum, "Non-Jewish Perspectives on German-Jewish History. A Generational Project?," in Aschheim and Liska (eds.), *The German Jewish Experience*, 193–205, 199.

Introduction

and politically successful segment of the population, it was now argued. Colonial peoples, as well as some non-European nations – many of whom have had rich and eventful pasts, often intertwining with major affairs in European history – were no more than roughly mentioned in it. Women played no role at all in such "his-story," unless, of course, they happened to be powerful monarchs, spouses of equally powerful monarchs, or some other exceptional figures. Jews were absent from all of these narratives.

Gender history, indeed, could serve as a model in analyzing the problem of Jewish marginality in history. Beginning as women's history, the purpose of this new scholarly field was mainly to add a forgotten or neglected chapter to our vista of the past; telling the tale of women, in the hope of saving them from oblivion. But, while doing so, one also wished "to transform the way *all history* was written," it was added.[9] In fact, this was clearly reminiscent of Eric Hobsbawm's earlier claim, promising to write a new social history. He then spoke not only about providing a research platform for the study of workingmen and the lower classes, but also in favor of changing the discipline of history as a whole, reshaping the way it had been written in a radical way.[10]

A project of this sort had succeeded only once before, namely in the hands of Karl Marx, whose shifting of focus to the working class and to class struggle had brought about not only the introduction of additional chapters into existing historiographies, but also the construction of an altogether new narrative, a comprehensive alternative to the history written and propagated before him. The appearance of the *new* social history in the later decades of the twentieth century, perhaps the second chapter of this development, may not have figured as a farce, to follow Karl Marx again, but it was surely less comprehensive than the first, and eventually, so it seems, less successful. Marxism gave rise to an altogether different kind of history writing, indeed, based on economic determinism and focusing on a different social milieu. Social history, heavily relying on economic history as well, clearly widened the interest of historians to the tales of lower-class groups, their interrelations, and their political effects, but its limitations soon became apparent. Some felt it was too dry and technical, moving into obscure corners and losing sight of large-scale, mainly political developments. Others remained unconvinced by its disregard for the role of outstanding personalities or for ideas and ideologies.

Women's history likewise ran under two headings. It wished both to introduce the story of women into the overall narrative of the past and at

---

[9] Joan Wallach Scott, *Gender and the Politics of History*, New York, 1999, ix.
[10] E. J. Hobsbawm, "From Social History to the History of Society," *Daedalus*, 100(1) (1971), 20–45.

the same time to transform and renew that narrative – its premises, methods, and overall direction. In the end, while it did bring the life of that neglected half of humanity somewhat more to the fore, women's history changed, but changed only marginally, the way one was writing history as a whole. More was apparently needed for such a transformation. The turn to cultural history helped, no doubt; the move from Europe to the global scene proved important too, and the combination of the two *did* bring about a somewhat different kind of history writing today. Could the place of Jews in it be likewise altered? Now that so much has been achieved in studying the history of German Jewry in isolation, with combined history having occasionally been written for some of the chapters along their joint route, this book attempts to tell a complete tale of the two, with many issues left out, to be sure, but with others woven together.

In fact, the book suggests another perspective on German history, observed – this time – through Jewish eyes, from their unique place in German society.[11] After all, we are constantly learning to recast the presumably outdated narratives in different contexts and provide new dimensions to familiar themes. Observe Dan Diner's history of the twentieth century, for instance, seen – as he explains – from a very concrete and unusual perspective. Europe is to be looked at in his book neither from Paris nor from Berlin, neither from London nor from Rome, but from the famous flight of steps in Odessa, site of the 1905 failed Russian revolution.[12] This, moreover, has a clear methodological advantage, too, since on these famous Odessa steps sits, so it seems, a *single imagined* observer, applying a single alternative gaze to the Europe of his time. Women, or, for that matter, Jews, are varied and their gaze varies, too. Women could be of working-class or middle-class origins. Their perspective could reflect their gender, but it could also be disengaged from it and be based on their economic position, their level of education or their unique cultural position. Jews too had never had only one viewpoint or one gaze. Like women, their look could reflect their life in rural or urban environments, while many of them became increasingly "metropolitan" towards the end of the nineteenth century. They could be poor or rich, religious, even orthodox, traditional or secular. Jewish women surely had

---

[11] See and compare now especially with Till van Rahden, "Germans of the Jewish *Stamm*: Visions of Community between Nationalism and Particularism, 1850 to 1933," and Yfaat Weiss, "Identity and Essential: Race, Racism, and the Jews at the Fin de Siècle," in Neil Gregor, Nils Roemer, and Mark Roseman (eds.), *German History from the Margins*, Bloomington, IN, 2006, 27–48 and 49–68, respectively.

[12] See Dan Diner, *Cataclysms: A History of the Twentieth Century from Europe's Edge*, Madison, WI, 2007.

a different perspective than Jewish men, and in every period their point of observation would have certainly shifted. Sometimes, it was not even clear: Who actually looked at whom; where, in fact, was this imagined social location occupied by Jews, and what in the end was Jewish about this or that particular kind of look?

Despite these complexities, I suggest that German Jews, taken as a whole, were observing events always from a unique perspective, or at least from yet another unique perspective. They were particularly sensitive to some aspects of the society within which they lived and perhaps negligent of others. At least one aspect of German history often attracted their special attention, namely the inherent ambivalence in the way this society handled a great many themes, its permanent double-faced subtext. Sometimes it was easy to feel the wings of progressive winds, the promise of a better future. At other times, other winds were blowing – reactionary, hateful, even dangerous, and finally disastrous. Not only Jews could observe this duality, of course, but it had for a long time had a particular effect on them, and it is through their eyes that one can observe it particularly well.

During most of the nineteenth century, following the Napoleonic Wars, times were relatively peaceful. But, in times of growing tension, such as during the 1840s or in the pre-1914 years, Jews could, in contrast, be comforted by their sense of achievement and miss the signs of danger. In rare times of domestic conflict, during the 1860s, for instance, *their* fate clearly improved, and while Germany experienced three wars as a prelude to unification, one German state after another completed the legalization of their civil equality. When, towards the end of the 1870s, a new wave of antisemitism erupted, first in Berlin and then, sporadically, elsewhere too, Jews were – just then – energetically climbing up the social ladder and could begin to count their blessings. Despite the animosity, they enjoyed extraordinary success not only in their old traditional economic niches, but now also in culture, science, and the arts. Thus, they often saw another face of Germany, and, following their vision, we too can benefit from applying it.

True enough, that unique Jewish observational point is not always unproblematic. The Jews, unlike many other minorities, moved quickly from a position of relative isolation in pre-modern times to an increasingly more central spot in modern times. Their economic success in Germany and then their rapid entry into the culture of their surroundings have often been commented upon with unconcealed admiration. This, however, could produce a skewed perspective. While individual Jews did, no doubt, experience unusual success, and while only a few of them were poverty-stricken even as early as the middle of the nineteenth century, a majority remained consistently anchored in the lower middle class, occupied in small-scale commerce, experiencing little or no social mobility. Who then was in the center? Who in the margin? Where were the Jews, as such, located? Did such a common spot exist?

The American sociologist Thorstein Veblen tried to explain the achievements of outstanding Jews by invoking the advantages of their presumed marginality.[13] Sigmund Freud apparently saw things in this way, too: "Because I was a Jew," Freud wrote, "I found myself free of many prejudices, which restrict others in the use of their intellect."[14] However, many successful Jews in Germany of that time did not *feel* marginal and would not have appreciated the possible advantages of such a position. Still, whether they realized it or not, they too must have seen things differently than others; they too had a special angle from which to experience and observe events, and their unique standpoint enables us, in the end, to consider familiar events, structures, and long-term developments in a different light.

I have chosen twelve chronologically ordered chapters of modern German history and tried to reconstruct them by using a Jewish perspective. This, it must perhaps be repeated, is not a Jewish-history book. Nor is it a complete history of Germany. When a number of various Jewish perspectives played some role in a single period, I tried to preserve this array and faithfully represent it, and the effort may have allowed me to tell a different story, woven into a different context. I have also tried to evade the almost inevitable pitfalls in this case, namely that of telling the story from its tragic end backward. While history is to some degree always told from the standpoint of a particular historian backwardly, this can be fatal in this case. Thus, even if I may have only partially succeeded, I will at least have tried to offer my own way of looking at Germany, surely seen from my own point in time, but without letting the tragic chapters of this tale dictate its entire unfolding. In this way, I may perhaps be able to throw *some* new light on the familiar chronicle, perhaps even bring the two histories – the German and the German-Jewish – together, turning them into a single, new narrative.

---

[13] See Thorstein Veblen, "Intellectual Pre-eminence of Jews in Modern Europe" (1919), in Max Lerner (ed.), *The Portable Veblen*, New York, 1950, 467–479.

[14] Ernst L. Freud (ed.), *Letters of Sigmund Freud*, New York 1960, 367.

Part I

Learning to Know Germany: 1780–1840

1 Enlightenment without Toleration

We begin with the Enlightenment. And why not? After all, when *does* the modern era begin? Where and when can one identify a clear break and a new beginning? Where could one identify a cluster of events that might be important enough to mark a new age? Furthermore, does such a new age begin at the same time for Europeans in general and for the German-speaking population across mid-continent in particular? Or, further still – for Germans in general and for the Jews, who were living among them, in particular?

Modern European history is usually said to begin with the French Revolution. This *was* no doubt a world-shaking event, one that even proclaimed itself as such, then and there, and could easily be shown to be one when seen from a distance, too. Americans would have probably preferred to begin with their own revolution and with the formal establishment of the United States. English historians, usually excluding their own history from that of the neighboring continent, often begin the story of modernity with Waterloo and the fall of Napoleon. Another starting point for modern history could be set according to one or another event along the route to industrialization, sometime in the middle of the eighteenth century. But present-day historians, attempting to write a history of modern Germany, where and when should they begin?

"In the beginning was Napoleon" – this is Thomas Nipperdey's resounding first sentence at the opening of the first volume of his grand history of modern Germany. "In the beginning there was no revolution" – wrote Hans-Ulrich Wehler, indicating with this sentence both his critique of Nipperdey and his own approach to modernity, focusing on matters of social history.[1] Interestingly, however, he did this only at the opening of his *second* volume – though the first to appear – while the entire magnum

---

[1] Thomas Nipperdey, *Deutsche Geschichte 1800–1918*, 3 vols., Munich, 1998 [1983–1992]; first volume in English, *Germany from Napoleon to Bismarck*, trans. Daniel Nolan, Princeton, 1996; Hans-Ulrich Wehler, *Deutsche Gesellschaftsgeschichte*, Vols. 1–5, Munich, 1987–2008.

opus begins rather unassumingly in 1700, suggesting a prolonged, chronologically not very precise starting point, defined by an equally suggestive subtitle: *From the Feudalism of the Old Reich to Defensive Modernization during the Era of Reform.* One is reminded of Heinrich von Treitschke's *History of Germany in the Nineteenth Century*, a classic as soon as it had begun to appear in 1879, opening with a longish introduction, taking the reader back to the Peace of Westphalia, signed in 1648, over 150 years earlier, to his real starting point. In fact, Treitschke's text begins even earlier, as he briefly tells Germany's tale since the Lutheran Reformation and the early political consolidation of the Prussian monarchy. Different kinds of histories, all chose a starting point unashamedly according to their ideological needs. For Treitschke, who strove to legitimize German unification under the Prussian crown, the beginning had to be placed within the context of north German Protestantism and the Prussian success story. For later narrators of the German nation-building process, sometimes called upon to rehabilitate it in the aftermath of the First and then the Second World War, a beginning with the collapse of the old "Holy Reich" and the early efforts at building a new all-German confederation offered a better fit. And, since the process of modernization was always considered an essential characteristic of that era, itself called "modern," one sometimes sought a fitting starting point along this route. Finding a convincing opening for the modern era has always been far from obvious.

In any case, during the time of Friedrich II, his victorious Silesian wars and his success in consolidating Prussian power – territorially, militarily, and politically – the Berlin Enlightenment, in which he was himself interested and personally involved, could not yet be perceived as a historical turning point, despite its brilliance. Still, even though it had always been so ambivalent, to the point of timidity, some of the early all-German histories could not but rely on the literary achievement of this age and made it into their starting point. Georg Gottfried Grevinus published his *Geschichte der poetischen National-Literatur der Deutschen* between 1835 and 1842, shortly before the major works of the Prussian Historical School began to appear, and for the following half century it dwarfed all other types of historical presentations.

Meanwhile, even the French Enlightenment, surely the most intensively studied of all European Enlightenments, has with time lost its status as a true forerunner of the Great Revolution and as the intellectual bedrock of those world-shaking events associated with it. While its significance had always been a matter of controversy, much of its splendor has been dimmed at least since the publication of a few path-breaking articles by the British historian Alfred Cobban, over fifty years ago. The influence of the Enlightenment on the Revolution, Cobban stated, could not be entirely disregarded, but "the revolutionaries never acted according to its principles," nor did they find "clear directions for action *in them*."[2] A couple of decades later, Robert Darnton managed to refocus our attention further away from the oeuvres of those great enlightened minds in the direction of what he then called *The Forbidden Best-Sellers of Pre-Revolutionary France*, or – more generally – *The Literary Underground of the Old Regime*, to cite the titles of two of his books.[3] The turn to politics in the last third of the eighteenth century left behind much of the intellectual baggage assembled earlier in order to take on a new and usually more radical ideal of Liberty, Equality, and Fraternity. From that point onward, the Enlightenment has had a great deal of bad press, and was criticized on philosophical, ideological, and especially political grounds.

The controversy for and against the Enlightenment ran through the entire nineteenth century and continued well into the twentieth, but it was only rarely disputed on purely historiographical terrain.[4] Its first renowned modern historian, Ernst Cassirer – a German Jew, writing in the fateful year 1932 – made the tension between Reason as a tool of critique and Reason as an instrument of practical politics the center of his interpretation. Other scholars were inclined to search the Enlightenment for the sources of the old ideals of *Bildung* – individualism, humanism, and moral devotion. Having experienced the force of National Socialism and by then living for a number of years in exile, within an entirely different intellectual milieu, this time on the American continent, Max Horkheimer and Theodor Adorno published their *Dialectic of Enlightenment*, adding a clear moral tone to what had previously seemed to consist of strictly academic interventions.[5] The Enlightenment *did* serve as a starting point for these two authors, though not only for progress and liberation, but also, perhaps primarily, for all modern forms of oppression. It was the root of fascism in general and of National Socialism in particular, they argued, and in its heart lay the source of all modern evils. Its false discourse on toleration and equality

---

[2] See Alfred Cobban, "The Enlightenment and the French Revolution," in Alfred Cobban, *Aspects of the French Revolution*, London, 1968, 18–28; Roger Chartier, *Les origines culturelles de la Révolution française*, Paris, 1990. For a different line of argument, see Jonathan Israel, *Radical Enlightenment*, Oxford, 2001 and Jonathan Israel, *Democratic Enlightenment*, Oxford, 2013.
[3] Robert Darnton, *The Forbidden Best-Sellers of Pre-Revolutionary France*, New York, 1996; Robert Darnton, *The Literary Underground of the Old Regime*, Cambridge, MA, 1982.
[4] See Zeev Sternhell, *The Anti-Enlightenment Tradition*, New Haven, CT, 2009.
[5] The book was first published in German, Max Horkheimer and Theodor W. Adorno, *Dialektik der Aufklärung*, Amsterdam, 1947; first English edition *Dialectic of Enlightenment*, trans. John Cumming, New York, 1972.

only meant to fortify the appeal for more effective control – firstly over nature, with all its resources, and then over man, too. It could be and was easily misused as a manipulative tool, enforcing alienation and increasing social disintegration, leading to moral decline and eventually to totalitarianism.

By the 1960s, this critique had been translated into the post-modern idiom, for instance by the sociologist Zygmunt Bauman. While historians such as Peter Gay continued to see the Enlightenment as the glorious opening of modernity, it gradually became ever more difficult to reconstruct what had once been its positive side, worthy of admiration. Horkheimer's and Adorno's judgment had still been ambivalent, but in Bauman's thinking or in the texts of some other post-modern authors, past appreciation was lost. From their perspective, the Enlightenment no longer served as a starting point for a tale of liberation, initiating a chain of further improvements, called "progress" in the language of the time. Instead, that progress tended to disappear from contemporary discourse altogether, and – having not had even a revolution at its peak – the *German* Enlightenment in particular lost its radiance. Despite its having been the bedrock of a new era under the pen of almost all nineteenth-century historians, its achievements turned out to be barely sufficient for marking an epochal turning point.

Furthermore, as the significance both of earlier periods and of cultures outside Europe has lately been rediscovered and is being stressed in much of the relevant historiography, it further diminishes the light of the once-so-prominent late eighteenth-century European Enlightenment. New continuities are now replacing old ones, and this, to be sure, is true for general European history and for Jewish history alike.[6]

All this, however, had only a limited effect on the writing of German *Jewish* history. Here, in fact, the Enlightenment continued to serve as *the* moment of Jewish regeneration, a time of dramatic emergence out of darkness into light, just as its name suggests. It marked a new beginning in the life of an entire *Volk*, indicating an end to centuries of oppression. German Jewish historiography usually recognized no Renaissance and for a long time perceived no early-modern period as such. Thus, the place of the Enlightenment as an epochal turning point, at least insofar as

---

[6] For moving the beginning of modernity to earlier times in general history, see, for instance, Brad S. Gregory, *The Unintended Reformation: How a Religious Revolution Secularized Society*, Cambridge, MA, 2012. For the same in Jewish history, see David B. Ruderman, *Early Modern Jewry: A New Cultural History*, Princeton, NJ, 2010. For widening our geographical horizons, see also Sebastian Conrad, "Enlightenment in Global History: A Historiographic Critique," *American Historical Review*, 117(4) (2012), 999–1027. Finally, for an attempt to save the Enlightenment from its critics, using an entirely different perspective, see Steven Pinker, *Enlightenment Now. The Case for Reason, Science, Humanism and Progress*, New York 2018.

German-speaking Central European Jewry was concerned, has remained virtually uncontested within it, designating the beginning of the modern era.

As a paradigm, this was outlined by Heinrich Graetz in the eleventh volume of his massive *History of the Jews from the Earliest Times to the Present Day*, published in 1870. Accordingly, the *Jewish* Enlightenment – or, under its Hebrew name, the *Haskalah* – focused more upon *Bildung* and erudition than on the metaphor of light or the centrality of Reason, and, in order to further elucidate this view, Graetz finally placed the figure of Moses Mendelssohn in the center of his narrative. He and a long list of Jewish historians, all the way to Jacob Katz in the second half of the twentieth century, some 100 years later, presented the Enlightenment as a clear turning point, albeit with changing particular stresses and the introduction of a few additional points.

Interestingly, one of the more recent volumes, offering a long-term historical overview, this time written originally in English and concentrating specifically on Prussia since 1600, namely Christopher Clark's *Iron Kingdom* of 2006, underlines the Berlin Jewish *Haskalah* in the context of other, parallel movements of religious and later political regeneration at the time. While, for Prussian history, Clark stresses the monarch and his bureaucracy, treating in a less detailed fashion the enlightened production of that blooming contemporary Republic of Letters, the Jewish achievements he describes are intellectually distinct, and – once again – center upon the figure of Moses Mendelssohn.[7]

At that time, Jews were already among the "movers and doers" in the new economy and began to develop an ever greater interest in the bourgeois culture evolving in the world around them.[8] Simultaneously, the rabbinical elite, being weakened by the intervention of the absolutist state, was losing its position of exclusive power. It was facing an emerging younger leadership – cautiously secularizing and generally well versed both in Jewish and in German scholarship. Moreover, this bourgeois society, gradually taking shape everywhere in the German lands, seemed ready to allow at least some measure of Jewish "entry." Thus, the lives both of Jews and of Germans were by then believed to have taken a turn, while Moses Mendelssohn's biography could be perceived as a fitting model, representing this double turn. He stands for the presumed move from darkness into light in Germany as a whole, and from isolation into integration for its Jews. This is surely not an unproblematic line of

---

[7] Christopher Clark, *Iron Kingdom*, Cambridge, MA, 2006. See especially pages 257–267.
[8] This phrase was introduced by Mack Walker, *German Home Towns. Community, State, and General Estate*, 1648–1871, Ithaca NY 1971.

interpretation. Still, I would like to follow it, at least in that I, too, would like to begin with the Enlightenment and with Moses Mendelssohn.

The future German-Jewish philosopher had been born in 1729 in Dessau, some sixty miles from Berlin, and was at first given an extensive Talmudic education, as was the custom among Ashkenazi Jews everywhere in Eastern and Central Europe at the time. He had apparently showed unusual intellectual prowess from the start. At the age of fourteen, so runs the attractive tale, having walked on foot for five days, this unassuming hunchback figure arrived at the gates of the Prussian capital, and, on being questioned by the guards, announced his intention "to learn." He was hoping to join his teacher, Rabbi David Fränkel, who had just been appointed a chief Rabbi of Berlin, and – according to the law of the land – was allowed, though only temporarily, into town. In fact, he would learn there much more than he had hoped for or had even thought possible. Within a short time, the young Mendelssohn became a regular visitor in many of the elegant salons of the wealthy Jewish elite of Berlin, while he was perfecting his knowledge of the German language and learned Greek and Latin besides, as well as English and French. Central to his later curriculum was mathematics and philosophy; he read Leibniz and Wolff and then Shaftesbury, Locke, Voltaire, and many others. At the next stage, the young Moses started translating Rousseau's treatise on the "Inequality among Men" and began publishing his own philosophical essays, in German as well as in Hebrew.[9]

By the mid 1760s, while Mendelssohn was taking on his role as intercessor on behalf of various Jewish communities, he already belonged to the educated elite of Berlin, being a leading figure both in the Jewish *Haskalah* and in the German Enlightenment. He befriended Lessing, Nicolai, and Gleim, and in 1763 won the first prize for a philosophical essay on metaphysics, awarded by the Prussian Royal Academy of Science, leaving the second place to Immanuel Kant. Eight years later, his candidature to the academy was unanimously approved by its members, but it was thereafter repeatedly blocked by the king, for whom accepting a Jew into this elevated body apparently seemed a step too far. In any case, Mendelssohn – sometimes known as "the German Socrates" – was by then clearly considered an established philosopher, the first Jew ever to reach such a status in Germany, a man of European fame.

---

[9] The most comprehensive biography of Mendelssohn is Alexander Altman, *Moses Mendelssohn: A Biographical Study*, Oxford, 1973. See also Dominique Bourel, *Moses Mendelssohn: La naissance du judaïsme modern*, Paris, 2004. For the following, I have used with great benefit Shmuel Feiner, *Moses Mendelssohn: Sage of Modernity*, New Haven, CT, 2010.

One could see in his achievements a sign for a new chapter in Jewish history, or even – despite the king's disfavor – a new era for Prussia. Such parallelism was made especially compelling by later events. The *Berlinische Monatsschrift*, one of those new bourgeois journals, handling issues of public interest and contemporary relevance, published in the fall and winter issues of 1784 first Mendelssohn's and then Kant's essays, replying to the question posed by its editorial board, namely "What Is Enlightenment?"[10] This was a hotly discussed matter among club members associated with this journal, worthy of a competition that would involve the best minds of the land. It was also a difficult question to answer, particularly in view of the monarchic censorship heavily imposed upon all scholarly works written in Prussia. Thus, both finalists – once again Kant and Mendelssohn – found themselves entangled in some hopeless contradictions. They wished to criticize the ills of their time, but could not touch upon the shortcomings of the regime. They wanted to fight prejudice, superstitions, and fanaticism, but were careful not to endanger the social order of the day. As a result, Mendelssohn got trapped in efforts to differentiate between Enlightenment and its common synonyms, namely *Bildung* and culture, while Kant sought in vain to define the distinction between private and public reason under conditions of absolutism. Both sought ways of propagating the free expression of opinion, or what Mendelssohn cherished as "liberty of conscience," without threatening the powers that be. Their respective discourses, unfolding less than five years prior to the revolution in France that would forever shake the old order, manifested the mildness of the German Enlightenment, if not always its deviousness. It surely demonstrated the conservatism of the two contestants and their adherence to the principles of this old order, as was common among many thinkers everywhere in Europe at the time, but perhaps especially in Germany.

The differences between Mendelssohn's approach and Kant's were clear. Kant's opening sentence, frequently quoted by contemporaries and future commentators alike, elegantly transports us from the practical to the theoretical sphere. "Enlightenment is Mankind's exit from its self-incurred immaturity," he writes. "'Sapere aude! Have the courage to use your own understanding!' This is the true motto of the Enlightenment," he concludes. It is thereafter disappointing to read how the author of the

---

[10] Both texts are available in numerous editions and reproduced in many publications. See Immanuel Kant, "Beantwortung der Frage: Was ist Aufklärung?," in *Kants Gesammelte Schriften. Akademie-Ausgabe*, Berlin, 1904ff., Vol. VIII, 33–36, and Moses Mendelssohn, "Über die Frage: was heißt aufklären?," in Alexander Altmann (ed.), *Moses Mendelssohn: Gesammelte Schriften. Jubiläumsausgabe*, Stuttgart-Bad Cannstatt, 1971ff., Vol. VI/1, 115–119.

Critique of Pure Reason quickly retreats to the practical sphere and plunges into what seemed, both at the time and in years to come, a tortuous effort to explain why reason should not be given free reign. Following his profound, even poetic starting point, Kant comfortably turns to what apparently most interested the members of the Mittwochsgesellschaft (Wednesday Society) in Berlin, for whom his essay was written – a mix of the educated and some highly placed state bureaucrats. In fact, the essay competition followed weeks of deliberations among them on issues of censorship and on various proposals for legal reform. Significantly, at the center of their secretly discussed concerns were the dangers of what was considered by them "too much Enlightenment." They wanted to find ways of embracing Enlightenment and delimiting it at the same time; to set its boundaries so as to preserve public order and prevent what they considered its adverse effects on society.[11]

Kant obliged by arguing for absolute freedom of thought and speech in the public sphere, while demanding full obedience in carrying out one's civil duties, as part of what he called the private sphere. The public use of reason, according to him, must always remain free in order to further Enlightenment among men; private use of that same reason, however, may be restricted for the benefit of society. Mendelssohn, for his part, began by trying to clarify the differences between Enlightenment, *Bildung*, and Culture, but – like Kant – being under pressure to sketch the *limits* of Enlightenment – insisted on the principled differentiation between "man as man" and "man as citizen." He then proceeded to define what truths ought to be conveyed to man as man, and especially what truths ought *not* to be conveyed to man as citizen. Within the discursive context of the time, the two attempted to achieve the same. Both sought Enlightenment without reaching too far and advocated the use of Reason without jeopardizing the existing order.

The members of the Mittwochsgesellschaft were apparently enlightened enough to consider the contributions of both authors without taking into account Mendelssohn's Jewishness. At the time, his book "Jerusalem," attempting to define the essence of Judaism, had just been published, and the public controversy over demanding his conversion was neither forgotten nor yet resolved. Moreover, Christian Wilhelm Dohm's extensive essay on the "Civil Betterment of the Jews," initiated by Mendelssohn at the request of some Alsatian Jews, had by then become a cause célèbre even beyond the borders of Prussia. Interestingly, however, it was Kant who placed the issue of religious Enlightenment at the center of

---

[11] See James Schmidt, "The Question of the Enlightenment. Kant, Mendelssohn and the Mittwochsgesellschaft," *Journal of the History of Ideas*, 50(2) (1989), 269–291.

the latter part of his essay, while Mendelssohn, probably intentionally, avoided this side of the problem completely. To be sure, both the Jewish and the German Enlightenment were integral elements of his intellectual make-up, and, although he did not deal with it openly in his Enlightenment essay, this must have been very much on his mind as well as on the minds of his readers – Jews and non-Jews. Mendelssohn took a moderate position in dealing with matters related to the general Enlightenment just as he took a moderate position on matters of the *Haskalah*. It made him, indeed, as Graetz later argued, a fitting figure to mark a new beginning in Jewish history. Could he also serve to mark a new beginning in German history?

Exactly 200 years later we can still hear echoes of the affinity between Kant and Mendelssohn in another essay, carrying the same title, namely "What Is Enlightenment?" This time it is a piece written by a twentieth-century French author of great fame. "With the two texts published in the *Berlinische Monatschrift*," wrote Michel Foucault in 1984, "the German *Aufklärung* and the Jewish *Haskalah* recognize that they belong to the same history." And, while we may question the final clause of this sentence, in which Foucault claims that the two also seek "to identify the common processes from which they stem" while accepting "the common destiny that unites them," one could still affirm his conclusion that "We now know to what drama that was to lead"; a joint drama that, according to him, linked German and Jewish history for inestimable future time, going back all the way to the Enlightenment.[12] This seems to be a good starting point for a "German history though Jewish eyes."

If the German *Aufklärung* and the Jewish *Haskalah* belong in the same history, then it may not be unreasonable to use the starting point of the one for telling the tale of the other and to open *modern* German history, together with *modern* Jewish history, at the same point in time. This, however, has been repeatedly contested. From the Jewish side, critique first stemmed from historians who preferred to place more stress on the history of Eastern European Jewry and not primarily on the Jews of Germany. A generation after Graetz, Simon Dubnow added Polish Jewry to the tale of their German brethren and, from his overall perspective, preferred to begin with the enactment of Jewish civil equality during the French Revolution. This was the critical step towards Jewish modernity, according to him, everywhere in Europe – East and West. Among others, especially the more nationally oriented historians during the early

---

[12] The full text was first published in English. See Michel Foucault, "What Is Enlightenment?," in Paul Rubinow (ed.), *The Foucault Reader*, New York, 1984, 32–50.

twentieth century, Mendelssohn was often considered the voice for assimilation, indicating decline rather than rejuvenation, not a brave new world, but the end of Jewish pride and the beginning of a disintegration of the centuries-old separate Jewish identity. There are also those who have tried to date the turn to modernity earlier than Mendelssohn, during the first half of the eighteenth century, while a few have preferred a later date, which would be independent of Mendelssohn's tale altogether. Jacob Katz, for instance, stressed the collapse of traditional Jewish society during the last two decades of the eighteenth century, heralding a new tale, indeed, but by no means a positive or promising one. Jonathan Israel, in a book published in 1985, described a process of decline that he considered characteristic of Jews and Judaism throughout the eighteenth century, while David Ruderman retells the history of a comprehensive transformation among Jews in that century without using the paradigm of progress and rejuvenation at all.[13] Meanwhile, the evident link between an overall Jewish and an overall non-Jewish narrative, for a while slowly becoming looser, has begun to be stressed again during the last few decades. In addition to Ruderman's encompassing cultural history, one could name the historians Jonathan Hess and David Sorkin as representatives of a new effort at joining the two historiographies – the German and the German-Jewish.[14] Still, perhaps a variation on this theme could be taken up again. After all, the Jewish enlighteners themselves, the "Maskilim," considered themselves representatives of a new age. Moses Mendelssohn may not have been very active in propelling the *Haskalah* among the Jews beyond its very first stage, but others, such as Naphtali Herz Wessely and Isaac Abraham Euchel, were more active in this respect. Finally, it was Mendelsohn's life-story that brought out – though perhaps only symbolically – both the potential and the limitations of this new beginning – for Jews and non-Jews alike.

Mendelssohn's fame quickly grew during the 1760s, and, by the end of the decade, his salon at 68 Spandauerstraße in Berlin served as a meeting point of enlightened personalities, including visitors from across Germany and from abroad. Goethe, curiously enough, is the only celebrity who tells of his unsuccessful attempt to visit Mendelssohn there on his

---

[13] In addition to Katz's work mentioned above, see also his earlier work, Jacob Katz, *Tradition and Crisis: Jewish Society at the End of the Middle Ages*, Cambridge, MA, 1993; see also Jonathan Israel, *European Jewry in the Age of Mercantilism, 1550–1750*, London, 1985, and David Ruderman, *Early Modern Jewry: A New Cultural History*, Princeton, NJ, 2010.

[14] See Jonathan M. Hess, *Germans, Jews and the Claims of Modernity*, New Haven, CT, 2002, and David Sorkin, *The Religious Enlightenment: Protestants, Jews and Catholics from London to Vienna*, Princeton, NJ, 2011.

only trip to the Prussian capital in 1778. At the same time, the Jewish sage was traveling widely himself, while maintaining an extended correspondence and continuing to publish philosophical essays both in German and in Hebrew. But, having stressed his achievements, of which he himself was surely aware, let us now observe the sources of his disappointments. Shmuel Feiner's biography of Mendelssohn dwells upon these, and I follow him closely in what follows.

Accordingly, Mendelssohn's career as a polemicist on the non-Jewish scene begins with his response to a harsh review of Lessing's early theatrical piece *The Jews*, written by Johann David Michaelis, the renowned theologian at the University of Göttingen. Mendelssohn was insulted. Here and now, in the midst of enlightened Germany, one should not expect to find such prejudices, he felt. Later on, however, and throughout his life, such prejudices resurfaced repeatedly, and often just when he had expected them the least. Being a deeply optimistic philosopher, this hit him hard.

Probably the worst case was the following. Among the occasional guests at Mendelssohn's home was a churchman from Zurich, Johann Caspar Lavater, somewhat later to become famous for his studies of physiognomy and to whom the host had apparently disclosed in a private conversation his fundamental respect towards Christianity. Soon thereafter, Lavater published a translation of a book by his French colleague Charles Bonnet entitled *La palingénésie philosophique*, later partly translated into English as *Philosophical and Critical Inquiries Concerning Christianity*, and – unexpectedly – dedicated it to none other than his Jewish friend, challenging him to either disprove Bonnet's contentions or accept them and convert to Christianity. Mendelssohn was insulted again. He felt betrayed, pushed into a corner and forced to defend his faith against his expressed wishes. Since he nevertheless felt forced to answer, he then openly rejected the millenarian enthusiasm of Lavater and insisted on his right to remain Jewish. Moreover, Mendelssohn now chose to principally defend Judaism as *the* religion of tolerance, compatible with the demands of Reason and of the modern state, a true "natural religion", in the language of the time, "founded on the providential justification of diversity."[15]

The issue of toleration then became a major theme in almost all of Mendelssohn's publications from that point onward. Negative attitudes to Jews and Judaism, even among his enlightened friends, blood-libel accusations in various forms throughout Europe, and widespread prejudices concerning their life and habits – all seemed to shake now his initial

---

[15] In this and many other respects, I have learned much from David Sorkin, *Moses Mendelssohn and the Religious Enlightenment*, London, 1996. For the quote see page 142.

faith in the victory of rational humanity. In fact, Lavater had turned his missionary zeal not only towards Mendelssohn. At some point, he also considered approaching Rousseau on this issue and later did in fact approach Goethe, who actually liked and respected him, but easily waved off his proselytizing efforts. Mendelssohn found it all very disturbing. Despite the fact that Bonnet himself and many of his enlightened acquaintances distanced themselves from Lavater both privately and publicly, Mendelssohn fell physically and mentally ill and consequently withdrew from much of his activities for years. Even in 1781, as he was reading Christian Willhelm Dohm's book on the "civil betterment of the Jews," written in response to his own instigation, he remained far from reassured and could not conceal his irritation.[16] An introduction he then wrote to a translation of the seventeenth-century English diplomat and author Menasse Ben-Israel, *Vindiciae Judaeorum*, served him as a platform on which to expose his aggravation. He admitted that Dohm did take an important step forward, especially in beholding "in man *man* only," as he then put it, but there were sections in Dohm's book that he felt compelled to reject. Most objectionable according to him was Dohm's description of contemporary Jewry. His assumptions regarding the Jews' sinister behavior and their presumably backward culture only served to recapitulate old prejudices, Mendelssohn felt. The notion that they ought to "improve" as a precondition for being granted civil equality was an affront to true Enlightenment. Granting them civil equality ought to be based on the principles of justice, he further insisted, and not be handed out as a prize for "good behavior."

Mendelssohn was becoming desperate. Despite all efforts, he felt, the Enlightenment had failed to free men from "barbarism," namely – in this case – from age-old Jew-hating. During the Middle Ages, their not being Christians was sufficient for pronouncing Jews "a useless burden on society," attaching to them "every possible horror and infamy," and subjecting them to the "contempt and abhorrence of the rest of mankind." Now, in the age of Enlightenment, Jews were being accused of being unfit for citizenship, for not sufficiently practicing the arts and sciences, and simply for not working in useful trades. "They tie our hands," Mendelssohn summarized, "and scold us for not making use of them," and, finally, he ironically added: "Reason and Humanity raise their voices in vain; for hoary Prejudice has completely lost its hearing."[17]

---

[16] See Christian Willhelm Dohm, *Über die bürgerliche Verbesserung der Juden*, Berlin and Stettin 1781–1783.
[17] All quotes are from Feiner, *Moses Mendelssohn*, 144.

In the end, Mendelssohn managed to revive, while others, who perhaps never hoped for so much, felt quite hopeful all along. To be sure, Dohm's book, reflecting a typical mix of enlightened thinking and bureaucratic Étatism, was mainly intended to reform the Prussian state. Nevertheless, it seemed to have carried a positive message for Jews as well as for those who supported the demand for granting them civil equality. In wide-ranging circles, it became ever clearer that toleration as such was not enough. It was often seen, indeed, and not only by such enthusiasts as Lavater, as no more than a tool for achieving conversion. Both Christian and Jewish voices demanded instead legal rights, a policy measure rather than an expectation of virtue. Surely, many still objected, both Jews, who feared the loss of communal privileges and the inroad of too many dangerous modern ideas, and Germans – old and new opponents of extending to Jews pronounced rights, manifesting their equality not only in a more or less restricted social sphere, but even within the overall reformed modern state as such.

Interestingly, it was Michaelis, the Göttingen theologian again, who voiced the strongest opposition to Dohm's proposals from the Christian side. In the aftermath of the controversy over his critique of Lessing's *The Jews*, Michaelis had seemed impressed by Mendelssohn's early philosophical work, and the two had enjoyed a friendly correspondence for several years. Now, once again, Michaelis' prior opposition to any kind of Jewish entry into German society, not to mention granting them equal rights, surfaced with a vengeance. Because of their religion, he wrote in reply to Dohm, Jews could never turn into reliable, loyal citizens. It was now above all their self-identification as a separate nation that stood in the way of their equal citizenship, he was quick to add.[18] Mendelssohn, going through Michaelis' objections to Dohm, felt that his late-life pessimism was being reaffirmed. Toleration was no doubt preached and professed by enlightened Christians – both Catholics and Protestants – but, since old prejudices were stronger, this turned out to be only a sham, he felt. No matter what the exact argument for achieving Jewish equality was, these prejudices proved stronger and ever more persistent.

To make things even worse, intolerance within the Jewish communities themselves meanwhile became a full-blown publicly debated issue. A number of Christian observers had noticed ongoing contemporary controversies within Jewry – in Prague, Hamburg, and especially in

---

[18] On Michaelis' life and work and especially on his comments with regard to contemporary Jewry, see Ofri Ilani, *In Search of the Hebrew People: Bible and Nation in the German Enlightenment*, Bloomington, IN, 2018, and Anna-Ruth Löwenbrück, *Judenfeindschaft im Zeitalter der Aufklärung: Eine Studie zur Vorgeschichte des modernen Antisemitismus am Beispiel des Göttinger Theologen und Orientalisten Johann David Michaelis*, Frankfurt am Main, 1995, 158f.

Berlin. Particularly embarrassing were disclosures that came from the satirical Deist August Cranz, he too a one-time friend of Mendelssohn. In a series of publications, Cranz demanded that his enlightened Jewish idol finally take a clear stand against intolerance among Jews; that he admit the problem existed within their own ranks and show that he was capable of distancing himself publicly from intolerance in this context as well.

Late in 1783, Mendelssohn could no longer evade a response to the renewed challenge. Once again, under pressure from others, he finally wrote and published what later became his most influential book, *Jerusalem, or on Religious Power and Judaism*. Defending his unshakable loyalty to Judaism, he was intent on showing that as a religion it was entirely compatible with Enlightenment, a fundamentally tolerant creed, stressing practical commandments and the historical tale of ancient Israel without introducing any dogma of faith. Despite appearances, he now claimed, Judaism represented the best of the Enlightenment. It embodied the spiritual ideals that a Christian enlightener ought to practice, not only proclaim: Rationality, Humanism, and Tolerance.

Few were convinced. After all, Mendelssohn himself was by then a veteran of many intra-Jewish battles, arguing against a number of community rabbis who showed no sign of tolerance towards deviating positions on various halachic issues and repeatedly threatened their opponents with excommunication. Toleration by no means characterized intra-Jewish discourse, he knew all too well, just as it had proven to be rare among Christians. The gap between ideals and reality was just as apparent with regard to and within Judaism as it was with regard to and within Christianity. Religious toleration was being discussed everywhere, as Mendelssohn correctly commented; but it was rarely practiced.

The deficit of toleration in the Enlightenment, especially of religious toleration, is not unknown. It was a topic of repeated exhortations since the late seventeenth century, when John Locke published his *Letter Concerning Toleration* in response to religious conflicts he had observed first in Holland, between Catholics and Calvinists, then in France after Louis XIV had revoked the Edict of Nantes, and of course in England between Catholics and Anglicans. Toleration remained on the agenda of the Enlightenment all over Europe, while the need to recapitulate the arguments supporting it was proof of the difficulty in its implementation. Finally, in Germany, where enlightened philosophy was especially entangled with arguments concerning religion, this theme gained particular significance. Usually, the Jews played a minor role in the relevant debates since the central conflicts were, indeed, the ones between Catholics and Protestants. Still, their case seemed to highlight the problem – from the margin to be sure, but with unique intensity. Old prejudices proved stronger than tolerant thinking, even in the case of outspoken defenders of the Enlightenment and even supporters of Jewish rights. Recapitulating what had for generations been considered the repugnant aspects of Jews and Jewish life was a routine matter, practiced by theologians of both Christian confessions and by many secular bureaucrats. The principle of toleration, even if accepted for issues arising between themselves, hardly applied to the Jews.

In the end, Mendelssohn had a moment of satisfaction. One of the main advocates of religious toleration in Germany was, indeed, his friend Lessing. His own past controversies with the church often involved matters of tolerance. In 1779, rounding up his thought on the matter, Lessing completed the manuscript of a verse-play entitled *Nathan der Weise*, premiered to great acclaim in Berlin, in 1783, a couple of years after the author's death. The play was set in twelfth-century Jerusalem, and its major figure was a wise old Jew who was unquestionably modeled upon Mendelssohn. Despite the fact that the two friends met only rarely during the last decade of Lessing's life, and although Lessing gave no sign of supporting Mendelssohn during the Lavater affair, he did seem to try to console his friend at this later date, as he was again under pressure in the aftermath of the Cranz affair.[19] On the stage, Nathan manages to send a message of toleration and bring Jews, Moslems, and Christians happily together. Still, in the end, while "everyone hugs one another," as we read in the original stage directions, Nathan stands alone, and as the participants in this tale turn out to belong to one happy family, Nathan remains the exception. He stands on his own, a tragic figure, perhaps even contrary to the intention of his benevolent literary creator.

---

[19] See Andree Michaelis-König, "Mendelssohn, Lavater, Lessing. Von Freundschaftskreisen und stützenden Netzwerken," in Lore Knapp (ed.), *Literarische Netzwerke im 18. Jahrhundert*, Bielefeld, 2019, 269–294.

2   Benevolent Autocracy

The concentration on Mendelssohn in the previous chapter brings to the fore a major difficulty in the handling of my topic. Naturally, individuals who document their life, leaving us written texts and a more or less complete private correspondence, are prime witnesses, both of their life and of their times. Mendelssohn is clearly such a prime witness. While there is more than one way of understanding even this singular tale and assuming we have understood him correctly, is he, being such an unusual personality, a reliable source for the position of his Jewish co-religionists? Can one deduce from his testimony a single "Jewish perspective" on German affairs during his lifetime? Was there ever such a single "Jewish perspective"? And if Mendelssohn represents, indeed, at least one such legitimate perspective, what were the views of other Jews at the same time, what were their own individual experiences and their own points of view?

To be sure, the majority of the Jews at the time, like the majority of all Germans, never heard of the "Enlightenment," nor did they care about its principles or vision. For Mendelssohn's religious brethren across Prussia and throughout the German lands, toleration was neither known as a concept, nor experienced as part of their daily life. Discrimination, on the other hand, was well known and easily perceived. It was interwoven into their life, an everyday occurrence.

The legal status of Jews in much of old Prussia was by then based on the Revised General Code of 1750, and the gradual relaxation of this strict code could not really have been felt before the late 1780s. During Mendelssohn's lifetime, the real turning point in this respect still lay far in the future, to be finally manifested in the emancipatory legislation of 1812. Meanwhile, Prussian Jews were being divided into five categories, as befits this highly bureaucratic state. The first and highest category included Jews holding *general privileges*, who could live anywhere they wished and could usually be employed in most vocations as long as they contributed handsomely to the state's coffer. By contrast, the last and lowest category included all who were *unprotected*. They needed permission for every change or move – personal, geographical, or vocational. All other Jews – those in between, so to speak – lived under various constraints and were expected to pay fees and duties to each and every authority they encountered.[1] Mendelssohn, to take this example again, was at first only temporarily admitted into Berlin. Later on, he had to wait almost a full year for permission to marry his chosen bride and bring her over from Hamburg, and, to the end, his *privileges* were limited and never extended to his family members. Meanwhile, during his many trips throughout Germany, he was only rarely exempt from paying the degrading *Leibzoll* (body-tax) and that too happened only upon special requests by his well-placed benefactors. Thus, despite repeated hymns of flattery to the gracious king in synagogues up and down the country, enlightened monarchy was for Mendelssohn, as well as for most other Jews, in and outside of Prussia, nothing but an empty phrase. One suspects that it was an empty phrase for most non-Jews too, of course. The bureaucracy's heavy hand was felt everywhere; its rule only became stricter and more effective as time went by.

Gradually, though, beginning in the mid 1780s, the atmosphere began to change. By 1781, as we saw, Christian Wilhelm Dohm's book *On the Civil Betterment of the Jews* was being read and discussed even beyond the Prussian borders, especially in Austria and in France. Listing the numerous presumed flaws of the Jews, Dohm nevertheless concluded that "[t]he Jew is yet more a Man than a Jew." He seemed even willing to acknowledge that those typical character flaws were the result of the Jews' age-old subjugation, partly – though by no means wholly – balanced out by their proven talents, and in any case "improvable" by proper education. Mendelssohn was not convinced, but many – including many contemporary Jews – were. It is true: Dohm did not call for a radical social or political change. After all, his was the voice of the Prussian establishment, seeking ways of strengthening the state by making it more inclusive and even-handed, forever prospering under its royal sovereign. Likewise, the new Edicts of Toleration, enacted at about the same time by Kaiser Joseph II, head both of the Habsburg Monarchy and of the then still functioning Holy Roman Empire, were only timid steps forward. The particular edict concerning the Jews opened with a declaration that "We have no intention of principally changing the limits of toleration between Christians and Jews," and by clearly stating that the new measure ought *not* to be used for abolishing the social boundaries separating them.[2] Still, the fact that such

---

[1] The best summary of this legal situation in Germany as a whole is Stefi Jersch-Wenzel, "Legal Status and Emancipation," in Michael A. Meyer (ed.), *German-Jewish History in Modern Times*, New York, 1997, Vol. II, 7–49.
[2] See Josef Karniel, *Die Toleranzpolitik Kaiser Josephs II.*, Stuttgart, 1986.

a law was now being considered and implemented was a hopeful sign. Soon, the French Revolution radicalized the situation in this as in all other spheres of life and then, somewhat belatedly, took on the task of making Jews full and equal citizens.

In fact, religious toleration constituted a challenge for the *French* Enlightenment no less than for the *German Aufklärung*.[3] Voltaire's contempt for the Jews – biblical as well as contemporary – had been well noted at the time. Only the revolution itself brought *Radical Enlightenment* to the fore, to use Jonathan Israel's fitting term. On January 28, 1790, the so-called Portuguese Jews in France were granted full civil rights, and on September 27, 1791, the French National Assembly decreed that all Jewish individuals who had taken the civic oath were thus committed "to fulfill all the duties that the constitution impose[d] upon them," having access to the various advantages it ensured as well. It had been on a somewhat earlier occasion that Count Clermont-Tonnerre declared in the Assembly that "We must refuse everything to the Jews as a nation and accord them everything as individuals,"[4] and this remained the basis of Jewish emancipation everywhere in the years to come, in Germany no less than in France. Individual rights were granted; community rights were at least restricted.

Jewish reactions, first to the careful efforts at reforming them and then to the revolutionary acts of accepting them, were understandably varied. Some tended to oppose change in whatever form. The majority, however, accepted – often with enthusiasm – what were by then the terms of a new contract, so to speak, between them and the Christian state that had hosted them for so long. Moreover, in many cases this strengthened from the *outside* the Jews' own efforts at reforming Judaism and at entering non-Jewish society, coming from the *inside*.

Mendelssohn did not live to see all that. He died in 1786, just as things began to change both in Prussia and elsewhere in Germany. As Napoleon and his troops crossed the Rhine, the ground was set for welcoming his imposed, revolutionary legal order, including its new measures with respect to the Jews. Their equal rights were then quickly introduced in the areas annexed or reconstituted by the French, such as the Kingdom of Westphalia, or only partially and to varying degrees in other occupied areas of Germany. Even though *some* restrictions on *some* Jews were re-introduced by Napoleon himself following an edict of 1808

---

[3] See the comparative discussion in David Sorkin, *The Religious Enlightenment: Protestants, Jews and Catholics from London to Vienna*, Princeton, NJ, 2011.

[4] For this chapter in French-Jewish history, see Ronald Schechter, *Obstinate Hebrews: Representations of Jews in France 1715–1815*, Berkeley, CA and Los Angeles, CA, 2003, especially pages 151–156.

known as the *décret infâme*, the march of emancipation, both in France and in Germany, did not come to a halt.

In Westphalia, in fact, local Jews embraced far-reaching communal reorganization and even attempted to modernize their religious life. Soon, too, the Duchy of Baden – not directly ruled by the French – likewise tried to introduce the principle of equal rights, albeit with some remaining restrictions and not without stressing the need to first "improve" the Jews and turn them into "useful" citizens. In Bavaria, a gradual revocation of various restrictions upon the Jews, including an end to the hated *Leibzoll* in 1808, culminated in the edict of 1813, acknowledging the principle of equal rights while upholding some older prohibitions and occasionally imposing new ones.

Achieving the right mixture of old and new constitutional arrangements with regard to the Jews proved particularly difficult in the city of Frankfurt am Main. There, a large Jewish community had previously enjoyed the principled protection of the Kaiser and the practical goodwill of the city council. Still, Jews were allowed to reside in town only within the limits of a narrow *Judengasse* and, while fulfilling various commercial functions, had always lived under burdensome and humiliating constraints up until 1806. In the past, the few privileges granted them in return for large payments to city authorities had to be repeatedly negotiated. And then, with the arrival of the French, while changes in the status of the city itself initially brought about hardly any improvement for the Jews, later on, as all other subjects were granted full civil rights, these were conferred upon the Jews, too. To be sure, all this occurred not without prolonged negotiations and – again – not without the payment of large sums of money on the part of the Jews. But in any case, as soon as the French had been defeated, the city took every possible measure to revoke Jewish rights – one by one.[5]

Developments in the three Hanseatic northern towns ran along similar lines. A combination of French intervention and the ever larger sums of money paid by local Jews enabled the latter to improve their status. In Hamburg, they managed to enjoy a short period of full equality. In Lübeck, they were even granted the right to buy an urban lot and build a synagogue. And finally in Bremen, where no Jew had previously been allowed to settle at all, local authorities were forced to accept a few Jewish families during the French occupation, though with the retreat of the French armies the city council, supported by the guilds and a number of

---

[5] See Rachel Heuberger and Helga Krohn, *Hinaus aus dem Ghetto: Juden in Frankfurt am Main 1800–1950*, Frankfurt am Main, 1988.

local dignitaries, managed to revoke all Jewish rights. While Enlightenment and Revolution somehow coexisted for a while with old forms of petitioning and bribery of officials in the interest of the Jews, the Germany of the post-Napoleonic times seemed unresponsive to both.

The complexity of the situation is well exemplified by the story of emancipation in Prussia, where Jews were, in fact, the first to be officially made citizens rather than subjects. "Those who now reside in our state, with general privileges, patents of naturalization, protection papers, and concessions, they and their families are to be considered as *Einländer* and Prussian citizens," read the law of 1812 concerning Jewish status. Further down in Paragraph 7, it was also explicitly stated that as such they ought to enjoy the same "civil rights and civil liberties" as the Christians. This law, however, was characterized by a mixture of principled statements and concrete instructions, intent on achieving Jewish "improvement" before further "concessions" were to be applied. That not all was well even with this piece of legislation is clear from the fact that the relevant law encompassed some thirty-nine paragraphs, in contrast with the clear, simple, one-sentence-long French emancipatory edict or the equally straightforward legal measures that were intended to conclude the process of emancipation in Germany during the revolution of 1848.[6]

Still, it was a remarkable achievement. After all, it was the same bureaucracy that had previously mounted restriction upon restriction on the Jews everywhere across the land that now figured as the scion of progressive, even enlightened reform. In view of the French show of success, first in war but then – no less strikingly – in forging a united, powerful nation of equal citizens, ready and willing to join forces in fighting for their fatherland, the need for fundamental renewal of Prussia, and if possible even of the entire German system of government, seemed more urgent than ever. Even contemporaries diagnosed this bundle of reforms, initiated by the highest echelons of government and led by the duo Karl Freiherr vom Stein and Carl August Freiherr von Hardenberg, as a significant turning point. It was a *revolution from above*, initially directed at modernizing the ruling bureaucracy itself and then reaching outwardly, to achieve a restructuring of the entire ruling system. The independent and semi-independent towns up and down the country received new constitutions; the countryside and agricultural land experienced the so-called peasants' liberation, limited as it finally was in

---

[6] For Prussia, the indispensable source is still Ismar Freund, *Die Emanzipation der Juden in Preußen*, 2 vols. Berlin, 1912. For more recent accounts, see Irene Diekmann, *Das Emanzipationsedikt von 1812 in Preußen: Der lange Weg der Juden zu "Einländern" und "preußischen Staatsbürgern,"* Berlin, 2013, and Marion Schulte, *Über die bürgerlichen Verhältnisse der Juden in Preußen*, Berlin, 2014.

concrete terms; some components of economic freedom were enacted, later to be complemented with tax reforms and an overall financial modernization. Eventually, one also took on the reform of the antiquated Prussian army and a reconstruction of the educational system – masterly carried out by Wilhelm von Humboldt and culminating in the establishment of the new University of Berlin. It was he, indeed, who initiated the changing legal status of the Jews, too.

The entire country felt the shock waves of reform. It was all the more felt since it had often been carried out against the opposition of the monarch and large sections of the one-time unconditional rulers of the land – the Junker aristocracy. In the case of reforming the status of the Jews, however, opposition came from below too. Jews were everywhere emancipated against a chorus of objections from the newly enfranchised local citizenry; the local bureaucracies piled up endless objections and half-hearted reforms often meant very little in practical terms. In Saxony, which preserved much of its independence during the Napoleonic era, little had been changed in respect of the Jews. Elsewhere, some restrictions remained in force even when and while far-reaching reforms were being introduced. In Prussia, but also in Bavaria or in Mecklenburg-Schwerin, Jews were explicitly disqualified from taking on state offices, and in Austria, neither the famous *Toleranzpatent* nor the highfaluting talk about equality in various other contexts did much to change their actual position. Signs that a reversal of emancipatory legislation was everywhere a distinct possibility could not be mistaken.

As soon as Napoleon seemed to be in retreat, both Jews and non-Jews entered a phase of intense activity. The former were determined to uphold their newly won rights, while among others the drive for repeal gained ever sharper momentum. Following a period of enthusiasm at the outset of the revolution in France, a prolonged military occupation gradually brought about opposition to everything French throughout the German lands. The move from cosmopolitan and humanitarian premises back to old Christian values and then to new national principles was felt everywhere. It clearly threatened to affect the fate of the Jews. And then, when Napoleon's defeat was sealed, the controversy concerning their status – along with many other unsettled issues – was brought before the Congress of Vienna, to be resettled there.[7]

---

[7] Much of this chapter relies on my article "Bitten und Streiten: Die Emanzipation der Juden auf dem Wiener Kongress," in Thomas Just, Wolfgang Maderthaner, and Helene Maimann (eds.), *Der Wiener Kongress: Die Erfindung Europas*, Vienna, 2014, 236–253.

Among the many delegates to this impressive all-European Congress in Vienna, Jewish representatives began to arrive, too. Being refused a full hearing in their own home towns and failing to organize a joint Jewish delegation, only a number of delegates from Frankfurt and then a few individuals from the northern Hanseatic towns reached Vienna on time for the opening events. In fact, their presence in town had initially been considered illegal, and the president of the city police had at first insisted on expelling them immediately. However, the delegates seemed to have had sufficient contacts with high-ranking personalities and various officials in town, some even with Metternich himself, and so they were finally allowed to enter and to stay indefinitely – or at least for as long as the congress was in session.[8]

There is no need to provide a full account of the controversy over Jewish rights at the Congress of Vienna and the zigzag fortunes of this matter there. It all ran parallel to the deliberations over other issues, usually of presumably far greater weight as far as the gathering representatives of the European powers in Vienna were concerned. But, while this seemed no doubt a minor point on their agenda, it brought forth – directly and indirectly – some interesting and principled issues.

To begin with, Jewish interests were taken up by a mixture of individuals using various tactics, sometimes applied for conflicting purposes. Prominent throughout were the men from Frankfurt, including Jacob Baruch, a wealthy merchant with worldly experience and aristocratic contacts, who was later to be known as Ludwig Börne's father. Together with his equally well-placed colleagues, the Frankfurt delegation insisted on representing only the Frankfurt community, while the men from the northern cities took a more comprehensive approach and presumed to be speaking for German Jewry as a whole. In fact, it was the small Lübeck community that had intended to organize a combined Jewish delegation from the outset. Accordingly, it had first turned to David Friedländer in Berlin, a disciple and colleague of Mendelssohn, with strong ties to well-known Jews in Hamburg and elsewhere, but these feelings quickly came to naught. The three northern cities then compromised on sending a single delegate, Dr. Carl August Buchholz – a non-Jewish advocate, who consistently showed interest in all matters Jewish. An opponent of the French rule from the start, Buchholz was a typical national-liberal. He took it upon himself to represent the Jews in Germany, according to his conception of a single Germany and in line with his liberal trust in equal civil rights.

---

[8] To this day, the best description of the handling of the Jewish issue in the Congress of Vienna is Salo Baron, *Die Judenfrage auf dem Wiener Kongress*, Vienna and Berlin, 1920.

In fact, the contrasting views as to the desirable constitution for the new German Confederation proved as important for deliberating the Jewish case as the contrasting views concerning their civil rights. And approaching the matter as a local affair had the advantage of arguing a more limited case, independent of more far-reaching decisions concerning Germany, acceptable to men of various political and ideological creeds. It opened up the possibility of achieving special favors in the spirit of previous eras, depending – in the best case – on the good will of local sovereigns and – in the worst case – on the familiar effect of ever larger sums of donations. By contrast, approaching the matter as an all-German project assumed the establishment of a joint German authority that would supervise the overall situation and act, partially at least, upon modern, liberal principles. This dualism was central to all the intra-German deliberations in the Congress of Vienna and influenced in its turn the handling of the specific Jewish case.

In this context, there was yet a third party playing a role upon this stage, namely the wealthy upper crust of Viennese Jewry, who often served as hosts to the rich and mighty and financed many of the social events during the deliberations of the Congress. Foremost among these was the Arnstein–Eskeles circle, led by Nathan Adam Freiherr von Arnstein, who had been ennobled in 1795, surrounded by his wife and two daughters, all of great charm and *Bildung*. Arnstein's partner and son-in-law Bernhard Eskeles was the most outstanding figure in this circle. He was a man of many talents and by then chief financial adviser to the crown and a *Ritter von*, of course, as well. With the single exception of the monarch himself, everyone enjoyed the hospitality of these men: the Prussian princes on a mission to Vienna and many other German delegates of the highest ranking, the various Russian diplomats, Lord Wellington and his entourage, cardinals and ambassadors, Austrian and other generals, all topped by an assortment of writers and intellectuals – local and international. Metternich, who apparently was not among this particular lot – though, curiously, his father was – had instead contacts with other Jewish magnates, especially with Leopold Edler von Herz, a financial aid to Austria during the latter part of the war against Napoleon and his own trusted associate. The Austrian foreign minister was a frequent guest, bringing with him some of the most illustrious and powerful visitors in town.

These wealthy members of the elite shared a long tradition of representing Jewish interests, but seemed indifferent to the issue of civil equality. This, after all, hardly concerned them. Thus, the particular case of Jewish equality in the Habsburg monarchy as well as in other parts of the old Reich and now also in the new Confederation had to be taken over by others, usually by equally or almost equally rich Jews, coming from elsewhere and more attentive to the needs of their less fortunate co-religionists. Simon von Lämel and Lazar Auspitz, both ennobled and involved in commercial matters of all kinds, especially in supporting the Austrian state, came from Bohemia and Moravia in order to observe developments in Vienna and work for Jewish interests wherever and whenever possible. These, like the wealthy Viennese elite, were men who belonged to the older tradition of Jewish politics, experts in lobbying for their co-religionists. They were at first responsible for a handed-in *Bittschrift* (petition), in which Jewish achievements, loyalty, sacrifice, and services were recalled as reasons for granting them equal rights. Unsurprisingly, in this case too, *they* were particularly concerned with rights in the areas of commence and property ownership, and that too only for Jews of the old Reich and not for those living in Hungary, for instance, or in Galicia. Eventually, no action followed upon the handing over of this petition and the respectable petitioners were forced to retreat shamefacedly. They must have realized by then that their political style had become obsolete and that it was no longer relevant for the purpose at hand.

That such old-fashion tactics were no longer useful could be seen by reviewing the tragicomic epilogue to this part of the story. It was apparently Simon von Lämel that decided to try yet another old-style tactic: bribery. He took it upon himself to offer his thanks to Wilhelm von Humboldt for the latter's continuous support of the Jewish cause, and Humboldt describes this episode in a letter to his wife, written June 4, 1815: "Yesterday came the old man again, thanking me endlessly and offering as gift three rings, emeralds with large brilliant-cut diamonds and a note explaining that if I did not want them, I could count on more than 4000 Dukats saved for me in his coffers."[9] Humboldt had refused the offer, as he rather proudly reported to his wife. But, while his integrity is clearly apparent here, it was the futility of von Lämel's gesture, its inappropriateness, and its anachronism that are so evident in this affair. The men who represented the Jews in Vienna were not always aware of the changing times. This was at least one reason why they eventually remained irrelevant to the deliberations, despite all their efforts.

The matter was now taken up by others. While Jewish pressure through one channel or another may have forced the issue on the decision-makers in Vienna, it was kept for so long on their agenda because some of the most important figures at the Congress hoped that at least this relatively

---

[9] *Wilhelm und Caroline von Humboldt in ihren Briefen*, Berlin, 1915, Vol. IV, 565.

side issue could finally be decided on an all-German level basis and not left once again to local sovereigns or to locally elected bodies. Jewish emancipation, not too crucial in itself for most Germans perhaps, could surely be seen as a test case, and the failure to decide upon it manifested the fundamental division on a great many other issues dealt with in the Congress. Thus, the leading Prussian and Austrian statesmen seemed to have often been here too on the same side, while representatives of the smaller German states took the opposite one. After all, the two major German powers wished to provide for as tight a bond among all German states as possible in the future confederation planned at Vienna. This meant, as far as they were concerned, exerting more influence on all matters of joint German interests, and it could have likewise offered a way of positively responding to some popular demands along national-liberal lines as well. By contrast, Bavaria and Württemberg, for instance, which had become much larger under Napoleon – both geographically and demographically – were now more interested in upholding and strengthening their own sovereignty and in handing over as little power as possible to the planned federal body. Under the circumstances, their representatives in Vienna had to be particularly attuned to voices from their constituencies and, with regard to the Jews, these usually demanded an immediate return to pre-revolutionary days and opposed emancipation. In the end, one continued to discuss the matter as long as the Prussian and Austrian delegates saw in it a matter of principle, and it was finally dropped when they lost interest in the constant haggling with the smaller states over details or wording and began to sense that the wind in their own countries, too, was now blowing in a different direction.

Support for the Jewish cause thus sometimes came from the most unexpected quarters and was being expressed in the most unexpected forms. At this point, Wilhelm von Humboldt's principled promotion of legal equality among all enfranchised citizens, including the Jews, came as no surprise. The young Humboldt had for a long time had many personal contacts with the Jewish elite of Berlin. He had good knowledge of the Jewish situation in Prussia, writes historian Salo Baron, "as only a few Christians of his time had."[10] Nonetheless, it was only much later, once he had become head of the Section for Religious Affairs and Education in the Prussian government, that he had an opportunity to put together his thoughts on this matter. In an extensive memorandum, he then expressed his astonishment at the long history of Jewish discrimination and called for the introduction of "full and unrestricted equal rights" for all Prussian Jews, as the only way of correcting the situation in ways that would be

---

[10] Baron, *Die Judenfrage*, 82.

"just," "prudent," and "consequent," as he then put it.[11] Although education and, indeed, *Bildung* were so central to his overall humanistic position, in this case he did not put the emphasis on the demand for so-called Jewish "betterment," arguing instead that, since the state is not an educational institution but a legal body, Jewish emancipation should follow immediately, irrespective of any educational measures, as a matter of pure legal principle. It had to be applied everywhere and without delay, he believed, and, as an all-German issue, it had to be settled for the German Bund as a whole. Somewhat later, however, in a letter to his wife from Vienna, explaining his insistence on finding a just solution to the newly defined Jewish question, he added that he was insisting upon this measure being applied everywhere in Germany not on grounds of some liberal principle, but lest all Jews would otherwise now be "streaming towards us."[12]

As Humboldt was an outspoken supporter of a tight all-German constitution, the initial draft laid down by him foresaw no reference to religious diversity in it and the formulation "[e]very subject of the Bund will be granted full civil rights" was sufficient as far as he was concerned. This formulation would have made a separate discussion concerning the status of the Jews superfluous, but by then, while Metternich was immediately prepared to accept this solution, representatives of the various middle-sized German states fiercely objected. The matter was left unresolved for many months, and with time, while agreement on other points in the constitutional draft became ever more difficult to achieve too, Humboldt was finally ready to compromise on this issue. By the beginning of April 1815, in a last effort to avoid mentioning religious diversity in the constitution, he was ready to include a promise of "uninhibited religious practice" for all citizens of the Bund, and, when even this failed to win sufficient support, he seemed to have given up.

By that time, because of the major territorial controversies between Prussia and Austria, it was becoming increasingly more difficult to uphold the spirit of cooperation between the two German superpowers with regard to internal German affairs, too. And by the summer of 1815, the deliberations on these matters, as against the all-important foreign ones, were also placed under an increasing pressure of time. One had to quickly reach an agreement if the establishment of the Bund were to gain international legitimacy at all through being a part of the so-called Viennese Acts. In view of the consistent opposition from several members of the

---

[11] The text of this memorandum can be found in Tilman Borsche, *Wilhelm von Humboldt*, Munich, 1990, 51–54.
[12] Cited in Baron, *Die Judenfrage*, 173–174.

future Bund to the introduction of Jewish equality as a principle of the new constitution, Humboldt could only conclude that there was apparently no way of achieving it at the present moment. Even the rights granted to Jews under the French occupation, he now realized, could not be upheld, nor could the rather incomplete Prussian legal compromise be agreed upon as a model for future legislation. As one formulation after another was watered down in the relevant committee deliberations, Humboldt lost ever more ground. The Jewish issue, he discovered, was a serious obstacle to a final agreement among the German states. It had to be abandoned, or at least postponed.

Humboldt was surely seen as a liberal among his governmental and administrative colleagues, despite the fact that he had for a long time been serving an authoritarian monarch, ruling over a strictly autocratic state. His immediate superior in Vienna, however, the Prussian *Staatskanzler* Hardenberg, could hardly be suspected of similar liberal inclinations, despite his patriarchal humanism and, indeed, his prolonged efforts at reform in the service of the crown. Unexpectedly, however, his record on the issue of Jewish emancipation was quite impressive. To begin with, his support of the emancipatory legislation of 1812 had by then become well known, and it had been consistently upheld by him despite the stark opposition from other peers of the lands. At the time, Friedrich August Ludwig von der Marwitz, for instance, attacked Hardenberg for what he saw as turning "our old, respectable Brandenburg-Prussia" into "a newly fashioned 'Judenstaat'"; and vom Stein, his predecessor at the head of the Prussian government and his associate in introducing many other reforms, repeatedly expressed his views concerning "the perniciousness of the Jewish horde" and the need to restrain their malicious influence.[13] In Vienna, to be sure, Hardenberg always had Humboldt on his side, but in the end he himself took a middle-of-the-road position on the Jewish question. Having meanwhile been convinced of Jewish loyalty and usefulness during the Wars of Liberation, he settled on upholding the concept of "Betterment," in contradistinction to Humboldt, but still consistently supported legal emancipation in collaboration with him.

On January 4, 1815, in the midst of the toughest conflict among the great powers with regard to the so-called Polish–Saxon question, Hardenberg found time to approach the Prussian emissary in Hamburg, clearly stating his position on the matter of revoking Jewish rights in that city: "Prussia cannot remain indifferent to the fate of the Jews in the other

---

[13] Cited from Karl Freiherr vom Stein, *Briefe und amtliche Schriften*, Stuttgart 1983, Vol. V, 512, by Francis L. Carsten, *Geschichte der preußischen Junker*, Frankfurt am Main, 1988, 90.

provinces and cities of northern Germany," he explained. One could not "improve" them by granting equal rights while discrimination and humiliation continued unabated. Impressed by the participation of the Jews – men *and* women, as he stressed – in the last war, he voiced his conviction that emancipation would turn them into useful citizens and that their dynamism would eventually benefit the Christian population too, adding to the wealth of the trading city in the north.[14]

It was apparently possible to support equal rights for the Jews with a minimum of reference to liberal high principles. Hardenberg insists on the upholding of civil rights for Jews, since "they have the right to demand it '*als Menschen*,'" (as people) and he attacks in no uncertain terms the prejudices against them. But the crux of his argument was his view of Prussia's *raison d'état* and his conception of the interdependent interests of the various German states, particularly in the north. Later on, when Jewish interests no longer corresponded to these interests, or even collided with them, he – like Humboldt – found that it was necessary to compromise on this issue, giving up the argument concerning the fate of the Jews in Germany.

Prince Metternich's attitude in this regard seems at first sight to be even less consistent with his image in much of modern historiography.[15] Metternich was clearly no liberal, nor was he known to be a man of reform. However, during the Congress of Vienna, he proved a consistent supporter of Jewish rights. Throughout the deliberations, Metternich had been involved in every detail and commented on every draft concerning the Jewish issue, just as he did, in fact, with regard to every matter dealt with there and then. For him, as for the Prussian delegates to the congress, the negotiations regarding the establishment of a new German Bund were of paramount importance. Like Hardenberg, he too insisted that the extension of equal rights to the Jews ought to be seen within this context and eventually solved on a unitary basis, for Germany as a whole. But this only partially explains his view on the matter. Like Humboldt and Hardenberg, Metternich too was sensitive to the humanitarian aspect of Jewish emancipation and felt that particularly in this case one had to rectify a long-lasting injustice. From his position of authority and his overall *Weltanschauung*, he took a moral stand on this matter – openly and emphatically.

---

[14] Quoted in Hans-Werner Hahn, "Judenemanzipation in der Reformzeit," in Thomas Stamm Kuhlmann (ed.), *"Freier Gebrauch der Kräfte": Eine Bestandsaufnahme der Hardenberg-Forschung*, Munich, 2001, 141–162, on page 141.

[15] For an unconventional but convincing view of Metternich, see Wolfram Siemann, *Metternich: Strategist and Visionary*, Cambridge, MA, 2019. Siemann, however, does not refer to the Jewish affairs discussed here.

Some three weeks after Hardenberg, Metternich too reacts to the evolving situation with regard to Jewish rights in the three northern hanseatic towns. This is what he writes to his business representative in Hamburg, on January 26, 1815: "Since that moment, when the Jewish faithful have truly expected that the Congress assembled here would rule upon their situation according to Liberal principles, I could not remain indifferent to the rumors about the oppression suffered by the Jewish inhabitants of Hamburg, Bremen, and Lübeck. I feel myself especially called upon to be involved in their fate," he added, "since their status in the Austrian monarchy and in a number of other German states had in fact already been decided upon in keeping with the demands of the time, of humanity, and of a paternal ruling system they had always enjoyed." Mistreating the Jews elsewhere, he wrote in closing, would have a deleterious effect on Jews living "under the protective scepter of Austria", and this clearly applied to the affairs of the three northern towns as well.[16]

The passage quoted above presents a Metternich that is little known to later generations. But the epilogue to this episode is perhaps even more telling. It seems that the two most influential German politicians at the time, representing the two German superpowers, Hardenberg and Metternich, even while bringing their full weight to bear on some of the much smaller and weaker political units in Germany, achieved in the end almost nothing. In Lübeck and in Hamburg, decisions on the Jewish issue were, indeed, postponed. The Bremen authorities, insisting on the expulsion of the newly settled Jews from their town, finally agreed to grant a short provisorium. But, considering the heavy artillery that was used in order to prevent a total reversal of the Jewish situation in these three cities, the results were meager indeed.

Meanwhile, in the Congress itself, things were moving from bad to worse, and here too the pressure from the highest echelons seemed to have had little effect. Negotiations concerning the paragraph dealing with Jews in the draft constitution of the new Bund dragged on for weeks, and the regulations to be included in it were made ever less concrete and less binding. On June 1, 1815, a formulation acceptable to all was finally found. In the first half of the relevant article it was stated that the matter of Jewish rights would be subject to future deliberations by the confederal assembly to be convened in Frankfurt and that it would there be clarified "how the civil betterment of believers in the Jewish religion in Germany would be most effectively achieved, and how they could be granted equal

---

[16] Quoting this letter, Baron cites some handwritten comments by Metternich which he found in the Austrian Staatsarchiv. See Baron, *Die Judenfrage*, 92–93.

civil rights as well as be subjected to all civil duties, everywhere in all the States of the Bund."[17] Furthermore, in the second half of the same paragraph, it was added that rights already acquired by Jews "*in* single states of the Bund" would be upheld until such deliberations took place. Thus, while all the elements of the pre-revolutionary discourse concerning Jewish emancipation resurfaced here, the ground for a return to older restrictions was likewise prepared. Finally, the closing sentence was construed to order the upholding of prior legislation enacted "*by* the states," presumably prior to the introduction of other regulations by the French occupiers "in" them. In the confusion of the closing days of the Congress, not everyone noticed the change from "*in*" to "*by*" in this sentence, though at the same time everyone could observe the failure of the two German superpowers to impose their view regarding the character of the future Bund upon the medium-sized and small states soon to be included within it.

Disappointment, perhaps even frustration, drove the entire top leadership in Germany to ever more reactionary steps. Everywhere, in fact, the old aristocracy reorganized its members and consistently opposed all liberal demands. Especially in Austria, modernization was blocked by conservatives, while particularism with all its ills – especially among the smaller German states, but also in Prussia – grew ever stronger. It became quite impossible to enact further reforms, while, in south-western Germany and sometimes in Prussia too, a few of the reforms, such as the freedom of occupational choice, were wholly preserved and others, such as the peasants' liberation, remained a torso. The window of opportunity for emancipatory, liberal reforms on an all-German scale – for Jews most particularly, but by no means only for them – was for now shut. Issues that were referred by the Congress to be further handled by the assembly of the Bund, such as some common provisions of defense, a variety of economic policies, and many more – including the issue of Jewish emancipation – were hardly touched. In a letter to his wife, Humboldt wrote that all this was merely "a shadow" of what he had hoped for. Not in vain was the confederation identified with reaction in the eyes of so many liberals. Reformers came under pressure now both from a strengthened aristocratic opposition and from widespread popular protest. Particularly in Prussia, the central government could not overrule local objections, and its further reform efforts were unevenly continued.[18] Provinces in the east, where previous reforms could not be instituted even

---

[17] Baron, *Die Judenfrage*, 152.
[18] The classic description of this ambivalent development in Prussia is surely Reinhart Koselleck, *Preußen zwischen Reform und Revolution*, Stuttgart, 1967.

previously, were most particularly disadvantaged. The efforts at changing the status of the Jews in these provinces miscarried, and an all-German solution could not be applied. Even an all-Prussian solution had to be postponed. The legal situation of the Jews in the years to come was evidently paradigmatic; it manifested the weaknesses of the domestic solutions arrived at in the Congress of Vienna and indicated the difficulties that would be faced by states and society in the decades ahead.

3 The Half-Open Society

The legal arrangements agreed upon in Vienna with regard to the Jews were only one side of the picture. Only a few Jews and perhaps even fewer non-Jews were by then aware of the intricate maneuvering that had taken place there, as one argued the pros and cons of granting civil rights to all. Most, however, were well aware of the repeal – in full or in part – of the legal arrangements imposed by the French and of the governments' failure to continue carrying out this – though by no means only this – reform and bring it to a conclusion. These reforms were all planned as steps on the road to the construction of modern German states, perhaps even leading to the construction of a single modern national state, fully and truly replacing the old Holy Roman Empire.

By then, that part of Germany directly ruled by and from Vienna had in fact failed to introduce *any* reform. After 1815, it was once again tightly in the hands of a reactionary aristocracy, and the option of radical change seemed more distant than ever. Even Metternich's tactical wisdom and his long political experience did not suffice to overcome this aristocratic hold on power. At the same time, however, under the impact of its humiliating defeats by Napoleon's army in 1806–1807, Prussia did manage to draw some lessons from its vulnerability and to introduce a number of important reforms, especially by modernizing its ruling bureaucracy – local and central, civil and military. While this bureaucracy soon developed into an actively reforming body of the state financial, military, agrarian, and educational systems, opposition both within and from without did not always allow the reforms to be fully accomplished or successfully implemented. Still, it was possible to see in them, considered as a whole, a veritable move towards modernity.[1]

As mentioned in the previous chapter, a bill making the Jews in the various Prussian territories full and equal citizens was finally enacted on

---

[1] See the details for the Prussian Reform Era in Christopher Clark, *Iron Kingdom: The Rise and Fall of Prussia, 1600–1947*, Cambridge, MA, 2006, Chapter 10, 312–344, and on further reforms passim in Chapter 12, especially pages 408–427.

March 11, 1812. And, following years of gradual easing of the restrictions upon the Jews, this bill was conceived as part of the overall reform process, crowning all previous efforts. In the end, however, it too – like other reforms – remained a torso. Typically, while the bill abolished some *old* restrictive measures, it strengthened *others* and opened the door for the introduction of new limitations at a later stage. The legal doors, so to speak, leading to full emancipation remained half open. As it turned out, even Jewish volunteers' enlistment in the so-called War of Liberation did not extend measurably their options for entry into Prussian society and, in the aftermath of the Congress of Vienna, in an increasingly conservative atmosphere, it became ever more difficult to achieve further formal changes, though some informal ones were by no means entirely impossible.

At the same time, in the "Third Germany" – though conditions differed greatly among the various middle-sized and small states – a measure of constitutionalism seemed to be gradually replacing absolutism, and far-reaching reforms were gradually being enacted by the established parliamentary institutions. After 1815, the newly consolidated states in this region continued to reinforce their sovereignty and buttress their relative independence from and within the German Bund. They also experimented with extending Jewish rights. Thus, while old prohibitions on Jewish residence and limitations on the choices of occupation available to Jews remained in force, some further emancipatory legal measures were cautiously introduced, and not only the ones dealing with Jews. In Baden, for instance, as progress in the matter of equal state citizenship had been achieved, local and urban prohibitions of all sorts remained in force. In Bavaria too, while the state parliament debated emancipatory legislation, the old "Jewish list" (*Judenmatrikel*), entailing strict bureaucratic monitoring of the Jews, their families, and their occupations throughout the land, was merely refreshed, adding new measures intent upon pressing the Jews to assimilate. And finally, in Prussia, the new legislation failed to apply to a great many Jews who lived in its newly acquired provinces, especially in Posen, while numerous restrictive measures were still applicable even in the old territories. On the whole, all central governments were now forced to maneuver – on this issue as on many others – between their own modernizing ambitions and opposition from the aristocracy and some local activists, often supported by large sections of the populace.

In the meantime, no one could mistake the hostile atmosphere that surrounded the Jews and became ever more threatening. It had already been the case in the years just *before* the Congress of Vienna too, and despite the pressure of the French, Jews – everywhere in Germany – must have later felt rejected even more intensely than before. Perhaps the

Enlightenment was, indeed, not what a man like Mendelssohn had hoped for, but there had surely been some positive signs associated with it. The last decade of the eighteenth century and the beginning of the nineteenth century were, after all, the years of the Jewish Salonnières both in Vienna and in Berlin. The entire urban elite of the two capital cities – the rich, the educated, and the politically influential – were happy to meet at the more or less elegant salons of a few energetic Jewish hostesses. This was a joint affair of Jews and Christians, aristocrats and bourgeois, men and women. They all met at the modest salon of Rahel Levin, later Varnhagen, or in the pretty rooms of Henriette Herz, whose husband – a student of Kant and a well-known physician – held lecture series on scientific themes and was a gracious host in his own right. Further south, the Viennese Jewish hostesses, usually richer and grander, sometimes even played some role in politics, as during the all-European Congress of Vienna. But all that was relevant only for the life of a tiny upper crust and eventually proved to be a passing matter. Just as the court Jews of the previous century did not really herald a new era, the famous Salonnières, too, did nothing of the sort. Their success may have signaled Jewish acculturation on a somewhat greater scale than in Mendelssohn's days and perhaps also a hesitant opening of the general German upper-class circles in urban central Europe to individual Jews, who were by then seen as "sufficiently acculturated." It may even have indicated an attempt to overcome old prejudices among members of that elite, perhaps somewhat reducing its sense of Christian exclusivity – but no more.

Then, with the surge of anti-French feelings and the growth of national consciousness, together with the rise of a new religiosity and of some cultural and literary romantic notions, it seemed that the brotherhood of men – a concept belonging to the receding Enlightenment – was losing its allure. The short moment of rapprochement – limited as it had been – seemed to be over. As early as 1799, David Friedländer, Mendelssohn's pupil and one of his early associates, approached the provost of the Protestant Church in Berlin, offering "in the name of some Jewish heads of families" to join the Lutheran church on the basis of shared moral values. The condition was that they were to be exempt from proclaiming faith in the divinity of Jesus and allowed to skip certain Christian ceremonies. But, while this may have been a serious offer in the better days of the Enlightenment, it was now clearly a "non-starter." Friedrich Schleiermacher, to take the most prominent voice in the following exchange, had no hesitation in branding this suggested procedure "a sham conversion." For him, Protestantism was by then no longer a religion of Reason, as one had tried to make of it during the heyday of the Enlightenment, but one of passion and of private, spiritual, even mystical experience. Meanwhile, more or less at the same time, frequent Christian visitors to Rahel's salon began to keep their distance, and within a few years her copious correspondence, too, was "reduced" – as she put it – to Jews only.[2] Her much coveted acculturation and what had seemed like her successful entry into high society could no longer save her, or her salon, from what she then acknowledged as a humiliating downward plunge. On the eve of Napoleon's defeat, the life that she, alongside other Jews and Jewesses like her, had for some time enjoyed was no longer sustainable. Hateful publications concerning Jews were by then flooding the market, reaching a peak as early as 1803. Jews must have felt betrayed and disappointed. Just as they began to experience improvement in their *formal* civil status, they had to face clear signs of a worsening of their *informal* social position.

This was the beginning of what could be named the zigzag course of Jewish emancipation. And it did, indeed, run parallel to the zigzag course of reform and modernization in Germany as a whole. Hope and disappointment followed each other throughout the first half of the century on a wide front and with regard to many issues. The alternations between reform and restoration were typical of this entire era – not just in matters concerning the Jews, but also, for instance, with regard to essential questions of constitutional arrangements or in handling the various administrative or agrarian reorganizations. Demands on the part of the bourgeoisie sometimes combined with the efforts of upper-echelon aristocratic bureaucrats, but most of the nobility usually took a more conservative line, while the various German lands struggled for compromises, seeking generally acceptable, practical solutions.

Immediately after 1815, liberals – everywhere in Germany – experienced a dimming of their hope for a constitutional Germany that would be both progressive and united. In the aftermath of the Congress of Vienna, their hopes were dashed first by aristocratic reaction and then by the violence of students' national associations, bringing about Metternich's quick and aggressive response. When he mobilized the various German governments of the day to act according to the Carlsbad Decrees of 1819, any progress in the direction of constitutional government seemed to have been crushed – together with the hope for a deepening of liberal rights, such as freedom of the press or of association as well as further legislation in the direction of Jewish equality.[3] Gradually, it became obvious that the course of Jewish

---

[2] On Rahel's changing fortunes, see – despite later critique – Hannah Arendt, *Rahel Varnhagen: The Life of a Jewess*, London, 1957.
[3] For a full presentation, I have relied upon Wolfram Siemann, *Vom Staatenbund zum Nationalstaat: Deutschland 1806–1871*, Munich, 1995, 29–81, 320–337.

emancipation ran parallel to other principled issues, so that, by following it, some of the inner paradoxes of contemporary society could be revealed.

To be sure, voices of opposition to Jewish advancement into the various tiers of bourgeois society were of various shades. Some protestors were staunch conservatives who refused to accept any change in whatever sphere of life. Others, some of whom welcomed the French Revolution and even supported its conquering armies, nevertheless remained wavering on the theme of reforms, specifically with regard to the Jews. Somehow, *they* did not fall under the guidelines of the modern, liberal principles now otherwise and elsewhere applied. Accepting Jews, surely accepting them as they were – unreformed and unchanged – seemed to be simply too much.

Especially interesting is the early case of Johann Gottlieb Fichte – initially one of the most respected public supporters of the French Revolution in Germany. In his anonymously published *Contributions to Correcting the Views of the Public Concerning the French Revolution* (1793), in which he comes out against oppression and exploitation, he insists on granting Jews "human rights" but at the same time criticizes their behavior and speaks out against granting them "citizens' rights." Then, in a spell of unexpected rage, this is how he concludes the section concerning the Jews: "I see no other means of giving them civil rights," he wrote, "than to chop off their heads in one night and replace them with new ones that contain not even one Jewish idea." And "in order to protect ourselves from them," he added, "I also see no other means than to conquer their promised land and send them all over there."[4] A small library of books and essays has since been written in order to explain away these sentences. At the time too, it caused much acrimony and, a year after its publication, gave rise to a fulminating reply by Saul Ascher, in his "Eisenmenger the Second." Comparing Fichte to this well-known antisemite of 100 years earlier, Ascher firmly placed the prominent philosopher, soon to become rector of the new University of Berlin, within the history of antisemitism. But later on, just as his revolutionary fervor was cooling off, Fichte proved he could also be careful with issues of human rights and even ready to protect the civil rights of individual Jews. At a certain point in his career, he was ready to resign his post as rector of the university, following a heated controversy with both students and faculty members over his defense of a single Jewish student against his fellow-student detractors. Interestingly, both Fichte's offending statements and his later insistence

---

[4] Quoted from Johann Gottlieb Fichte, *Sämtliche Werke*, Berlin, 1845, vol. VI, 149–150.

on upholding equal rights for Jews were true expressions of his position. The first were neither mere witticisms nor a slip of the pen. They were excessive, but not entirely out of line. After all, we had previously witnessed vom Stein's animosity towards the Jews and noted *his* suggestion to populate the northern coasts of Africa with them. And the second – his decent stand on equality and his insistence on orderly behavior within the university – was surely perceived by him as a prerequisite of his position as rector. He could detest Jews as "*Bürger*," but his position as a public figure, in the service of the Prussian state, required full obedience to its rules. Echoes of Kant's directives a generation earlier could easily be heard in his case.

The case of Wilhelm von Humboldt reflects a different but still similar duality. To be sure, Humboldt always acted consistently – often against powerful opposition – in his efforts to achieve equality for Jews. Nevertheless, he too must have had conflicting thoughts on the matter. Originally, we find him expressing his views about the Jews' "nomadic national character," somewhat in the tenor of Michaelis during Mendelssohn's days. And, while he apparently found it "purely logical" that the state should legalize their equal status, *civil* institutions, he insisted, ought to take the necessary steps in order to "improve" them – a demand often stated by other reformers, before and after him. Furthermore, in private letters Humboldt explained that, while he did love the Jews *en masse*, *en détails* he rather preferred to avoid them. His friendship with Rahel, for instance, did not last longer than that of other celebrities that had previously been guests at her salon. Like them, he too could apparently not stand her "Jewishness," as he put it, while at the same time he continued to socialize and to regularly correspond with Henriette Herz, whom he considered – in contrast to Rahel – "almost a Christian."[5]

These conflicting attitudes reflected, in his case too, the contemporary rift between state and society, typical of that *Sattelzeit* (saddle period), reaching well into the first half of the nineteenth century. Both Fichte and Humboldt could express a stark lack of sympathy towards Jews *as members of civil society*, but – while holding administrative posts, high or low – felt obliged to obey the law of the land and act accordingly. In Prussia, indeed, where an enlightened bureaucracy was dedicated to comprehensive reform, men like Fichte or Humboldt found themselves in a predicament and had to steer a complex, ambivalent course.[6]

---

[5] On Humboldt's views concerning the Jews and for the quotes here, see Werner Treß, "Liberale Politik im christlichen Staat? Wilhelm von Humboldt und das Bürgerrecht für die Juden," *Zeitschrift für Religions- und Geistesgeschichte*, 69(2) (2017), 193–207.

[6] See especially Werner Conze, "Staat und Gesellschaft in der frührevolutionären Epoche Deutschlands," *Historische Zeitschrift*, 186(1) (1958), 1–34.

Later on, following the French defeat, not everyone that participated in the debate on the now so-called Jewish Question could be considered merely ambivalent. Some were outright antisemites. One often mentions the two anti-Jewish works by Friedrich Christian Rühs, a historian at the University of Berlin, published in 1816. Their titles denoted their content and reflected their overall tenor. The one read: "On Jewish Claims to Acquire German Civil Rights," the other "The Rights of Christianity and the German Volk against the Claims of the Jews and Their Advocates." An enthusiastic review of these works, written by Jakob Friedrich Fries, was entitled "On the Endangering of the Well-being and Character of the Germans by the Jews." While Fries, like Rühs, was a respected university professor, he was also known as an outspoken liberal. Still, among the numerous antisemitic pamphlets that were flooding the market at the time, *his* stood out in its radicalism and callousness. The Jews had no interest to "better" themselves, he argued. They constituted a "State within a State" – a common claim that had been earlier applied to various groups and corporations at least since the Great Revolution – and must be seen as "*Volksschädlinge*", a term used previously too, but one that would curiously be reapplied by the Nazis, a century later. They ought to be banished, he insisted, if they did not renounce their religion as well as the "indecent" patterns of behavior contingent upon it.[7]

In the immediate post-Second World War years, the historian Eleonore Sterling collected many private letters and diary entries, written by young German intellectuals during the years just before and just after the Napoleonic defeat of 1815. Following her untimely death in 1968, Uriel Tal, an Israeli historian, set out to analyze this material and flesh out its characteristics. It proved to be a real treasure.[8] Here, for instance, is a relevant quote, typical for many other passages in this collection: "I hereby swear," writes one student, "that my whole life would be dedicated to the revival of our Reich. The memory of old days makes me now realize how evil, disgusting and amoral, how disastrous was the Jewish influence over our life. French rationalism, Prussian petrification, western skepticism and Jewish intellectualism have all poisoned the Germanic soul, our rivers and forests, our youth and our spirit." Thus, not only the Jews, but most particularly the Jews, were the reason for past defeats and the present misery in the eyes of these young men. The hoped-for

---

[7] See Jacob Katz, *From Prejudice to Destruction: Antisemitism 1700–1933*, Cambridge, MA, 1980, 78–92.

[8] The following quotes are from Uriel Tal, "Young German Intellectuals on Romanticism and Judaism – Spiritual Turbulence in the Early Nineteenth Century," in Saul Lieberman (ed.), *Salo Wittmayr Baron: Jubilee Volume*, 3 vols., Jerusalem, 1974, Vol. I, 919–938. The original documents he cites are here translated by Ulla Höber.

rejuvenation of national life was clearly linked in their minds to a strong antisemitic sentiment. "Jewish dirt should never again be allowed to stain and sully our grandiose future," summarized yet another one of them his heartfelt patriotic convictions.

Naturally, fellow *Jewish* students, now permitted to study at universities up and down the country, must have suffered a painful reawakening. A letter from a Jewish student, also found in Sterling's collection, described their deep disappointment – the insult, the frustration, the humiliation. And finally, during the Wartburg festival, national and national-liberal students did more than merely agitate against the Jews. They publically burned some of the published replies to Rühs and Fries, such as – and most famously – Saul Ascher's "Germanomanie," manifesting their unequivocal anti-Jewish stand. Somewhat later, in 1821, Heinrich Heine, enraged at what had taken place at that festive Wartburg celebration, high point of the German liberal tradition, penned this memorable prediction in his tragedy *Almansor*: "This was a prelude only," he prophesized. "There, where books are burned, in the end people will be burned, too."[9]

While hate pamphlets could be either ignored or openly countered – either by Jews or by their supporters – it was difficult not to take offense at the violent anti-Jewish riots occurring immediately afterwards. In the summer of 1819, yet another series of events erupted, deepening Jewish insecurity and underscoring the difficulties on their road to full, equal citizenship. While the Bavarian *Landtag* was debating some new regulations concerning the Jews and the matter was likewise being discussed in various local councils and assemblies, violent assaults on the Jews took place – first in the city of Würzburg, then in Bamberg, Bayreuth, Regensburg, and a number of smaller towns and villages. The riots then further extended to Frankfurt am Main, to various locations in the Duchy of Baden and in the Rhineland, and then to Hamburg, Breslau, Danzig, and Königsberg. In some cases, the unrest did not go beyond loud verbal attacks. In others – as, for instance, in Hamburg – Jews who set out to defend themselves seem to have only caused further irritation, provoking even more violent confrontations.[10]

---

[9] Heinrich Heine, *Almansor*, lines 243f.
[10] The riots were fully described and analyzed first in Eleonore Sterling, "Anti-Jewish Riots in Germany in 1819: A Displacement of Social Protest," *Historia Judaica*, 12(2) (1950), 105–142, and later in Jacob Katz, *Die Hep-Hep Verfolgungen des Jahres* 1819, Berlin. 1994. On these and later anti-Jewish riots, see especially Stefan Rohrbacher, *Gewalt in Biedermeier: Antijüdische Ausschreitungen in Vormärz und Revolution (1815–1848/49)*, Frankfurt am Main, 1993.

In any case, the initial events in Würzburg were drastic enough. The mob raged for a number of days, attacking the homes of local Jews, members of the small but well-established Jewish community in town, who were frightened, severely beaten up, and finally forced to flee to nearby villages. The rage was then turned against the apparently insufficient army and police troops that had been sent to restore order, and one soldier was killed. In Frankfurt, home to one of the oldest and largest Jewish communities in Germany, the police force was likewise unable to control the situation, while neither the local senate nor the Bund authorities, convening there, could calm things down.

Contemporaries as well as later historians disagreed about the causes of these so-called Hep-Hep riots. To be sure, the atmosphere at the time, everywhere in Germany, was generally volatile. The same social elements that had been marching to the Wartburg in 1817, expressing disappointment at the failing reforms following the Congress of Vienna, were protesting violently during the spring and summer months of 1819, too. In March, August von Kotzebue, an author known for his opposition to liberalism, was murdered at his home in Mannheim by a member of the Jena *Burschenschaft* (student association), and, while tension was rising everywhere, the authorities were placed under unusual pressure. It is possible that the riots against the Jews developed as part of this general unrest.

More direct and no less powerful, however, was the influence of two additional factors. First, there was the exasperation of town merchants, often still organized in guilds, directed against Jews that were suddenly allowed to enter their protected professional sphere. They also organized to oppose Jewish peddlers, adding – as many believed – to the spreading of "unfair competition." Secondly, there was the effect of hostile propaganda against the Jews, disseminated by an army of speakers and writers, popularizing the more sophisticated antisemitic literature and making it available to the entire public. To be sure, some contemporary observers, noticing this poisonous atmosphere, warned against its consequences. In a letter of August 29, 1819, Rahel – by that time converted and married to Karl August Varnhagen von Ense – recapitulated how, upon reading the works of Fries, Rühs, and others, she had everywhere and repeatedly warned that Jews would soon be physically assaulted, too.[11]

Thus, a combination of irresolute behavior at the top and social unrest from below was apparently sufficient to cause the conflagration, and, as a result, the joint, dual experience of apparent progress towards civil

---

[11] Cited in Karl August Varnhagen von Ense, *Denkwürdigkeiten des eignen Lebens: Die Karlsruhe Jahre 1816–1819*, Karlsruhe, 1924, 370.

equality and increased antisemitism continued to characterize the following years, too. While the Hep-Hep riots were raging, discussions about further improving the status of Jews continued unabated, both in Bavaria and in Baden. Violent expressions of opposition to Jewish "entry" – formal and informal – occurred again during the revolutionary upheaval of 1830, in Munich, Hamburg, Breslau, Mannheim, and Karlsruhe. Then they happened yet again in 1834, especially in the Rhineland, and during the 1840s, in Berlin, Paderborn, Regensburg, and even Vienna. While in some locations Jews were forced to flee for their lives, in others they continued their project of integration, moving closer towards their non-Jewish neighbors, joining in their cultural life, assimilating their habits and norms, and trying to live *with* them and become more and more *like* them.

Not everyone was busy writing or reading antisemitic books and pamphlets at the time, of course. Neither was everyone busy measuring the extent of Jew-hatred in German society, then and there. Not everyone, not even every Jew, was interested in the success or failure of the various equal rights legislations. For most Jews, reforms had little practical meaning. Moreover, they were by then no longer comparing their situation with the grand promises of the Enlightenment. Jewish life, like the life of non-Jews everywhere on the European continent, was changing most dramatically and in many different ways during these years. It was a period of extreme uncertainty. The dangers were many, but so were the chances and the opportunities.

By the middle of the eighteenth century, as we have seen, Jews began to take part in the cultural life of those around them. In fact, recent research tends to stress that multiple links between Jews and non-Jews had always existed, even throughout the Middle Ages and during much of the Early Modern period. Rich Jewish merchants or bankers, for instance, could not have avoided such links; neither could vagrants or peddlers, on the other end of the social ladder. But, by now, Jews of the middling ranks were also beginning to show more interest in the life of their neighbors. German *Bildung* and the life of the *Bildungsbürgertum* (educated bourgeoisie) attracted educated Jews even more powerfully now than ever before, and what had been at first a matter for small elites – Jewish and Christian alike – was, since the early decades of the nineteenth century, a relevant matter for an ever growing segment of the population. To be sure, expressions of antisemitism continued to be common; efforts and calls for the conversion of Jews continued as well. But the entry now offered to Jews, into a new social segment that no longer rejected them, was extremely attractive. Optimism could not be damped, as the prospects for the future were all too promising.

Here is how one observer described the new situation in the year 1833: "Let us perceive the unimaginable changes that occurred in [Jewish] language, fashion, and life-style; in necessities and pleasures, in behavior and habits! ... Could one have really seen thirty years ago a Jew in restaurants and eating-halls, sharing a table with Christian guests and freely talking with them?" Jews were now to be seen, he added, "in concerts, evening parties, dances, and popular festivals ... in coffee houses, and in the stock exchange, in the theater, in scientific and in various other educated circles."[12] In fact, Jews were to be seen in the stock exchange much earlier, whereas in the "eating halls" they were probably still a rarity. Thus, writing about a somewhat later period, the historian Jacob Toury stressed that "full social integration, symbolized by the possibility of eating and sleeping together, remained an exception."[13] And this was certainly true for the restoration years as a whole. Jewish "entry," to apply Toury's terminology again, was a clear sign of the time. Many closed doors were now being opened – though surely not all.

Outside the aristocratic milieu, a growing bourgeoisie – in numbers and in cultural achievements, if not always in matters of politics – produced a new public sphere that had by then much to offer, no doubt. Theater and music provided the most attractive platforms both for light entertainment and for the seriously creative contents of the time. And it was an open platform, at least for all who could afford its pleasures. As listeners, well-off Jews were welcome in concert halls and the theaters. At the very least, they could not be excluded. As men and sometimes women of talent, the requirements imposed upon them may have been somewhat stricter than for others, but the exceptionally creative could now achieve at least some measure of "entry." In addition, access to higher education became available. Bourgeois students were by then entering the universities in great numbers. Only now, and for the first time, were Jewish bourgeois students too allowed to join in growing numbers. They could now enter, and not only through the doors of the medical faculties. Other doors were finally beginning to open, and there seemed to be a rush of Jews to enter all faculties. They seemed to have been just waiting for this opportunity.

---

[12] Cited from Michael Benedict Lessing, *Die Juden und die öffentliche Meinung im Preußischen Staate*, Altona, 1833, by Jacob Toury, "Der Eintritt der Juden ins deutsche Bürgertum," in Hans Liebeschütz and Arnold Paucker (eds.), *Das Judentum in der deutschen Umwelt 1800–1850: Studien zur Frühgeschichte der Emanzipation*, Tübingen, 1977, 139–242. The quote is from 199.

[13] Jacob Toury, *Soziale und politische Geschichte der Juden in Deutschland 1848–1871*, Düsseldorf, 1977, 123.

Eduard Gans began to study law, history, and philosophy as early as 1816, first in Berlin and then in Göttingen and Heidelberg. Later on, back in Berlin, by then already known as an extraordinarily brilliant scholar, he hoped to launch a university career, but there were still many who found fault in his success and could not imagine a Jewish colleague. Eventually, Gans was barred from advancement by a special royal edict, to be known as *Lex Gans*. It was a procedure reminiscent of the royal intervention in the case of Moses Mendelssohn, prohibiting his entry into the Prussian Academy of Science. At the time, this was a great disappointment for the Jewish philosopher, but now it must have been an even greater shock both for Gans himself and for his co-religionists.

Gans then tried other tactics, looking for parallel routes to reach his goal. After all, in the past, too, Jews – and even converted Jews – were often excluded from intellectual groupings of all kinds, such as the Christlich-Deutsche Tischgesellschaft in Berlin or its successor association, the Christlich-Germanische Tischgesellschaft. They were more often than not kept out of less distinguished groupings, such as reading societies – common platforms for joint reading during the late eighteenth and early nineteenth centuries, where reading Germans used to meet. In all these cases, Jews responded by establishing their own societies, thus building up a separate Jewish public sphere, one that could function in parallel to the emerging German *Öffentlichkeit*. The community in Frankfurt, to take only one example, was known for its lively Jewish Reading Societies, and, in Berlin, the Jewish Society of Friends, established as early as 1792, fulfilled varied social and intellectual purposes at the initiation of its members, in parallel to similar activities among non-Jews.

Other groups that were excluded from the by-now blooming bourgeois public sphere – lower-class men, or women of *all* classes – often used the same tactics. They established their own cultural associations, and their activities within them differed only marginally from the activities of the original associations. The same books were read and discussed now in Jewish reading societies as in non-Jewish ones; the same theater pieces were staged; the same music was rehearsed – only in separate choirs and in separate halls. Historians sometimes called this tactic "negative integration."[14]

Thus, Gans and a number of his associates, facing closed doors despite legal promises, responded – like others before and after them – by

---

[14] This term was first introduced by Guenther Roth, *The Social Democrats in Imperial Germany: A Study in Working-Class Isolation and National Integration*, Salem, 1963, and then applied by Dieter Groh, *Negative Integration und revolutionärer Attentismus*, Frankfurt am Main, 1973.

establishing an exclusively *Jewish* association, the Verein für Cultur und Wissenschaft des Judentums (Association for Culture and Science of Judaism). Here they could decide upon their own agenda and create their own scholarly environment, a platform for their academic work outside the university and beyond its discriminatory rules. At first the Verein proved effective, indeed, but in the end it turned out to be disappointing and above all short-lived.[15] Despite its brilliant membership and the truly promising teaching and research program presented by its energetic members, it was abandoned within only a few years. At first, to be sure, members met frequently, holding lectures followed by spirited discussions, in which they were trying to rethink the meaning of Judaism and contemplate its place within and in relation to European culture. For the first time, these men were openly searching for a modern form of Jewish identity extending beyond and outside religion; an identity that would serve them in their efforts to enter non-Jewish society while remaining Jews. Soon, however, they began to lose heart. Despite its promising beginnings, the Verein did not manage to offer a satisfying alternative to full scholarly life. In 1825, Gans abandoned this route and decided to convert. Immediately thereafter, he launched himself upon a meteoric career, finally becoming dean of the law faculty in Berlin in 1832, four years before his untimely death.

Such a career was doubtless exceptional. Still, Jews could now study everywhere in Germany, hoping to move both upwardly and inwardly within the academic establishment. But, while for Christians a degree usually meant the start of a life-long employment in town or state administration or the launching of an academic career, both routes were closed to the unconverted. A position of authority in the state was denied Jews by law, and achieving a proper position in the universities proved impossible, as we saw, too. Even accomplished Jewish students found themselves jobless, despite their academic achievements.

This could have been the fate of Leopold Zunz, the first practitioner of what soon became known as *Wissenschaft des Judentums* (Jewish studies), which had originally been contemplated and propagated under his leadership by the defunct Verein.[16] In fact, Zunz began to publish carefully researched studies on various aspects of Judaism and on the Ashkenazi literary tradition since the Middle Ages even before its establishment, in response to various antisemitic publications circulating by then in Berlin, partly written by his own university professor, Friedrich Rühs. Later on, as a member of the Verein, he was responsible for its academic journal,

---

[15] I rely here on the detailed description of Rachel Livneh-Freudenthal, *The Verein: Pioneers of Jewish Studies* [in Hebrew], Jerusalem, 2018.
[16] See his full biography, Ismar Schorsch, *Leopold Zunz: Creativity in Adversity*, Philadelphia, 2016.

which published three issues during 1822 and 1823. Thereafter, following the dissolution of the Verein, Zunz was among the few members who remained loyal to its original aims. Until his death in 1886, at the age of ninety-one, he produced a string of scholarly works on Judaism, while subsisting on meager salaries gained in various teaching jobs in half-defunct Jewish educational institutions. An independent scholar, he usually worked alone and gradually became bitter and frustrated.

Bitterness and frustration, to be sure, could also be the fate of those who, like Gans and unlike Zunz, *did* convert but still remained outsiders. Most famous again is the life-story of Heinrich Heine, himself also a one-time member of the Verein. Despite his harsh criticism of Gans' conversion at the time, Heine soon chose the same route – even though, in his case, no special career opportunities lay ahead. Conversion, he then tried to explain, was an "entry ticket to European culture," but for him even that promise remained unfulfilled. Acquiring all the nuances of the German language and then adopting all of the habits and manners of the non-Jewish bourgeois world clearly sufficed neither for Heine nor for other Jews of his generation – baptized or not.

No one wrote as extensively and as passionately about Germany as Heine. When he was not obsessed with Jews and Judaism, he seemed preoccupied with Germany and the Germans. Soon he wrote the first version of his *Rabbi von Bacherach*, perhaps his most Jewish piece, which was to be published only later, in 1840, together with his earliest poetry cycle, *Die Heimkehr* (*The Homecoming*), in which he introduces himself to that young, black–brown-eyed girl, watching him silently from her window, simply as "a German poet." Gradually, the Jewish component of his identity became rather negligible, already playing no role in that most gentle and most emotional of his works. But there was a highly impressive poem, entitled "An Edom!" ("To Edom!"), sent by Heine, just three months before his conversion, to a friend in Berlin; a poem that remained unpublished until long after his death. It begins as follows: "Brotherly forbearance/ Has united us for ages;/ You, you tolerate my breathing/ And I tolerate your rages." And it ends breathtakingly so: "Later we became more cordial/ Day by day our friendship grew – / For I also started raging/ And I almost seem like you."[17]

In parallel – how typical for him, indeed – Heine somehow upholds his Jewish identity while he develops a unique poetic genre that defines his sense of patriotism and his love for Germany. It is a genre based on

---

[17] In a letter of October 24, 1824, in Heinrich Heine, *Rabbi of Bacherach: A Fragment*, trans. E. B. Ashton, New York, 1947, 72–73. Here I have used the translation of the poem by Amos Funkenstein, "The Dialectics of Assimilation," *Jewish Social Studies*, 1(2) (1995), 1–14, from pages 13–14.

childhood memories and the attraction to nature, to landscape and cityscape, to local food and local colors, to mountains and the northern sea shores. The combination of early life excursions in nature with strong family attachments is perhaps best presented in one of his most well-known romances. It begins with that suggestive line: "At night I think of Germany," presumably indicating a longing for his homeland; but further down he hastens to correct this impression: "I should not thirst for Germany so/ Did I not there my mother know." This, Heine seems to indicate, is above all a personal poem, expressing longing for his mother, whom he did not see for twelve long years. And Germany, he explains, "will ever stand/ It is a strong and healthy land/ And with its oaks, and linden trees/ I'm sure to find it, when I please."[18] It is a poem of longing, we inevitably sense, both for the fatherland – so indelibly imprinted on his memory – and for the mother – real flesh and blood, aging silently far away.

Back in the fall of 1824, Heine published his impressions of the Harz, and a year later he described a vacation on the shores of the North Sea. He came back to this style much later, too, especially in his *Deutschland: Ein Wintermärchen (Germany: A Winter's Tale)*, where he dwells upon the German forests, beloved by the Romantics, the mountains with their many creeks, and the lonely huts, carrying a promise of young love. He was apparently enamored of the combination of ancient legends and dramatic seascapes and finally, it was the various German towns, with their towers and holy churches, that attracted his loving attention, together with local bars and their late night fun and vivaciousness. At this point in time, the bitterness of an exile – devoted to "the religion of freedom" and therefore banished from his homeland – common in Heine's later writings was as yet not there.

Living in Paris since 1831, Heine writes both for French and for German journals. In April 1835, he published his *L'Allemagne*, a combined edition of his essays on German Romanticism, its religion, and its philosophy. Heine took over the role of a mediator, explaining for the French the essence of Germany, looking – indeed, from the margin now – on his beloved, but at the same time deeply detested fatherland. Heine admires the Lutheran reformation, but he despises its belief in Satan and in the afterlife. He sings the praises of Kant, but laughs at his heavy style and the pomposity of his followers. Throughout this brilliant presentation, Heine repeatedly talks of "we, the Germans" and weaves a complex view of "us" for the benefit of his French readers. At the end,

---

[18] This translation is taken from *Lyrics and Ballads of Heine and Other German Poets*, trans. Frances Hellman, London, 1892, 129–131.

however, his prophetic sense gains the upper hand. He then talks of the "better" and the "worse" half of Germany, and most particularly of the dangers inherent in that "worse" half. Finally, "as on the steps of an amphitheater, the nations will group themselves around Germany to witness the terrible combat," a drama "compared to which the French Revolution will seem but an innocent idyll."[19]

Is he back at the scene of Edom that made him tremble more than a decade earlier? Is that the Jewish Heine, no longer a member of that magic German "we" – neither of the good nor of the evil Germany? It is difficult to be sure. But clearly, even the shrewd Heine could not extricate himself from the German double-edged dilemma of a society that was only half-open, promising freedom and enforcing new prohibitions, imagining modernity and imposing censorship, planning reforms and practicing restoration.

---

[19] See Heinrich Heine, *Religion and Philosophy in Germany: A Fragment*, London, 1892, 177.

Part II

Liberty, Unity, Equality: 1840–1870

4 Pogroms and Revolution

Meanwhile, despite the absence of political unity, a compound new national consciousness in Germany was slowly maturing. At the same time, moreover, notwithstanding the humanitarian pathos of liberalism, "otherness" continued to be considered a threat. Equality for Jews, aside from its legal connotations, was conceived by many as an offer made by society to individual Jews, as individuals, an offer with unequivocal conditions attached. Jews were now more or less formally allowed entry into bourgeois society, but they could not do so collectively, nor – and in the long run this point was ever more important – could they accomplish such entry unless they, in fact, "stopped being Jewish."

The phrase is taken from a debate in the General Estates of the Duchy of Baden in the early 1830s, analyzed by the historian Reinhard Rürup in a path-breaking article of 1966.[1] A somewhat earlier quote from the same article, coming from Württemberg, likewise stressed that, in the process of their so-called improvement, the Jew must first be made un-Jewish (*entjudet*). Such radical demands were especially – and somewhat unexpectedly – prevalent in the southern and south-western middle-sized German states. These were states where a budding constitutionalism could be detected early on, and there, the controversy over the changing position of Jews, like other controversies on the agenda, had for some time been expected to be decided not solely from above, by the state bureaucracy, but by the combined forces of state and society. Representative bodies were here fully responsible for new legislation. But parliamentarians were, in fact, more responsive to popular opinion and to the mood in small towns and especially in the countryside than appointed officials. And in these areas, crowds everywhere and repeatedly expressed their views in verbal and physical attacks upon the Jews. The hopes of achieving

---

[1] The quotes in this and the following paragraph are from Reinhard Rürup, "Die Emanzipation der Juden in Baden," and "Judenemanzipation und bürgerliche Gesellschaft in Deutschland," both in Reinhard Rürup, *Emanzipation und Antisemitismus: Studien zur "Judenfrage" in der bürgerlichen Gesellschaft*, Göttingen, 1975, 10–36 and 37–73, respectively.

"fusion" through emancipation seemed at this point rather illusory. Demands for the advancement of a process by which Jewish uniqueness would be obliterated, not just restrained, were being propagated from all sides.

In a speech of 1833, Karl Rotteck, a prominent liberal voice during the years preceding the 1848 revolutions, or what one often calls the Vormärz (pre-March period), again in Baden, explained that the state, after all, required a "certain uniformity," so that fusion between Jews and non-Jews meant not only the dismantling of old Jewish special rights and duties but also "the end of their history," even "the death of their nation."[2] One senses a certain loss of patience here. There were more important issues at hand, Rotteck felt, namely "the emancipation of the Christians and the emancipation of the Germans," and these were in any case preconditions for emancipating the Jews. Other speakers – and Rürup quotes here from the Bavarian Landtag, too – listed in this context the many additional objects of emancipation that ought to be handled: children and youth, army officers, land property itself, even commerce and the press.[3] In fact, some such statements, intent on relativizing the case of the Jews or perhaps just insisting on seeing it in context, were aired by some Jews, too.

Heine's case is – as always – particularly telling. In answering the question concerning the "task of our times," he had first employed the term "emancipation," giving it the most inclusive meaning. Emancipation is the main task of the day, he argued, not only with regard to "the Irish, the Greeks, the Frankfurt Jews, the West Indian blacks and other oppressed people," but of "the whole world, indeed of Europe ... [freed] from the iron shackles of the privileged aristocracy."[4] Clearly, granting equal rights to the Jews could only be considered as part of a larger project, though it nevertheless had a particularly paradigmatic meaning and a special resonance.

Jewish "otherness" had been and remained an irritation, bringing out the worst in most commentators, even in men who could hardly be considered antisemitic. Some were hoping – as in discussing toleration half a century earlier – that a long process of assimilation would bring about the erasing of Jewish identity; others hoped that conversion would finally achieve it. Like Humboldt at the beginning of the century, Karl August Varnhagen von Ense, in a diary entry of October 20, 1842, despite

---

[2] Quoted in yet another important article: Reinhard Rürup, "The Tortuous and Thorny Path to Legal Equality: 'Jew Laws' and Emancipatory Legislation in Germany from the Late 18th Century," *Leo Baeck Institute Yearbook* 31 (1986), 23–24.
[3] Rürup, "Die Emanzipation der Juden in Baden," 35–36.
[4] Heinrich Heine, *Sämtliche Werke: Düsseldorfer Ausgabe*, vol. II, 85.

his apparent long-term loyalty to liberalism, light-heartedly answered the question "what do the Jews actually want?" with the maxim "that one allows them time to become Christian."[5] This could have been the lesson he drew from the experience of his by-then-deceased wife Rahel, though it was not generally reflected in reality.

It has been roughly calculated that, between 1800 and 1850, some 5,000 Jews in Prussia converted to Christianity, mostly in Berlin. By the end of this period, some 200,000 Jews lived in this major German state, half of all the Jews in Germany, not including the Habsburg Empire. This number may have been sufficient for some non-Jews to feel vindicated in their expectations. Others remained skeptical and continued to seek various solutions to the vexing "Jewish Question." Among these, many still insisted that integration could not be achieved at all – reactionaries of all sorts, but not a few liberals as well. Thus, while most Jews believed that emancipation meant the ability to enter German society without giving up their uniqueness – be it their religion or their various secular traits, most non-Jews, even those who were in principle ready to accept them, required their total makeover, either as a precondition or as an aftereffect. For most Germans, integration meant the abandonment of Jewishness, regardless of its precise definition.

One could even make of this duality a kind of expurgatory theory. Eduard Gans, for instance, saw in the 1819 attacks upon the Jews the birth pangs of a new world, during which distancing and integration were acting together, as they should, indeed, according to the dialectics explicated by his admired university lecturer, Georg Friedrich Wilhelm Hegel. Ludwig Börne too, attempting to observe events "objectively," found the anti-Jewish attacks upon individuals unacceptable, but he was prepared to forgive "the German *Volk*" its prejudices as unavoidable on the road to true freedom and to mature national consciousness.[6] Jews were expected to understand the deep sense of the ongoing transformation and not let few incidents stop them from joining other Germans on their common route towards liberty and unity. Later on, Karl Marx, whose father had converted a generation earlier to become a successful lawyer, would argue in his "Zur Judenfrage," written in 1844, that Jews had a special role in the process of universal emancipation and that this more encompassing emancipation would mean in the end, for them too, a liberation not only *for* the Jews and *of* the Jews but *from* Judaism as well, for them and

---

[5] See Karl August Varnhagen von Ense, *Tagebücher*, Leipzig, 1861, Vol. II, 113 (my translation).
[6] See Ludwig Börne, "Eine Kleinigkeit," in Ludwig Börne, *Gesammelte Schriften*, Hamburg and Frankfurt am Main, 1862, Vol. II, 326.

for all other Germans.⁷ By then, however, among the many issues that called for resolution, their issue proved particularly vexing. Sheer Jewish existence in Germany made it necessary for non-Jews to take a stand on their own future, bringing to the surface deep German dilemmas. Above all, one had to weigh liberal principles against the rising tide of national, perhaps nationalistic, sentiments, while the very content of this nationalism had to be seriously reexamined. Taking a stand here on the Jewish issue had consequences for one's stand on various other issues, too: on citizenship as a whole, on the definition of German-ness, on one's own identity, on the standing of religion in modern society, and more.

The hostile atmosphere towards the Jews, but also – more generally noticeable and important – the general police oppression and censorship regulations were all losing some of their edge at the beginning of the century's fifth decade. "In sum," wrote the historian Stefi Jersch-Wenzel, "during the 1840s, the liberal-democrats clearly spoke out for complete emancipation of the Jews, which led to a certain improvement in their legal status. Above all, the 'Jewish Question' was now an integral part of liberal efforts in general."⁸

And further improvement was now particularly called for. To be sure, the new decade had opened with yet another disappointment – both for the Jews and for their old and new supporters. The legislation promoted by Friedrich Wilhelm IV, who succeeded to the Prussian throne in 1840, though at first generally liberal in tone, soon turned out to be rather reactionary, firstly, as usual, in all things Jewish. Like his presumably enlightened grandfather, known as "the Great," he too had always professed to be a man open to reform, and at the beginning of his reign he did, indeed, stop the persecution of the so-called demagogues, relax censorship, and rehabilitate political opponents. Already by the end of 1841, however, the king, and his legal advisers, were busy reconstituting Prussian Jewry as an old-style corporation. They formulated an anti-emancipatory argument that would not have surprised Jewish subjects of his great predecessor 100 years earlier, or – for that matter – Jewish nationalists 100 years later. Accordingly, Jews "represented a unique legal case in which peoplehood is identical with religion . . ., and where [sic] the

---

⁷ Karl Marx "Zur Judenfrage," in Karl Marx and Friedrich Engels, *Werke*, Berlin, 1959, Vol. II, 91–124.
⁸ Stefi Jersch-Wenzel, "Legal Status and Emancipation," in Michael Brenner, Stefi Jersch-Wenzel, and Michael A. Meyer, *German Jewish History in Modern Times*, Vol. II: *Emancipation und Acculturation, 1780–1871*, New York, 1996, 7–49. The quote is from page 49.

Jews alone have preserved their national peculiarity through their religious constitution."[9]

For Prussian Jews, who had been endeavoring now for some two or even three generations to prove their loyalty and show their sense of patriotic belonging, such a definition was nothing less than an insult. Once again, it seemed, their efforts at integration were being rebuffed, this time from above, endangering not only the further progress of their legal equalization, but also their efforts at becoming a legitimate part of society. Only this time, as the danger of yet another setback in the battle for emancipation seemed imminent, disappointment produced fierce opposition – in and outside of Prussia, and by no means only among Jews. The king's legislative intentions were leaked and then quickly – and rightly – taken as indication of his general anti-constitutional stand, leading to further opposition.

Meanwhile, reforms were gradually introduced elsewhere in Germany – in Hanover and Bavaria, for instance – seemingly in response to waves of protest throughout the country. Even though full equality was still far from being enacted and integration continued to be problematic, winning the battle seemed more likely now than it had ever previously been. Most liberals, even outspoken national-liberals, were distancing themselves from the attitudes of their predecessors. Equality for all, Jews included, became part of their political campaign, logically linked to their grand call for Liberty and Unity. In fact, winds of revolution were now blowing all around. The approaching upheaval of 1848–1849, often romantically called the "Spring of Nations," constituted the high point of a protracted anti-restoration movement everywhere in Germany. It had finally swept the country in the wake of many years of stagnation, carrying with it a feeling of a new beginning.

But, despite the liberal rhetoric that characterized the days of approaching revolution, it had actually begun with a series of spontaneous rural uprisings, reminiscent of the popular riots that were typical under the old regime. In February 1848, unrest began across the border, in French Alsace, directed against tax collectors, representing the central government, and against some of the wealthier Jews in towns and villages. Fleeing their assailants, many Jews crossed the border into Germany, but, by March, violence had spread to over thirty localities in the southwestern part of that country too; first to Baden, Württemberg, and Bavaria, then all the way to Westphalia, Upper Silesia, even Posen; finally to Bohemia, Moravia, and Hungary. Attacks on Jews were apparently part of riotous peasants' uprisings against the establishment as a whole, in

---

[9] Quoted by Jersch-Wenzel, ibid., 46.

France as well as in the various German lands, but they also sometimes appeared to be more like the familiar pogroms directed against local Jews, which had not been uncommon in the past. And, as during the old regime, Jews often fled, leaving their homes to the looters, who "threw [stones] through the shattered windows into the homes [of the Jews], screaming 'Money or Death.'"[10]

The atmosphere during these days was brutally antisemitic – not very promising as an opening act of an enlightened, liberally oriented revolution. Even less promising were the urban expressions of anti-Jewish sentiments common in many large cities. Handicraft masters with their journeymen were often among the active revolutionaries, and, although open antisemitism was rare in their public gatherings during this *tolles Jahr* (great year), there is enough evidence to show the prevalence of such sentiments among them everywhere across the land.[11] Late in 1848, a group of master artisans from Leipzig, for example, sent out a letter to all guild members in Germany, spewing a tirade of anti-liberal rhetoric against the intention to discard the guilds and the privileges attached to them, together with rabid attacks on Jews and against plans for their emancipation. Jews, argued the dispatch, were the archenemies of the German middle class, in fact of all hard-working Germans and therefore of society at large. They were the "hated strangers, who are nowhere at home and lack all compassion for the *Volk*, where [sic] they live."[12]

Rural attacks on Jews, when and if they appeared in descriptions of the revolution, are often explained away as an understandable reaction to Jewish moneylending in an impoverished countryside, while city rage against them is seen as a response to Jewish competition both in commerce and in the handicrafts themselves. But these are questionable claims. During much of the Middle Ages, a great proportion of rural Jews were, indeed, pawn-brokers, and in early modern Germany many continued in this line of business, often combining it with cattle breeding and with the running of slaughtering yards or small-scale retail of old garments. But, while it was surely unnecessary to explain to those involved the significance of the quick and flexible moneylending provided by Jews, especially in rural areas, many still found it obnoxious. And, even though, by 1848, only a diminishing section of rural Jews were actually engaged in moneylending, this continued to be a cause for unease among the populace.

---

[10] Cited in Stefan Rohrbacher, *Gewalt in Biedermeier: Antijüdische Ausschreitungen in Vormärz und Revolution (1815–1848/49)*, Frankfurt am Main, 1993, 208.
[11] This and the following are based on my *The Rise of Popular Antimodernism in Germany: The Urban Master Artisans, 1873–1896*, Princeton, NJ, 1978, 109–110, 215–229.
[12] Emil Ferdinand Vogel, *Offener Brief an alle Innungsgenossen Deutschlands so wie zugleich an alle Bürger und Hausväter*, Leipzig, 1848, 21–22.

Fear of competition was likewise unreal by then. German artisans only rarely encountered Jewish competition. Throughout the old territories of the Reich, Jews had normally been barred from the practice of most handicrafts. In Prussia, as early as 1817, less than 5 percent of all working Jews were occupied in them. Their number may have somewhat increased later on, but centuries-old prohibitions slowed down the rate of change, and even an influx of Jewish craftsmen from Eastern Europe, some of whom became Prussians following the Polish partition, could not noticeably alter the situation. Most Jews on the land and in small towns were occupied in small-scale commerce – especially peddling – and as such they could hardly constitute serious competition. In any case, hard facts were apparently irrelevant. Crucial was fear of change combined with a traditional and often revived fear of the Jew as foreigner, even if and when he or she was a familiar, old-time neighbor. Religious motivations continued to play a role too, of course, adding to the general disgruntlement. Thus, old and new reasons were combined to unleash anti-Jewish violence, manifesting a general dissatisfaction, propelled by fierce anti-establishment rage. As the ruling governments in Germany seemed no longer capable of preserving order or providing a sense of security, Jews were, as usual, the first to be pillaged and attacked.

Interestingly, it was not only later historians who paid little attention to the anti-Jewish side of that early stage of the revolution. Contemporaries too, Christians and Jews alike, were quick to offer reasons for minimizing or even fully disregarding these violent episodes. The riots, wrote the Jewish weekly *Der Orient* were no more than "wild weeds of freedom," or just "outbursts of the raging mob," to quote the Jewish scholar Leopold Zunz.[13] He, an exception among prominent Jews at the time, a radical democrat, repeatedly stressed the grand universal mission of the revolution. Jews could be freed, he believed, only as part of the whole, and they must accept as inevitable the attacks against them in the meantime, signs of age-old hostility: "The fury of the mob against the Jews in some regions will pass without a trace just like other disturbances," Zunz wrote in a private letter of March 17, 1848, "and freedom will remain."[14]

---

[13] For these and other Jewish reactions to the revolution, see Jacob Toury, "Die Revolution von 1848 als innerjüdischer Wendepunkt," in Hans Liebeschütz and Arnold Paucker (eds.), *Das Judentum in der deutschen Umwelt 1800–1850: Studien zur Frühgeschichte der Emanzipation*, Tübingen, 1977, 359–376. The quotes are from page 365.

[14] The letter is reprinted in Nahum N. Glatzer, "Leopold Zunz and the Revolution of 1848: With the Publication of Four Letters by Zunz," *Leo Baeck Institute Yearbook*, 5(1) (1960), 122–139. The quote is from page 132. The English translation is from Ismar Schorsch, *Leopold Zunz: Creativity in Adversity*, Philadelphia, PA, 2016, 164.

At the start of the revolution, the orthodox rabbi of the not-yet-German city of Altona, Jacob Ettlinger, argued that liberty must be "consecrated in blood," and the editor in chief of the liberal *Allgemeine Zeitung des Judentums* seized the opportunity to preach once again the need for "productivization," the best antidote to the rage of the rural mob, according to him.[15] In all of these texts, one finds a simplified dichotomy, stressing the difference between rural uprisings and the urban revolution, presenting the first as an echo of pre-modern popular unrest, not to be taken seriously, and the latter as a forward-looking modern struggle.

Moreover, Jewish active participation in the revolutionary movement seemed to most Jews – provided, of course, that they themselves were not directly hit by violence – far more important than the sporadic riots, seemingly quick to die out, against their co-religionists. After all, the voice of German Jewry was now heard from all revolutionary stages, and this alone represented success, short-lived as it eventually turned out to be, celebrating – in Jewish eyes, too – the heroic "Year of Freedom." From Berlin to Vienna, Jews actively participated in the opening days of the March revolution, hoping – together with their Christian comrades – that equality, too, would soon be legalized as a fundamental principle of a free, united Germany. The peak of this activity was the formulation of Article 16 of the new constitution drafted at the National Assembly with its seat in the Paulskirche in Frankfurt. It stipulated equal civil and political rights for all, regardless of religious affiliation, and was voted through practically without opposition on December 10, 1848. Several state parliaments adopted this or similarly worded paragraphs either immediately before or, more often, immediately after the historic vote in Frankfurt am Main. And in most of these state parliaments a number of Jews were by then sitting as elected delegates. The most well known of them were Jacob Jacoby of Königsberg and Gabriel Riesser of Hamburg, the first an outspoken democrat and the second a left-center liberal, both of whom were veterans of the fight for Jewish rights. They witnessed, together with others, the changing atmosphere in Germany and joined in constructing a just society of citizens that was sure to accept Jews as undisputable equals.

One often mentions the Constitutional Commission of the People's Chamber in Baden that approved a bill granting Jews equal rights as early as April 1848, adding that a detailed justification of such a step was a "waste of time."[16] The bill did, indeed, pass almost without opposition,

---

[15] Editorial, *Allgemeine Zeitung des Judentums*, 1848, 187.
[16] Rürup, "Judenemanzipation und bürgerliche Gesellschaft in Deutschland," 66.

but that was not everywhere the case, nor was this the final act in the unfolding drama even in the relatively progressive Baden. Soon, popular opposition resurfaced everywhere, forcing the reenactment of numerous old and new restrictions upon local Jews, as well as other edicts and acts, practically voiding the revolutionary achievements. In Bavaria, a storm of local protest and hundreds of petitions came out against Jewish emancipation, halting proposed legislation and turning the clock back, so to speak, against all hopes and expectations.[17]

At first, such steps were considered exceptions. The general feeling was that equality was winning the day. After all, at the start of the revolution, the old regime everywhere collapsed and new governments enacted liberal reforms in various parts of Germany. While the monarchies were not overthrown, conservative statesmen – such as Metternich in Vienna or Prince Wilhelm in Berlin – were forced to flee for their lives. The upheaval in the countryside had been calmed down, as peasants' demands were generally complied with, and moderate liberals seemed to be able to restrain the revolutionary crowd, guiding it away from violent action and in the direction of conciliation and compromise. Finally, an elected National Assembly was expected to provide Germany with a liberal constitution and – most importantly – achieve its political unity. This was a time of great hopes.

Soon, achieving national unity took center stage and then repeatedly seemed to touch upon those sensitive points that were inherent in the attempt to combine nationalism and liberalism. Among the many difficulties, the newly imagined Germany was faced with the need to handle minorities, men and women who were not initially seen as part of the nation. It also had to cope with the separate nationalisms of some of these minorities: Danes in Schleswig-Holstein, Czechs in Bohemia, Italians in Trieste and Tirol, Poles in parts of the Habsburg Empire, and the combination of Poles and Jews in the province of Posen, once more a part of Prussia after 1815.

At first, the minority issue, especially with respect to the Jews, seemed of light weight. To be sure, equality for Jews had been on the agenda at the outset of the revolution, and Jews made it clear they were patriots of the first order, German nationalists no less than their non-Jewish fellow revolutionaries. During the Vormärz years, many of them had actively endeavored to discard all reference to their own particular nationality. This was done with special eagerness in the various reform communities that insisted on seeing Judaism as no more than a religion, yet another denomination, and often even erased from the liturgy all phrases of yearning for Jerusalem or hopes of return to Zion. Abraham Geiger, the

---

[17] See the details in James F. Harris, *The People Speak! Anti-Semitism and Emancipation in Nineteenth-Century Bavaria*, Ann Arbor, 1994, 87–158.

main spokesman of Reform Judaism at the time, found it difficult to relate to Jews outside of Germany, especially those living in Eastern Europe, in the way one had usually done as a matter of course for generations. Now, belonging to Germany, being part of the German nation, increasingly became a more important aspect of Jewish identity in the various German lands, and it became all the more so during the revolution. Even orthodox Jews were by then animated by German national feelings, and these constituted a clear and resolute stand among liberal Jewish reformers of all kinds. "From now on, we no longer define our cause as a special one, it is now identical with the cause of the fatherland ... we are and want to be only Germans ... We are Jews (Israeliten) only by our faith," wrote Rabbi Leopold Stein of Frankfurt am Main.[18] Activists, such as Riesser, were dreaming of a politically unified Germany, convinced that Jewish emancipation would naturally be included as part of its social and political order.

But the combination of constitutional liberalism with nationalism and the need to act without giving up on either of them proved more intricate than one tended to believe. This was made particularly apparent in the controversy over Polish national rights in the province of Posen, where Jews constituted a significant part of a complex ethnic equation. In some ways, the Jews of the province of Posen made all the difference. Poles, to be sure, constituted the majority of the population in this province, and many of them surely hoped to live in a free Poland and not in a free Prussia or even in a free united Germany. Above all, they feared living in an authoritarian Prussia, where policies were decided by an austere bureaucracy in the best case or by harsh military rule in the worst case, and, as things stood at the time, Prussia used both in resisting the Polish national movement during 1848. Beyond military means, the administration sought to modify the numerical ethnic composition of the province by moving the border so as to weaken the relative size of the Polish population within it and as a rule count the Jews *en masse* together with the Germans.

This last measure was not in itself unreasonable. At the time, Jews in the previously Polish region spoke primarily German; often in addition to Yiddish, of course. Moreover, they often depended on the support of the ruling Prussian bureaucracy as against the local population and therefore usually preferred to identify themselves as Germans. They realized, no doubt, that this would become vital in the coming nationality contest and, as long as the revolution – liberal and national – seemed to be still marching on, they were eager to contribute to it in whatever way they could. They could not yet foresee that it would soon prove to be ever less

---

[18] Rabbi Leopold Stein, *Zuruf eines israelitischen Bürgers an seine christlischen Mitbürger*, Frankfurt am Main, 1848.

liberal and in fact more and more national, not to say nationalistic, and that, in whatever form it took, it was in any case soon to be crushed.

By the spring of 1849, with the revolution entangled in its own contradictions and losing support on all sides, both the Austrian and the Prussian monarchical authorities regained control over the situation. In December 1848, the Austrian Kanzler (Chancellor), Felix Prince zu Schwarzenberg, managed to achieve the abdication of Emperor Ferdinand and the ascension of his no less reactionary nephew Franz-Joseph. Soon thereafter, the army subdued the revolutionaries in Vienna, bringing this historical chapter – or perhaps only this historical interlude – to an end. By the spring of 1849, the Prussian king, too, felt strong enough to resist any cooperation with the National Assembly in Berlin or with the Parliament in Frankfurt. A delegation from the Paulskirche, including a number of Jewish delegates, traveled to Berlin and offered the king the imperial crown. He refused. The revolution was nearing its end. He did not need to make any concessions. Meanwhile, all other liberal hopes came to naught, too. Towards the end of the year, political reaction set in and, among all other steps reversing the achievements of the revolution, most of those that concerned the Jews were reversed, too. They could now once more observe, from the margin, how Christianity was being reinstated as a state religion in Prussia as well as in Austria, and bourgeois liberalism suffered setbacks on all fronts.

However, in the historiography, both German and German-Jewish, the days of 1848 were long remembered either only for their glory or not at all. Isaac Markus Jost, who wrote the first nineteenth century history of the Jews, ended it in 1847, and Ludwig Geiger's history of the Jews in Berlin "passed lightly over the events of 1848."[19] The first to give it the allure of a turning-point was Heinrich Graetz. Here, at some length, are his words in the last volume of his *Volkstümliche Geschichte der Juden (Popular History of the Jews)*, first published in 1870, a standard work of a "generalist" that has been intensively used and extensively quoted by many contemporary and later historians: "During the stormy years of the revolutions of February and March [1848], in Paris, Vienna, Berlin, in Italy and other countries, an intoxicating desire for liberty came over the nations of Europe, more overpowering and marvelous even than the movement in the years 1789 and 1830. With imperious demands the people confronted their princes and rulers. Among the demands was that of the emancipation of the Jews. In all popular assemblies and proclamations, the

---

[19] See the comprehensive article by Adolf Kober, "Jews in the Revolution of 1848 in Germany," *Jewish Social Studies*, 10 (1998), 135–164.

despised Jews of yesterday were admitted into the bond of 'Liberty, Equality, and Fraternity.' What the most sanguine observer had never ventured to hope for suddenly took place." Graetz goes on to describe how everywhere in Europe "the shackles of the Jews have fallen," clearly standing in awe before these glorious events.[20] And, indeed, similar awe was apparently felt by other historians at about the same time, too. Even Simon Dubnow, who moved the focus of Jewish history in modern times from Germany to Eastern Europe, treating only the major political aspects of the 1848 revolution, enthusiastically told his readers of those Jews who took part in the deliberations of the Frankfurt Parliament. He mentioned the Jewish radicals in the streets of Vienna, albeit only briefly, but the fierce anti-Jewish violence in the first phase of the revolution not at all.

Later on, moving about 100 years forward, Jakob Katz returns to its glories in his *Out of the Ghetto*, completely disregarding the popular manifestations of antisemitism. This is likewise true in his later more detailed, masterly *From Prejudice to Destruction*.[21] And he is no exception. German historians, too, usually mention only the matter of Jewish legal emancipation in 1848, since it falls easily into their overall positive, heroic story of the revolution. Its less palatable events and their apparently contradictory nature are all too often avoided. Even Veit Valentin, himself of Jewish origins, one of the few left-wing historians writing during the early twentieth century, known as an outspoken defender of the Weimar Republic and thus naturally interested in its precursors, avoided this theme. He too was still writing what was after all a history of the revolution "from above," and could therefore disregard the rural anti-Jewish riots and the stream of anti-Jewish petitions which flooded local assemblies during much of the *tolles Jahr*, voicing, no doubt, the popular sentiment. Even modern social historians, finally writing history "from below," on the whole did no better. While placing more emphasis on the popular aspects of the revolution, most of them tended to pass over the "Jewish connection." And historians writing in the Bundesrepublik, in full awareness of the significance of the Jews for contemporary German history, tended to ignore these matters, too. The anti-Jewish riots do not feature at all in Hans-Ulrich Wehler's *Deutsche Gesellschaftsgeschichte* (*German Social History*), for instance, nor in Thomas Nipperdey's *Deutsche Geschichte*. The latter mentions those "Jewish creditors" who

---

[20] Quoted from a later edition: Heinrich Graetz, *Volkstümliche Geschichte der Juden*, Munich, 1985, Vol. VI, 322 (my translation).
[21] Jakob Katz, *Out of the Ghetto: The Social Background of Jewish Emancipation, 1770–1870*, Syracuse, NY, 1998; Jakob Katz, *From Prejudice to Destruction: Anti-Semitism, 1700–1933*, Cambridge, MA, 1982.

were – among others – the targets of peasants' rage in March 1848, but he too does not go further into this topic.[22] Finally, among later German generalists, only Reinhard Rürup has given the matter his full attention. Rürup exhaustively treats this topic in an essay originally published in a volume dedicated specifically to Jewish aspects of the revolution. However, in his succinct *Deutschland im 19. Jahrhundert (Germany in the Nineteenth Century)*, one finds only a brief reference to "violence against Jews, against rich priests and other persons who were occupied as moneylenders."[23]

Thus, the best and most comprehensive study of anti-Jewish unrest in 1848 appeared as a small volume in Hebrew – almost an underground publication – printed by a minor publishing house in Tel Aviv, in 1968. Jacob Toury, by then already well known among historians of German Jewry, gave his book an elaborate and fitting title: *Turmoil and Confusion in the Revolution of 1848: The Anti-Jewish Riots and Their Influence on Modern Antisemitism*. A dozen years later, in 1981, a German version of this book was published, making the whole affair better known among specialists.[24] But in the end, more influential were historical surveys of antisemitism rather than the revolution, placing the riots of 1848 in this context, and, if the history of antisemitism were in itself to become an integral part of the overall German historical narrative, this subsection of the revolutionary saga might become indeed a true part of the whole.

What does that part in fact do to the whole? Perhaps, in the end, not too much. Perhaps it simply offers a chance for some contemplation, for reevaluating what we generally know so far, and for casting it all in a somewhat different light. The German Enlightenment, despite its rhetoric, never fully practiced religious toleration, I have claimed above. Neither did its presumed heir, the national liberal movement of the Vormärz years, find ways to accept those who until then did not belong – the strangers, the "others," the German Jews. They themselves first found *Bildung* a useful bridge and, since politically they did not have too many alternatives at the time, liberalism was self-evidently their choice. On the eve of the revolution, most of them were moderate liberals; only some were radical democrats. But, for the most part, their love of country, their true, fervent patriotism, remained unrequited. As much as they tried to

---

[22] In English: Thomas Nipperdey, *Germany from Napoleon to Bismarck, 1800–1866*, Princeton, NJ, 1996, 533.
[23] Reinhard Rürup, *Deutschland im 19. Jahrhundert*, Göttingen, 1984, 180.
[24] See Toury's article in *Das Judentum in der deutschen Umwelt, 1800–1850*, and Wolfram Siemann, *Die deutsche Revolution von 1848/49*, Frankfurt am Main, 1985.

"enter," they usually still remained on the margin, often hated and suspect, never fully allowed to join – even by many of their liberal comrades.

In rural society, among more traditional and less educated people, things were even worse. We have seen the widespread hatred directed at Jews, erupting repeatedly, manifesting the fact that they continued to be targets of humiliation, objects of exclusion, even of sporadic violence into the middle of the nineteenth century. The Germany of the first half of the nineteenth century, a land still deeply authoritarian, marked by what the historian Wolfram Siemann called "*staatspolizeiliche Verfolgungen*" (state-police persecutions) and strict censorship, appears even more unyielding and oppressive from our perspective. Finally, the revolution promised an overall change, including change in the relationships between Jews and non-Jews. Most liberals were now ready, perhaps even willing, to see Jews as comrades in arms and to enact their full and complete emancipation. But changes came more slowly than one expected. While there was some improvement in their status during the 1840s, no doubt, it was only a beginning, and even the revolution left untouched the basic asymmetry of this situation. It apparently lay too deep. Integration had been seen by the Jews as the ability to live and act together with non-Jews; it was seen by most Germans as a process by which Jews would gradually lose all signs of their "otherness." While German society as a whole no longer rejected the Jews, many sections within it were still far from ready to accept them. For the time being ambivalence, half-steps, and fear of too radical reforms continued to be the rule.

This was true not only with regard to the Jews. The revolution of 1848, despite its heroic narrative, was in the end frustrated on all fronts; none of its main goals was achieved. Germany was neither made liberal, nor was it nationally united. True Constitutionalism was experimented with, both within the various single German states and on the national level. Impressive acts of legislation were agreed upon. Even authoritarian monarchs yielded to their validity. But all this proved temporary. Soon, reaction set in, seemingly rolling back the march of progress, and, while the revolution at first seemed to succeed mainly because of the weakness of the restorative forces, it eventually failed because of the unexpected strength revealed precisely by the same old forces. Most issues remained unresolved, though none could now be completely discarded. Both liberal constitutionalism and national unification remained unfulfilled projects, but both remained on the agenda. Now, in fact, they had to be further handled by the victorious counter-revolution.

The story of Jewish emancipation well reflects this ambivalence. Revolutionary achievements were once more almost everywhere reversed. Old restrictions were reenacted, so that a state based on equality and a society characterized by open doors remained unfulfilled dreams.

All that is strangely reminiscent of the events following the Congress of Vienna. At that point too, the Jewish issue reflected the inability of the restoration regime to handle even relatively simple first steps in the direction of modernizing Germany. The Bund had been a weak compromise, while discussions of German unification were suppressed. The liberalization of the economy attracted the various state bureaucracies, and some of its principles were, in fact, gradually applied. But, on the whole, reforms in all fields stagnated or at best remained partial.

The failure of Jewish emancipation had clearly manifested this stagnation at that time. The project of building an independent citizenry, roughly sketched during the Enlightenment and experimented with under French occupation, remained in the hands of an indecisive bureaucracy and sometimes well-meaning but ineffective heads of states. Finally, the revolution took on all these projects again, trying to reshape them in an even more radical and more modern framework. Only it too ended in defeat. The issues were redefined, but in the end none of the goals, now better thought-out and better delineated, were practically achieved.

The 1850s were years of regrouping under powerful reactionary governments. Prussia, now in open conflict with Austria, at first still tried to change the status quo by using the advantages it had gained during the latter stages of the revolution. It cemented its power with the help or through the manipulation of the smaller states which made up the "third Germany." In the meantime, however, powerful economic changes, no longer controlled by the Prussian or any other administration, a force of a new quality, had set in. Only in the early 1860s did Germany seem ready to take on the challenges that had been left unanswered, like open wounds, by the failed uprising. By that time, all was set for the next stage in the effort to achieve the various required changes, and by then such changes were, indeed, needed more than ever.

5 Germany's Entangled Modernities

From early on in the nineteenth century, Jews were firmly associated with modernity. The leading anti-reform aristocrat in Prussia, Friedrich August Ludwig von der Marwitz, is known to have expressed his misgivings about what he saw as the emerging "modernized Jews' state." Presumably, Jews were threatening to take over aristocratic land properties and in the end destroy their "old honorable Brandenburg-Prussia" and its ancient corporate form. There were Conservatives, who tended to link all forms of modern living, as well as the general danger of revolution, with Jews and Judaism. Prussia's King Friedrich Wilhelm IV complained that Schiller's *Wilhelm Tell* was "a piece for Jews and revolutionaries", and Adam Müller, a well-known defender of the world of yesterday, feared that "merchants, artisans and Jews" would soon take over the then weakened "aristocrat's and peasants' corporation."[1]

Jews – or at least some Jews – seemed to have accepted this view of themselves, maintaining that they did indeed constitute a vanguard of modernity, for better rather than for worse. In one of his meandering commentaries on contemporary affairs, attached to his 1838 text on "Shakespeare's Maidens and Women," and while discussing Jessica, Shylock's daughter in the *Merchant of Venice*, Heine describes, perhaps for the first time, what he saw as the affinity between Germans and Jews, and then adds that, right from the beginning, "Jews always bore within themselves that modern principle, which is only now becoming visibly prominent in the nations of Europe." They had always adhered to republicanism, he goes on in the same vein, "their creed was liberty and equality." "Ah, the delusion of it!," he typically adds, preparing the ground for yet another twist to his argument. This "principle of modernity," he explains, manifested itself in the special Jewish "mercantile

---

[1] For the quotes in this paragraph, see Götz Aly, *Why the Germans? Why the Jews? Envy, Race Hatred, and the Prehistory of the Holocaust*, New York, 2014, 32–33. For the full context, see Marion Schulte, *Preußische Offiziere über Judentum und Emanzipation*, Berlin and Boston, MA, 2018, 269–278.

spirit," so perfectly developed because they had always been pushed out of all respectable occupations and practically forced to become "the cleverest bankers and merchants." The Jews "were forced into growing rich and their wealth made them hated"[2] was his conclusion. Only a few years later, Marx too stressed the link between Jews and capitalism, finally defining emancipation as liberation from Judaism itself. Similar statements, making Jews responsible for the modern production system and its evils, could be quoted from other contemporary authors – on the right and on the left; by no means only from outspoken antisemites.

For Heine, it surely was the Jewish milieu around his uncle in Hamburg, one of the richest men in Germany of the day, that served him in writing the passage quoted above. Perhaps it also was the Jewish community of Berlin that he still cherished from his time in the Prussian capital; a community whose sons – such as Eduard Gans, likewise the offspring of a rich banker's family – he had once befriended. But this was, on the whole, no more than a legend; a legend first adopted by antisemites, and then – curiously enough – by many Jews, too.

In fact, from the very beginning, the role of the Jews in the process of modernization has been wrongly appraised. Modernity, to be sure, meant different things to different people. Nevertheless, some of its common characteristics were usually agreed upon. Urbanization, for instance, has always been considered an important element within its overall portrayal, and in much of Central Europe Jews had been, no doubt, earlier and more intensively urbanized than others. This was the outcome of centuries of prohibitions on land purchasing, even on working the land, a systematic pushing of the Jews into a few, specific occupations, especially petty trade and moneylending – mostly on a small scale. Still, even by 1840, roughly at the time when Heine published his Shakespeare notes, only 56,000 Jews – 14% of the total – resided in the 24 sizeable communities within the borders of the old Reich, and in 1852, fewer than 40,000 Jews, or 9% of the whole, lived in towns of over 50,000 inhabitants. It is, however, true that while as many as 80% of the Prussian Jews lived in settlements of over 2,000 inhabitants, considered urban by the statisticians at the day, only 30% of the general population resided in settlements of this size. Clearly, Jews preceded others in becoming urban and then in moving to large metropolitan centers, though this later trend began only in the 1860s and gained real momentum no less than a full generation afterwards.

During the first half of the nineteenth century, most Jews still lived in small and middle-sized towns. In southern Germany, many of them had

---

[2] Quoted from Heinrich Heine, *Heine on Shakespeare: A Translation of His Notes on Shakespeare's Heroines*, trans. Ida Benecke, London, 1895, 136–141.

for a long time settled only in rural areas, as they were forbidden to move into towns until the granting of full emancipation in the 1860s. Even then, many were regarded as only "partly urban," since they usually served as middlemen between town and village, selling local agricultural products in nearby towns and bringing back for sale various town-produced articles or an assortment of colonial wares. On the basis of numerous Jewish memoirs, the historian Monika Richarz claimed that, in most rural areas, Jews seemed to have had "an urban touch." They did not fit the cliché image of "urban Jews, reading Schiller, Kant or Goethe," nor were they the rich, modernizing figures described by Heine. Nevertheless, they did gradually become ever more urbanized, together with many non-Jewish inhabitants of the region, though seemingly more rapidly and in some ways more completely.[3]

Jews showed other, related and unrelated characteristics of modernity earlier than others. This was particularly apparent in various aspects of their intimate life. Quite spectacular was the relatively lower Jewish infant and child mortality rate, to be perceived as early as the beginning of the nineteenth century, everywhere in and outside of Germany. Furthermore, while such diminishing child mortality is normally correlated with economic status, the data for Jews indicate low and steadily declining rates regardless of wealth or income. This phenomenon has been repeatedly recorded throughout Europe, in east and west, even where Jews were known to be particularly poor,[4] and, while this was in itself by no means sufficient for launching a full-scale modern demographic transition, it did play a not insignificant role in achieving it. Above all, it had an effect on the size of the Jewish family, at first larger than contemporary non-Jewish ones and then smaller and quickly shrinking. It also influenced the overall mortality rate of Jews, which was likewise lower and quickly declining, especially in comparison with non-Jews. Finally, one could indeed claim that the so-called demographic transition, of which lower birth rates and lower death rates were most clearly characteristic, occurred for the Jews in Germany a whole generation before it finally occurred for non-Jews.[5]

---

[3] For the data and the quotes in this paragraph, see Monika Richarz, "Emancipation and Continuity. German Jews in the Rural Economy," in Werner E. Mosse, Arnold Paucker, and Reinhard Rürup (eds.), *Revolution and Evolution: 1848 in German-Jewish History*, Tübingen, 1981, 94–116, and the response to this essay by Stefi Jersch-Wenzel, "Comment," in Mosse, Paucker, and Rürup (eds.), *Revolution and Evolution*, 117–122.

[4] See Usiel O. Schmelz, *Infant and Early Child Mortality among Jews of the Diaspora*, Jerusalem, 1971, 15–33, and Usiel O. Schmelz, "Die demographische Entwicklung der Juden in Deutschland von der Mitte des 19. Jahrhunderts bis 1933," *Zeitschrift für Bevölkerungswissenschaft*, 8 (1982), 31–72.

[5] Further data and literature on these themes, for Jews as well as generally for the population in Germany and in some of its major cities, are available in my "Die jüdische Gemeinde in Altona 1867–1890. Ein demographisches Profil," in Shulamit Volkov, *Das jüdische Projekt*

The changing Jewish occupational structure seems to have been even more spectacular and noticeable in its uniqueness. This was the most discussed feature of their peculiarity, especially since the late eighteenth century and throughout the debate on emancipation. To be sure, being more urban necessarily meant the practice of more typically urban occupations, too. Thus, in the Prussia of 1842, self-employed men in trade still made up some 40% of the overall working Jewish population, and these employed an additional 8% as shop assistants and clerks. By 1861, the figures for both categories were 45% and 12.5%, respectively, while at the same time only 20% of *all* working men were listed under the rubric of "commerce and services" – less than half the Jewish rate. The issue of Jewish "productivization," namely the presumed need to have them perform in other sectors that were considered more productive, came up repeatedly for decades. However, despite the pressure from outside, and the efforts to recruit the Jewish public sphere in favor of this cause from the inside, little was changed in this respect during the entire century. Commercial occupations became more rather than less attractive with the onset of industrialization, and it could hardly be expected that those who already had experience in these growing sectors and had wide-ranging, even international contacts, enabling them to work profitably in this field, would now seek other forms of employment. Typically, Jews remained almost always self-employed, thus independent of non-Jewish employers, who often resented their insistence on observing the Shabbat and the various Jewish holidays. They continued to develop their business with relatively little capital, while gainfully cooperating with family relatives – near and far. Some change did occur in this occupational structure during the century, of course, even some dramatic change towards its end, but this took place mostly *within* the commercial sector. By the later years of the nineteenth century, fewer Jews were itinerant vendors, while the majority had become established shop-owners of various size and some – very few, in fact – became heads of large commercial concerns.

Throughout these years, the fact that only a small section of the working Jews were working in agriculture or in industry remained the major difference between them and the rest of the population. During the third quarter of the nineteenth century, over 50% of all Germans were still employed in agriculture, the great majority of them as small peasants or as seasonal employees. At the same time, over 40% were industrial and

der Moderne, Munich, 2001, 97–117. This is recapitulated in my *Germans, Jews, and Antisemites: Trials in Emancipation*, Cambridge, 2006, 209–223.

handicraft workers, and the difference with the Jews remained conspicuous throughout the century. In the end, this did not considerably change even during intensive industrialization and – significantly – despite continuous migration of poor Jews from the East. Thus, while some Jews became exceedingly rich, the majority remained lower- or middle-lower-class people, living very modestly. Some 20% were for a long time even too poor to pay any taxes. Successful bankers, large-scale international merchants, and department-store moguls were very conspicuous, no doubt, but they were and remained the exception.[6]

Perhaps because of their conspicuous success in *some* economic spheres, one expected Jews to be a leading force in industrialization as a whole. This, however, was – once again – not the case. It was true that many Jews almost everywhere moved economically and socially upward throughout the years of gradual emancipation. It was also true that this upward trend was easily perceived and often gave grounds for envy, as the historian Götz Aly forcefully argues.[7] But actual figures paint a much more complex picture. In reality, only a small minority of German Jews ever reached the higher levels of the bourgeoisie, and only a few did so through active participation in industry. Below the few court Jews and some successful private bankers, often mentioned for the late eighteenth and early nineteenth century, we later encounter the group of the "recently *arrived*," mostly larger merchants, sometimes businessmen who often produced traditional articles, mainly in the clothing and textile branches, thus buttressing their income from commerce. In most cases, they were not full-time industrialists. Differently put, Jews were clearly becoming better off, but the most successful among them came from commodity trading; that is, neither from finance nor – more significantly – from industry.

Some individual Jews, of course, did become powerful industrialists even in the earlier stages of industrialization. In Silesia, for instance, some Jews were involved in coal extraction and in related branches of heavy industry. But, on the whole, as the historian Avraham Barkai wrote, "Jewish entrepreneurs in mining, smelting or machine-tool manufacture were exceptions," and these – not the textile industry – were, after all, the leading sectors of German industrialization. Jews, it appears, continued to be concentrated in their traditional branches: the clothing, food, and

---

[6] See Avraham Barkai, "German Jews at the Start of Industrialization – Structural Change and Mobility 1835–1860," in Werner E. Mosse, Arnold Paucker, and Reinhard Rürup (eds.), *Revolution and Evolution: 1848 in German-Jewish History*, Tübingen, 1981, 123–149.
[7] See Aly, *Why the Germans?*, passim. For a good critical review of Götz' argument see Steven E. Aschheim in *Holocaust and Genocide Studies*, vol. 30/2, 365–368.

tobacco industries. They hardly participated in the so-called German take-off.[8]

A more spectacular view of the Jewish case may emerge when one focuses on Berlin – an important, but clearly exceptional case – or when one chooses to stress the success of some exceptional figures such as Bismarck's banker Gerson Bleichröder, Bethel Henry Strousberg, known as the "railways king," or the Mendelssohn family, with its Europe-wide banking enterprises. These were probably responsible for the view that emerges from much of the older literature, in which one tends to overestimate the role of the Jewish minority, its success and its economic influence. A minority of some 1 percent, of whom quite a few were still poor and remained economically marginal for much of the century, states Avraham Barkai convincingly, could not lead an economy the size of the German one, even if they *were* disproportionally active within it. Basing his studies on the work of the American economist Simon Kuznets, who dealt with the economy of minorities in general, he concludes that Jews could not have changed the course of the German economy, despite all the talent, the hard work, and the typical consumers' modesty that they had brought to bear in abundance.[9]

The role of the Jews in the German economic growth during the nineteenth century became a topic of public and scholarly debate at the start of the twentieth century, following the publication of Werner Sombart's magnum opus, *Die Juden und das Wirtschaftleben* in 1911.[10] Sombart reacted to Max Weber's influential book *The Protestant Ethic and the Spirit of Capitalism*, published somewhat earlier, in which the up-and-coming sociologist described the small sectarian protestant minority in England who – according to him – initiated and propagated modern capitalist business practices as a whole. Sombart, in turn, stressed the role of the Jews in the development of latter-day capitalism and brought out what he saw as their unique role in industrialization. Being what one historian called "a media phenomenon," Sombart's arguments soon gained much publicity.[11] They were fiercely disputed by some, but a taste of his tale has never entirely vanished. In one of the fullest and most carefully worded presentations of the topic, Monika Richarz, showing the comparative success of Jewish entrepreneurs in the early stage of industrialization, still saw fit to remark that "the main features that characterized the Jews' acquired economic behavior were, above all,

---

[8] Barkai, "German Jews at the Start of Industrialization," 142.   [9] Ibid., 143–145.
[10] Werner Sombart, *The Jews and Modern Capitalism*, trans. Mortimer Epstein, London, 1913.
[11] See Derek Penslar, *Shylock's Children: Economics and Jewish Identity in Modern Europe*, Berkeley, CA and Los Angeles, CA, 2001, 165.

the courage to take risks, the readiness to be innovative, and the ability to attract customers."[12] Perhaps. Some Jews were surely ready to take risks, and some were doubtlessly innovative, attracting exceptionally many customers. But these were not the general characteristics of the Jews as such. We are on safer ground if we assume that, within the industrial sector, even in the unusual event of a Jew venturing into a modern branch of an experimental nature, he would behave more or less like his non-Jewish counterparts. With very few exceptions, Jews usually worked within the known parameters of their time.

An interesting example, demonstrating the complexity of the situation and neatly covering the entire nineteenth century, is the story of the Liebermanns.[13] The family, consisting of cotton and silk merchants, all strictly orthodox religiously, came from the West Prussian border town of Märkisch-Friedland. Some of its members settled in Berlin between the mid 1820s and mid 1830s, joining the intensive trade in the Prussian capital at that time. Berlin was by then a center of the textile branch, and they were determined to participate in developing it as gainfully as they could. England, being the main producer of various cotton articles, provided a good starting point, and it was from there that Josef Liebermann imported and then sold his wares, in and outside of Prussia. He did not directly participate in modernizing the process of industrial cotton production, but was always a reliable supplier of needed credit to bolder entrepreneurs working in the same branch. It was particularly cotton-printing that began to apply newly invented machines at the time, first in England and then in Berlin, too. The final, much-coveted "Prussian shawls" were sold by Liebermann not only in Eastern and Western Europe, but even in North America and as far afield as Mexico and Japan.

Younger members of the Liebermann clan made further steps into the world of industry. Through marriages with wives from other Jewish families in Berlin, Benjamin Joachim and then his brother Pincus, now fashionably called Philipp, became silk manufacturers and the latter also a "Councilor of Commerce" and even a "Kingly Councilor of Commerce." In the meantime, there were at least two large trading firms bearing the name Liebermann in Berlin, participating in a mercantile network with strong links to England. They all had a hand in production, but their main strength remained large-scale commerce.

---

[12] Monika Richarz, "Occupational Distribution and Social Structure," in Michael A. Meyer and Michael Brenner (eds.), *German History in Modern Times*, Vol. III: *Integration in Dispute, 1871–1918*, New York, 1998, 35–67, quoted from page 44.

[13] For the details below and the full story of the Liebermanns, see Regina Scheer, *"Wir sind die Liebermanns": Die Geschichte einer Familie*, Berlin, 2008.

One by one, the daughters of the family also married successful businessmen from central Berlin, though this did not always work out so well. In 1836, Therese – previously Teibchen – Liebermann married the sixteen-years-older grain merchant from the same social milieu Moritz Rathenau, but he turned out to be rather uninterested in business. It was only later on that their son Emil struck out in a successful business career, later followed by his son Walther. Other Liebermanns – and there were many, since orthodox Jewish women still had eight, ten, or even sixteen children at that time – all climbed upward noticeably. Some took side-lines, so to speak, and studied medicine or law; the majority stayed in business.

To be sure, not all remained in the *same* business. While cotton and silk were still – and would continue to be – in great demand, it soon became evident that the future lay elsewhere, and, by 1856, the old Josef Liebermann and two of his sons, Louis and Benjamin, first purchased the Wilhelmshütte, an old iron foundry in Sprottau, lower Silesia, and soon thereafter the Dorotheenhütte in a town nearby. They were producing various kinds of machines and metal parts for the quickly expaning railroad system. Emil Rathenau left some details concerning these iron foundries in his memoires, describing his four unhappy years there, working as an apprentice. Emil was required to work as "a blue-colored proletarian with battered hands," he remembered, while his local cousins remained in their comfortable business offices.[14] Moreover, they soon transferred all technical matters to their manager, one Adolf Mestern, who later became a partner, responsible for modernizing the foundries and managing the machine-building and iron-manufacturing firms, while the Liebermanns – once again – handled finance and trading matters, in which they had a long, in fact, a generations-long, experience.

Finally, the Liebermanns never left their hold on the Berlin's textile trade. They continued to expand there in parallel to their investments in Silesia, gradually becoming well known and even politically respectable. In 1857, intent on sealing his prestige in Berlin, Louis Liebermann purchased the family house at Pariser Platz 7, next to the Brandenburgertor, living now in the neighborhood of Prussian aristocrats and the French embassy. His son Max had been born ten years earlier, and it was perhaps not atypical for German Jewry that, of all the enterprising men in this impressive family, the most well known was to be this unassuming son, who never entered business at all but emerged as a famous artist, a leading impressionist painter.

Thus, while German Jews were energetically marching along the course of economic modernization, their uniqueness was probably

---

[14] Quoted from Felix Pinner, *Emil Rathenau und das elektrische Zeitalter*, Leipzig, 1918, 5.

nowhere to be observed more clearly than in their educational drive. This had slowly become apparent since the middle of the eighteenth century and came to full fruition towards the end of the nineteenth – presenting us once again with that gradual, slow movement, typical of their overall modernization.

To be sure, Jews always placed great emphasis on the education of their children, especially – of course – on that of their sons. Some historians have recently argued that, even in the early years of their diaspora, it was not only discrimination that held them away from the land. Rather, it was the fact that, for men who could read and write, it seemed irrational to labor as agricultural hands. After all, their skills were much sought-after elsewhere. Even their minimal educational head-start was often enough to equip them for better work – either in some of the more sophisticated crafts, when this was legally allowed, or in some branches of commerce, often in finance.[15] While their presumed educational advantage lost its edge in late medieval times, it regained its influence, limited as it had been, in early modernity and then during the nineteenth century. Earlier on, most Jewish children in the Ashkenazi European region learned in a traditional Cheder, beginning there at the age of three or four, and Germany was no exception. They learned Hebrew and the biblical tales, but, in any event, they always became at least literate. They also simply learned to learn, and this was surely unusual for the majority of rural non-Jews and frequently for urban non-Jews as well.

At the same time, Cheder education was by no means adequate for those who wished to enter higher non-Jewish schools, or even move further on along the route leading to university studies, perhaps eventually to one of the free professions. In the early years of the nineteenth century, Heine's mother, seeking more appropriate education for her son, entered him in a girls' school, and then, soon afterwards, in a school at an old Franciscan Closter, where he was beaten up and mistreated before later being admitted to the somewhat better Catholic Lyceum, within the same establishment, apparently just as far from being humane or inspiring. By then, Jewish children in Berlin and in Hamburg could already attend special Jewish schools that offered them a mix of religious and secular education. And although these "free schools" were initially intended for children of immigrants and the poor, they were gradually turned into educational institutions for middle-class Jewish boys – a model for many similar such schools that sprouted thereafter up and

---

[15] This process is described in a number of articles by Maristella Botticini and Zvi Eckstein and finally in their book Maristella Botticini and Zvi Eckstein, *The Chosen Few: How Education Shaped Jewish History, 70–1492*, Princeton, NJ, 2012.

down the country, in which secular subject matters were taught as an ever expanding part of the curriculum.

It is difficult to estimate the effects of traditional learning on Jewish educational modernization. Perhaps of greater import was the widespread appreciation of learning among Jews or the respect they tended to accord to scholarship as such. We have previously seen the eagerness of Jewish youth to enter the universities. Their motivation was surely twofold: interest in the sciences or the humanities and hopes for social betterment. That the latter could not always be materialized, we have also seen before, but, gradually, their academic drive did have an effect on the overall Jewish occupational structure. Exact numbers for the earlier period are hard to come by, but – once again – Barkai's calculations as well as his precise way of citing others serve us well in this case, too. Accordingly, while in the Prussia of 1852 some 2,300 Jewish men drew their income from the various free professions, in 1925 their number had risen to almost 19,000, about nine times as many within three-quarters of a century. By the latter date, over a quarter of all the independently employed physicians and 15 percent of all private lawyers in Prussia were Jews. In 1907, there were 526 Jewish lawyers in Berlin, who represented about half of all the attorneys in the Prussian capital, and the numbers for medical doctors, the preferred free profession for upward-climbing Jews and non-Jews alike, were no less remarkable. For decades, indeed, Jewish students focused primarily on medicine. Even relatively poor Jewish students, often coming from the eastern Prussian provinces or even migrating from Russia, studied medicine and then practiced it, in and outside of the German Reich. In Vienna, it was estimated that Jewish attorneys, physicians and journalists – all academically educated – made up more than half of these occupational groups in the years immediately after the turn of the nineteenth century.[16] The situation in Berlin was similar.

Naturally, all of this depended on a Jewish lead that was not confined to elementary schooling. Towards the end of the nineteenth century, one begins to notice the over-proportional participation of Jewish boys – and in fact of Jewish girls, too – in the Gymnasium and in high schools for girls. The gap between Jews and the rest of the population was – if anything – only growing. In Prussia, the proportion of Jewish children within these educational institutions was eight times larger than that of other children in the same age groups. In Frankfurt am Main, Jewish boys made up 14% of all high school pupils, when Jews in general made up 7% of the population. In Berlin, where they comprised just over 4% of the

[16] Richarz, "Occupational Distribution and Social Structure," 59.

population, a quarter of the Gymnasium pupils and one-third of those in the Realgymnasia were Jews, and this fraction remained virtually unchanged until the First World War.

We have previously mentioned the importance of *Bildung* in general, beyond school learning, even in the earliest stages of Jewish acculturation, and the pronounced Jewish interest in the German-speaking theater, in literature, and increasingly in music and the visual arts. Clearly, the high rate of Jewish urbanization supported these cultural trends. Conversely, urbanization had been so much speedier and so outstanding among Jews at least partly because they often tended to move to towns with better educational facilities. Sometimes, boys were sent over in advance of their families, to live with relatives and visit the better schools. It is again Avraham Barkai who indicated that Jews usually did not move to the great industrial centers in the Rhine and Ruhr areas, for instance, but rather to commercial and service centers. They did so mainly for economic reasons, but educational considerations were always there too, being carefully taken into account. In any event, even with their educational head start, Jewish prominence in education developed gradually and slowly, like the other legs of their modernization. It took almost a century to be fully manifested, though when it was, the effect was, no doubt, quite staggering. And this was true not just insofar as their sons were concerned, but often regarding their daughters as well.

Girls in traditional Jewish homes were by no means so energetically encouraged to study as their brothers. They were not supposed to learn in Torah schools, nor were they expected to show any proficiency in Jewish subject matters, except in the practice of Jewish everyday life. However, reading Yiddish literature, often in fact specifically written for them, was common among Ashkenazi Jewish women as far back as the sixteenth and seventeenth centuries. The most well-known example can be found in Glikl von Hamelin's extensive memoirs from the late seventeenth century, disclosing an astonishing level of literacy. While hers was apparently a unique case, it does point out that at least some women were by then no less capable of taking part in cultural activities than men. Less ambitious women too were often able to read one or another of the various Yiddish editions of *Tzena U'reina*, providing edited biblical texts and general Jewish education trimmed for women, as well as other literary and didactic books. Some women could read Hebrew, and even this proficiency provided them with a relatively superior starting point.

It is possible that, in the case of girls, there was even less continuity from traditional Jewish learning, limited as it had been, to the various modern forms of education. Thus, while initially women – Jewish or not – had usually helped their husbands in their work, on the land or in small handicraft and commercial shops, they normally no longer did so later on, as their families reached middle-class status. Bourgeois women were expected to stay at home, venturing outside solely in order to take care of the purchasing needs of their families or on social and festive occasions. It is likely that, as Yiddish now stood for backwardness, reading in this language too became inappropriate in bourgeois circles, while reading German gradually replaced it. Within the privacy of family and home, elementary reading and writing were once more required. Children's education had to be supported, and mothers were expected to display at least some minimal *Bildung* in society, too.

During the first half of the century, then, Jewish middle-class girls, like other middle-class girls, received limited education in special institutions, or, if the parents were better off, by private tutoring. One often thinks of the Salonnières in Berlin, so extremely well educated and often so eager to exhibit their *Bildung*, whereas the special drive for ever more systematic learning among Jewish women in general was a later phenomenon, typical of the latter part of the nineteenth century. By then, Jewish girls' enrollment in the various Prussian high schools was ten, twelve, and fifteen times higher than that of other girls in the same towns or provinces. In Frankfurt, to take this example again, where Jewish boys made up 14% of the high school population, as we saw, Jewish girls made up 24% of the pupils in parallel institutions.[17] In Berlin, one-third of all high school girls were Jewish. Later on, Jewish women were among the first to enter the universities, worked privately as physicians, and entered other free professions and other academic spheres, too.[18]

A more or less clear picture emerges from these selected and somewhat arbitrary data. While some Jews were leaving the fold and others made every possible effort to assimilate, the Jews as a whole continued to behave according to the written and unwritten rules of a distinct, separate minority. In many respects they also took a unique path to modernity. To be sure, both before the onset of modernization and during its course, some individuals and various subgroups behaved uncharacteristically. Still, it is easy to observe the uniqueness of the Jewish group and the distinctions between Jews and others in terms of their particular pattern of behavior,

---

[17] For the data, see especially Jakob Thon, *Der Anteil der Juden am Unterrichtswesen in Preußen*, Berlin, 1905, and, for much of what is discussed here with further sources and bibliography, see Chapter 10 of my book *Germans, Jews and Antisemites: Trials in Emancipation*, Cambridge, 2006, entitled "The Paradox of Becoming Alike," 202–223.

[18] On the early phase of Jewish academic studies, the best presentation is still Monika Richarz, *Der Antritt der Juden in die akademische Berufe*, Tübingen, 1974. For women in the later period, see Claudia Huerkamp, "Jüdische Akademikerinnen in Deutschland, 1900–1938," *Geschichte und Gesellschaft*, 19 (1997), 311–331.

and their way of adapting to change and of driving it forwards for their own benefit.

Recent historiography has modified the concept of modernity in a number of ways, especially by applying its plural form.[19] The grand generalizations typical of early modernization theories and many simplified historiographical texts based upon them no longer seem convincing. The old insistence – in fact Marxist in origin – on a repeated pattern of industrial growth, and the known syndrome of various developments attached to it, has not been borne out by the facts. The presumably inseparable link between industrialization and the progress of democracy had already appeared too facile as early as the heyday of Soviet Communism. Then, the effects of "backwardness" were introduced into the analysis and enabled the sketching of new paths to modernity, while regional and group histories with their manifold variety abounded. Furthermore, the experience of modernization in the colonial world and then under conditions of post-colonialism strengthened the impression of versatility, too. It thus became crucial to give proper weight to local ties of solidarity, stressing distinctions between metropolis and periphery and between internal, autochthonous pressures and influences from outside. Finally, within each unit of investigation – whether continental, national, or regional – inner differentiations and various patterns and constellations became ever more significant. One learned to name all these "entangled modernities."[20]

Having put together some aspects of the German-Jewish path to modernity, the overall process described for the entire country seems to have gained new contours. Differentiation along regional lines within the Central European, German-speaking area has, of course, often been noted. After all, this part of the continent had been divided into numerous political units through much of the nineteenth century, at least until the establishment of the Bismarckian Reich, and industrialization was never evenly stretched across these units, nor within them. Differences between town and countryside and between different agricultural setups across political borders emerged as critical for understanding future developments. Different reactions to economic change or to other aspects of modernization, characteristic for Protestants, on the one hand, and Catholics, on the other, could no longer be disregarded. They began to take center stage. Complex cultural elements had to be integrated into the now newly reconstructed view of events.

[19] See especially S. N. Eisenstadt, "Multiple Modernities," *Daedalus*, 129(1) (2000), 1–29.
[20] The phrase originated in Shalini Randeria, "Jenseits von Soziologie und soziokultureller Anthropologie: Zur Ortsbestimmung der nichtwestlichen Welt in einer zukünftigen Sozialtheorie," *Soziale Welt*, 50(4) (1999), 373–382.

The Jewish case, in the way it combined social, economic, and culturally unique elements, is perhaps particularly appropriate for breaking up the single perspective on modernization in the case of Germany, suggesting the many alternative paths to modernity that coexisted in an entangled way in that country as a whole.

On the religious-identity scale, the Protestant–Catholic divide was always more significant than the difference between Jews and Christians. The Jewish path to modernity, however, provides a useful angle of observation. It may be easier to comprehend the entanglement of the various paths to modernity in Germany by using the Jewish perspective. Owing to their population size, Jews could not possibly strike an entirely independent path. Every step on their part depended on the larger German context and the potentials available within it. Even geographical movements – from one village to another, from village to town, from one town to another, and then beyond local borders, from one state to another – had been strictly regulated for most Jews during much of the relevant period. Jews in Posen, for instance, at first lived under pre-emancipatory legislation even as their province became part of Prussia. They needed special permission for every move, at least until 1833. The Liebermanns, let us remember, had great difficulties in moving from their West Prussian province into the capital city of Berlin. Even though restrictions were gradually alleviated, they had for a long time constituted a powerful brake upon Jewish modernization. On the other hand, prohibitions imposed upon Christian residents of most European countries for much of the Middle Ages and the early modern period, especially in regard to the practice of financial businesses and some forms of commerce, enabled Jews to fill in the gap and therefore become particularly fit to enter the modern economic era. The Liebermanns showed great facility in expanding their business in view of economic change and developments both across the sea, in the British Isles, and in various parts of the European continent. They adopted new technical inventions, applied new machinery, and finally also tried their hand in heavy industry.

Indeed, Jews – or, at least, *some* Jews – had at least *some* head start for modernization despite all restrictions imposed from the outside by state regulations, and from the inside by their tradition. Finally, on the eve of the First World War, they were – on the whole – more fully modern than the majority of other Germans, but always in their own particular way. Other confessional groups adopted other modern characteristics, depending on their various starting points and cultural preconditions. Catholics, more than Protestants, often remained on the land. Jews increasingly preferred the cities. Industrialists of both Christian denominations – but in this case more the Protestants than the Catholics – chose mining and heavy industry, and moved more decidedly towards ever more modern forms of production. While lower-class men, both Protestants and Catholics – crowded the ranks of the industrial proletariat, Jews almost always worked as independent – usually small – employers. Besides, and perhaps most importantly, owing to their educational advantage, many of them were now well placed within the *Bildungsbürgertum*, preparing for future success in the professional and cultural spheres – in medicine and the law, in science, and in scholarship. Slowly, but surely, they moved along their own unique path, almost forcing others to notice their uniqueness, and all too often, no doubt, to find fault in it.

The Jewish case demonstrates how important were the different starting points of the various population groups; how both groups and individuals could and did adapt to change differently, using various strategies along the way. And, within the German mid-European sphere, the Jewish example focuses our attention on the numerous and different routes towards achieving prosperity and on the all-important cultural specificities that eventually dictated choices along the way. Observing modernization from a Jewish angle, we become aware of the multiple aspects of the process with which we are dealing and of how the different elements comprising it were interwoven and intertwined in many different and often unexpected ways.

6   Unification as Rupture

The cluster of issues that had determined the fate of the 1848 revolution soon came back to haunt Germany. But meanwhile, as we have just seen, the country had undergone dramatic changes. Rapid economic growth, achieved by ground-breaking industrialization, transformed rural areas and cities alike. It changed both the work habits and the life-styles of millions, and, while Jews were clearly a part of this overall transformation, they were neither a crucial part nor an indispensable part of it. Still, they quickly made the best of it. The historian Jacob Toury estimated that, in 1848, 15–30% of all the Jews in Germany could be considered "bürgerlich," whereas in 1870 as many as 60% were to be counted in this category. For 1848, he calculated, half of the Jews were living as "marginal existences," to use his own term, whereas in 1870 the Jewish poor constituted only 5–15% of the entire Jewish population, depending on the particular province or region.[1] This was an outstanding achievement, all within a relatively short period of time. It reflected the fact that the Jews were well prepared for the coming changes, that they were quick to adapt to them, and that they were sufficiently mobile, enterprising, and resourceful in exploiting them.

However, events in mid-nineteenth-century Germany were not dictated by the economy alone. The two decades in the wake of the revolution were no less stormy in the area of high politics and foreign affairs. The Italian "Risorgimento," leading to the unification of Italy into a single kingdom, occurred during this time and, while the Crimean War was clearly the most important event of the 1850s, the 1860s were years of intense international strife mainly in and around Germany, ending with

---

[1] His most detailed presentation of these data is to be found in Jacob Toury, *Soziale und politische Geschichte der Juden in Deutschland 1847–1871*, Düsseldorf, 1977. A more concise overview can be found in Jacob Toury, "Die Eintritt der Juden ins deutsche Bürgertum," in Hans Liebeschütz and Arnold Paucker (eds.), *Das Judentum in der deutschen Umwelt 1800–1850*, Tübingen, 1977, 139–242. See also my "Die Verbürgerlichung der Juden in Deutschland als paradigma," in Shulamit Volkov, *Antisemitismus als kultureller Code*, Munich, 2000, 111–130.

the Prussian victory over France in 1871. From this perspective, Jewish history seems entirely irrelevant. As a rule, Jewish politics was everywhere limited and local. Having no government, no armies, and no power ambitions, Jews did not play upon this stage. Their existence and their interests were only occasionally felt, and – as before – they continued to observe events and perceive their consequences from their own unique perspective.

Following a decade of repression and reaction in the immediate aftermath of the revolution, new political winds began to blow as the sixth decade of the century approached its end. In Prussia, a new king came to the throne, first as a regent in the fall of 1858 and then as a ruling monarch at the beginning of 1861. Wilhelm seemed willing to reconsider old and new demands coming from liberals throughout his land, and this accommodating spirit affected public discourse everywhere, in and even outside of Prussia. The so-called New Era – a prelude to an unusually eventful decade – had begun.

The new decade was especially eventful on the European military and foreign policy stage. Some three years after the end of the Crimean War in 1856, fighting broke out in Italy, ending in a humiliating defeat of the Austrian army at the hands of the French, allied to the movement for national unification in Italy. Unresolved problems in Schleswig-Holstein thereafter led an Austrian–Prussian alliance to engage in war with Denmark in the fall of 1864. Despite all the bad blood between them, the two Central European powers managed to fight together, though apparently for the last time. By then, tension within the German Bund was constantly rising, as the issue of German unification, ever more explosive, remained far from settled. The "Third Germany" continued to waver between the two "superpowers," Prussia and Austria, unable to decide which of them would better serve their purposes. Napoleon III in France was meanwhile observing developments from afar, and Europe, no longer functioning along the lines of the old Holy Alliance, was in a state of suspense. Later on, having defeated Austria in a quick campaign in 1866, the Prussian army went on to win a war against France too, and thus closed the cycle. Bismarck managed to fight three major campaigns without involving Russia or Great Britain and then move on to what he saw as a united Germany without raising too much alarm among these and other European states.

All this, while surely meaningful for individual Jews no less than for individual non-Jews in the different areas of Germany, surely for different reasons, did not seem relevant at first for the Jewish community in the German-speaking lands as a whole. This was not because its members were more apolitical than their non-Jewish neighbors. After all, intracommunal and intercommunal strife over power and influence had not been unknown to Jews in the German-speaking European lands. They had always practiced some form of politics both among themselves and in dealing with the non-Jewish world around them. On the international stage, however, or in the world of state diplomacy and military affairs, Jews never practiced politics on their own. Their joint efforts during the Congress of Vienna, as we saw, remained a rather unhappy episode, and it was only in 1860, with the establishment of the Alliance Israelite Universelle, attempting to organize a joint battle against antisemitism and for full emancipation, that a new move to give voice to Jewish interests had been initiated, this time not in Germany, but in France. It proved meaningful for German Jews only during deliberations at the Congress of Berlin in 1878, where and when demands for equal rights for the Jews in Romania required a united Jewish appeal on their behalf.

To be sure, a small elite of Jewish political figures in the various German states had by then been noticeably active in local assemblies and state parliaments. For a short and last time, it was once more the issue of full emancipation that gained priority, while gradually, indeed, this was achieved – first in Baden in the fall of 1862, then in Württemberg by 1864 and in Saxony by 1868. The various other German states were now legalizing full Jewish equality one after the other too, practically without opposition. The hated *Matrikel* in Bavaria, intent upon restricting the number of Jews in the monarchy, was expunged from the Bavarian legal system as early as 1861, and in the Habsburg monarchy equality was legislated as part of the Austro-Hungarian pact of 1867. Significantly, Prussia too finally legalized full emancipation at the establishment of the North German Confederation in 1866, and the relevant paragraph in its constitution was thereafter introduced unchanged into the constitution of the new Kaiserreich in 1871. Liberal principles concerning civil equality seemed to have by then gained the upper hand, and a debate of some ninety years concerning the civic status of Jews came to an end.

This, to be sure, was finally achieved not only as a result of an apparent liberal victory and not simply in parallel to Bismarck's pressure for unification, but also in conjunction with a triumphant national cause. It was particularly the Prussian Jews who seemed to be aware of this side of recent developments, and they indeed were by then clearly the ones that were giving the tone. Some prominent Jewish liberals, such as Gabriel Rießer and Moritz Veit, having been active during the 1848 revolution, were members of the influential Nationalverein, even participants in its constitutional assembly, as early as 1859. They enthusiastically supported – as they had already previously done – a "little-Germany" model of unification, to be achieved under Prussian hegemony and through the exclusion of Austria.

Among them were not only former participants in the revolution of 1848, but also a number of younger Jewish politicians. Some of them were by then partaking in the establishment of the Prussian Progressive Party and shortly afterwards in that of the National-Liberal Party, both standing for pronounced German nationalism. Apparently, this was the cause of widespread irritation, especially among conservatives. "Until now, we thought that you belonged to another nation," teased the *Kreuzzeitung*, the conservatives' leading daily.[2] But Jewish eagerness and their ever more pronounced patriotism – even nationalism – aroused unease in some liberal circles, too. August Lamey, Minister for Internal Affairs in Baden and an outspoken supporter of Jewish emancipation, admitted – though only in a private letter – that "of course, everyone must overcome a certain aversion in order to set them [the Jews] on an equal footing. They possess something foreign for us Germans, of an unpleasant kind."[3] There was, no doubt, more than a trace of antisemitism in the air. Richard Wagner, himself a 48er, published his *Judaism in Music* – first anonymously in 1850 and then again, under his own name that had meanwhile become famous, in 1869. Even so, Jews continued to fill the halls in the premieres of his operas following his return from exile in 1862, and Jewish musicians continued to perform his music with enthusiasm. They also continued to support national liberalism. In fact, these were the years in which Jews joined public life everywhere in Germany. By 1868, Moritz Elstätter had become the first Jewish minister in the same cabinet of Baden in which Lamey had served only a few years earlier. The orchestral conductor Hermann Levi, son of a rabbi, performed Wagner's operas, though all of them were steeped in Christian mythology.

By then, the main political question in Germany was no longer whether or not unification was needed or possible, but only – to follow the historian Wolfram Siemann's acerbic formulation – whether it would be achieved "with or without Austria."[4] This, after all, was on the agenda at least since the days of the revolution. In the spring of 1849, as mentioned above, the National Assembly offered the Prussian king the imperial crown and by doing so gave explicit legitimation to

---

[2] Quoted in Peter Pulzer, *Jews and the German State: The Political History of a Minority, 1848–1933*, Detroit, MI, 2003, 86, from the *Kreuzzeitung*, September 21, 1859.
[3] See Reinhard Rürup, *Emanzipation und Antisemitismus: Studien zur "Judenfrage" in der bürgerlichen Gesellschaft*, Göttingen, 1975, 70.
[4] See Wolfram Siemann, *Vom Staatenbund zum Nationalstaat, 1806–1871*, Munich, 1995, 244.

a solution along the lines of "little Germany," led by Prussia and excluding Austria. Having refused the offer, the king and his government were thrown back on cooperation with the southern monarchy, first in bringing the revolution itself to an end and then in upholding the uncompromising spirit of reaction during the following decade. Thereafter, with the beginning of the New Era in Prussia, the Habsburg monarchy too was finally being led by a liberal politician, Anton Ritter von Schmerling, and the atmosphere in Vienna was clearly not very different from that in Berlin. The two governments seemed capable of continuing their rather uncertain cooperation even after the appointment of Otto von Bismarck as chancellor in September 1862. He still considered Austria a more reliable ally on the outside than the Prussian liberals from within. Throughout this time, indeed, the latter were preoccupied with ongoing domestic strife rather than with international affairs. They were involved head over heels in what was soon to be known as the Constitutional Conflict and needed all their energy to withstand Bismarck's repeated attacks upon them. After all, he had been appointed in order to bring to an end precisely that parliamentary blockade which prevented the king from carrying out a fundamental reform of the army. In fact, however, even under these uneasy circumstances, joining Austria on the national question, working towards a "Greater Germany" solution, was no more than a remote option, appealing to some south-western liberals but to practically no one in Prussia itself. By then, the economic backwardness of the Habsburg monarchy had made such a solution all the more unpalatable, and Prussian advantages at leading an industrially advanced northern Germany could no longer be doubted. The *Zollverein*, from as early as 1834, had brought together Prussian interests with those of the other free-trading German states, mostly north of the river Main. Even the Prussian Junkers in the most outreaching eastern provinces learned to enjoy free-trade policies, amply gaining from their benefits. In 1862, the trade agreement with France strengthened Prussia's alliance with the south-western German states, too. Finally, what had not been achieved by peaceful means and consideration of economic interests was completed by the Prussian military, marching through Hannover, Hessen, and the streets of Frankfurt am Main on the way to a decided battle against Austria. Within a couple of years, the southern German states joined a newly established North-German Bund, basking in the glory of the Prussian victory at Königrätz and preparing for another spectacular Prussian victory, this time over France. On January 18, 1871, the new Kaiserreich was declared in Versailles. The "German Question" seemed to have been resolved.

Most German liberals found themselves supporting Bismarck. Now it could even appear as if it were not they who were capitulating before him, but the other way round. Among his eventual supporters, there were not a few Jewish liberals or perhaps – as one ought to call them now – liberals of Jewish origins. For the one-time Jewish activists in the Nationalverein, this was nothing but a follow-up to their previous politics. For other liberals, Jews and non-Jews, everywhere in the newly established Kaiserreich, it was an expression of their German nationalism, the new identity they had by then been adopting for some time. It was an identity that became increasingly more rooted, more palpable, and more powerful, and it was now a matter that concerned everyone, not only a few active politicians, and not only liberals.

Two long-term processes helped make possible the adoption of this identity by so many Jews: secularization and massive migration. The historian Michael A. Meyer, who more than anyone else investigated Jewish efforts to come to terms with modernity *without* abandoning Judaism, especially by inventing a reform version of the old faith, writes about his protagonists' changing identity during the 1860s, through which "the relegation of Judaism to the periphery of personal identity, if not to irrelevance, became ever more common among German Jews."[5] A great majority of them, especially in urban centers, no longer held to Orthodoxy; neither were they particularly interested in neo-Orthodoxy or in any other form of modernized Judaism. They often simply became indifferent to religion. Some kept a few rituals as part of their family tradition, conducting them behind closed curtains, like so much of bourgeois life at that time. Others did occasionally visit the synagogues, though often only once or twice a year. Some did not preserve even this minimum.

To be sure, secularization among Jews ran parallel to secularization of the majority Christian population – both Catholics and Protestants. However, today's historians tend to doubt both its extent and its depth during the nineteenth century. It is often no longer seen by them as yet another part of the process of modernization, running parallel to other trends associated with it. Secularization was apparently characterized by ebb and flow. Even in the wake of the rationalist Enlightenment, Christianity managed an impressive revival. While German Catholics formed a variety of social and social-welfare organizations, finally strengthening their community ties by establishing the Center Party,

---

[5] See Michael A. Meyer, "Jewish Identity in the Decades after 1848," in Michael A. Meyer and Michael Brenner (eds.), *German-Jewish History in Modern Times*, Vol. II: *Emancipation and Acculturation, 1780–1871*, New York, 1997, 319–348, quoted from page 319.

Protestants – stronger in urban areas, especially among the educated and the better off – achieved attractive new forms of piety. Religion was surely there to stay, although it lost some of its previous exclusiveness and prominence in the shaping of one's personal identity. During much of the nineteenth century, most people remained members of a confession, learning to live their everyday life without full compliance with its rules.

Until the late eighteenth century, all men – and probably all women, too – defined themselves primarily according to their religion. In a world of equal political rights – even if by no means fully realized – one tended to define oneself by one's citizenship or by what was considered by then one's national belonging. Religion may not have been weakened as such, but its power to define one's identity was much reduced. In the case of the Jews, but surely not only in their case, the receding significance of religion created a vacuum, into which a growing sense of pulsating national belonging tended to flow.

But, while distancing oneself from one's own religion was no doubt an important step upon the route to Jewish integration, it was not the only one. Another parameter, weakening denominational identity in a more indirect way, was geographical mobility, and this was particularly important in the case of the Jews. While considerable inner migration as well as some outward emigration could be shown to have taken place among Jews since the beginning of the nineteenth century, both types of movement quickly intensified after the middle of the century. "Mobility," wrote the historian Avraham Barkai, "was the most outstanding feature of German Jewish history in the nineteenth and early twentieth centuries."[6] And Uziel Schmelz, a demographer, also stated that "the overwhelming majority [of Jews during the period] 1852–1933 changed their domicile inside the country or emigrated from or to other countries."[7]

Somewhat forgotten are those who left Europe altogether, usually for the shores of America. Precise figures are hard to come by, but various methods of calculation always add up to tens of thousands of Jewish migrants. Some 30,000 left Prussia between the mid 1840s and 1871, and about 50,000 emigrated from Bavaria during the same period. Those who left were, of course, no longer a part of the new self-definition of Jewishness in the German-speaking world. But, for those who stayed, migration was critical. On the whole, Jews moved like non-Jews, from the

---

[6] See Avraham Barkai, "German-Jewish Migration in the Nineteenth Century, 1830–1910," in Jeffrey S. Gurock (ed.), *Central European Jews in America, 1840–1880: Migration and Advancement*, New York, 1998, 37–54.

[7] Uziel O. Schmelz, "Die demographische Entwicklung der Juden in Deutschland von der Mitte des 19. Jahrhunderts bis 1933," *Zeitschrift für Bevölkerungswissenschaft*, 7(1) (1982), 31–72, quoted from page 51.

agrarian east to the more industrialized west, from villages to small towns and later on to ever larger towns and to the metropolis. Thus, Posen lost between 1834 and 1871 over 50,000 Jews, half moving to Berlin and the rest abroad. Swabia lost a third of its Jewish population in the mere two decades between 1848 and 1868 – probably likewise divided between emigration abroad and movement into more or less nearby urban centers.

What did this mean in terms of identity change? For many, moving from one location to another often meant the loosening of traditional ties. Memoirs seem to substantiate this fact. We know, for instance, that many Jews, moving *en famille*, often decided on migration in order to provide their sons – and later on their daughters too – with better education; at first, better *Jewish* education and, later on, better general education in non-Jewish institutions. Some moved for economic reasons, mainly into larger centers of finance or commerce and sometimes, though not too often, as we saw, into promising industrial centers. Finally as a result of moving, old links, joint memories, and other common sources of identity were broken or lost. Thus, Jews became gradually ever more capable of adopting a new identity, in response to new circumstances and new emotional ties.

Yitzhak Lasker was born in Jarocin, a small town some sixty kilometers south-east of Posen, to strictly Jewish orthodox parents of relatively comfortable means.[8] Until the age of thirteen, he was taught by religiously well-trained teachers, both privately and in a traditional Cheder, located in the nearby town of Ostrowo. Then, as was not uncommon among the more open-minded Jews of the province, the talented youngster was sent to Breslau, to continue his schooling in the local Gymnasium. He soon changed his name to Eduard and launched upon a student career, studying mathematics and philosophy.

German students frequently moved from one university to another, and it had been among *them*, since the early nineteenth century, that a strong all-German identity, rather than local or provincial identity, easily evolved. Lasker's route, however, was particularly hectic. He had been studying for a while in Vienna and, as it happened, experienced much of the 1848 revolution there, being deeply influenced, molded, it could be said, by the events there. Returning soon thereafter to Breslau, he seemed to have decided to become a lawyer, but, having passed some of the necessary preliminary examinations and still being undecided as to

---

[8] For the biographical details and the short quotes here and in the following section, I have mainly relied on Rosemarie Schuder, *Der "Fremdling aus dem Osten": Eduard Lasker – Jude, Liberaler, Gegenspieler Bismarcks*, Berlin, 2008. See also James F. Harris, *The Theory and Practice of German Liberalism: Eduard Lasker, 1829–1884*, New York, 1984.

his future, left Germany for a three-year stay in London. Eduard's older brother was by then living in the British capital and provided him with a welcoming home and with help in adjusting to the new environment. Eduard, however, did more than enjoy life in this vivid international center. For three years, he had the opportunity to observe the workings of the British parliamentary system, which he did with characteristic intensity and ever growing appreciation. Upon returning to Germany, being now a man of strong liberal persuasion and – most outspokenly – a German nationalist, Lasker decided to settle in Berlin and, having meanwhile taken the remaining state examinations, normally allowing one to practice law, Lasker's rather smooth progression was for the first time blocked on account of his Jewishness.

To be sure, not much remained of this Jewishness. Nevertheless, discrimination against Jews aspiring to careers as judges, even at the beginners' level, forced the ambitious jurist to give up his plans for a legal career and turn first to journalism and then – ever more passionately – to politics. Lasker joined the Deutsche Fortschrittspartei (German Progressive Party), which had been established in 1861, and was soon elected to the Prussian Landtag. In 1867, he secured a seat in the new North German Parliament, together with sixteen other Jews, and chose to join the National-Liberal fraction within it. Though he at first strengthened its right-wing, later on he became Bismarck's most consistent and most principled critic, moving slowly but surely to the left. In his own eyes, no doubt, and probably in the eyes of his political colleagues too, Lasker was a true German liberal and outspoken patriot. In the eyes of his opponents – and these were by then numerous, no doubt – he was and remained "Lasker the Jew," or – more particularly – "the Stranger from the East."

At first, Lasker supported Bismarck's steps for a Prussian-headed unification of Germany. A centralized German state had, after all, been the hope of most liberals ever since the years before the 1848 revolution. Gradually, however, he found himself opposing the chancellor and his cabinet on almost all other matters. Like many of his liberal associates, Lasker had exchanged his religious belief for faith in freedom; and for him it was freedom of the kind he had learned to appreciate first during the revolution and then during his years in England. Even though he welcomed the approaching unification of Germany under Prussian hegemony, Lasker had an entirely different vision of the newly hoped-for state than Bismarck, and this difference became ever more pronounced, in fact unbridgeable.

The central issue on the agenda, just as he entered the political scene, was – as we saw – the king's insistence on the reform of the army against the clear opposition of practically all the liberals in the Prussian Landtag during the Constitutional Conflict. Bismarck, who believed that politics in Germany must be determined by princes and dynasties even against the wishes of parliament and surely against "the barricades," seemed to Lasker and his colleagues to be a source of clear and present danger. Both in parliament and in the press, the energetic Jewish parliamentarian was now coming out against the aristocratic presumption of the Prussian upper house. He used legal and historical materials to prove its members' unfounded arrogance and show their basic ineptness. Their insistence on the right to take the lead in all budgetary matters, in order to provide for the planned army reform, replacing in effect the lower house of parliament, enraged him. He did not hesitate to come forwards with his own firm views: defending parliamentary prerogatives, freedom of the press, and then also objecting to the death penalty, while Bismarck argued vehemently for it. It was, in fact, the "Jewish Nation," among all ancient cultural peoples, Lasker argued, that, despite "the barbarism of its legal system," had managed to make capital punishment impossible in practice, though not in theory. And it was entirely inconceivable that the Germans, such a "highly cultivated nation," would resort to such a measure, disregarding the highest value of human life. Lasker soon found himself fighting for the independence of the judiciary, too, even against the anti-Jesuit law, a major component of the soon to be launched *Kulturkampf*, in which Bismarck joined a majority of liberals in fighting the Catholic Church in Germany.

Until his untimely death in 1884, Lasker was the target of Bismarck's most vicious verbal attacks, aimed not only at his views but also at his personality. The battle between the two raged "with unsurpassed personal bitterness, irritability, and grim vindictiveness."[9] Even those who admired the chancellor found his attitude towards his liberal critic inexplicable. Bismarck must have sensed the principled contradiction between his and Lasker's political vision. Naturally, this became even clearer later on, with Bismarck's turn away from his liberal allies, abolishing free trade and forming a coalition with the conservatives and with the Center Party, his one-time enemies. The actual conflict with Lasker, however, was at its height before this political turning point. It ran through the entire decade between 1869 and 1879 and represented the tension between two different conceptions of the newly established Reich: an enlarged Prussia versus a truly united Germany; an absolute

---

[9] Johannes Ziekursch, *Politische Geschichte des neuen deutschen Kaisereiches*, 3 vols., Frankfurt am Main, 1925–1930, vol. II, 360, and quoted by Louis L. Snyder, "Bismarck and the Lasker Resolution, 1884," *The Review of Politics*, 29(1) (1967), 41–64, quote from page 43.

monarchy, supported by an army and an established landed aristocracy, versus a parliamentary monarchy, depending on a free civil society, itself inspired by a sense of nationalism and the basic principles of liberalism.

Most Jews probably supported Lasker's vision, even if not all of them could always sympathize with his fighting spirit. By then, most Jewish newspapers, organizations, and groups, as well as many individuals, expressed an outspoken German nationalism, no doubt. But, in fact, like Lasker himself, most Jews still maintained a kind of Jewish identity – dear to them despite successful acculturation and at least a measure of social integration. Many of them – like him – were ever more dedicated to the German side of their own self, their German self, so to speak. It was mostly a matter of *Bildung* and culture at the beginning of the century, but, by the 1860s, and ever more intensively thereafter, it was also a matter of politics.

Non-Jews likewise underwent a transformation during this time. Within a short period, the familiar, all-German, strictly cultural identity became more important than the particularistic states' sense of belonging. And, eventually, a majority of all Jews, like the majority of all Germans, seemed to have acquired that new, all-German identity, rejoicing in that heartfelt sense of unity offered them by the new Kaiserreich.

It was during the 1980s that historians learned from anthropologists to apply the term "imagined community" to the phenomenon of nation building.[10] Thus, one of the main features of new nations was brought to our attention, namely their being invented, in fact, and usually for some clear and discernible political purpose. Meanwhile, we have gradually learned to combine what was indeed imagined in the nation, having been invented and propagated by a relatively small elite, with what had always been real and concrete about it: a common language, a specific territory, and sometimes a more or less effective state.

The Jews, in the absence of a common territory, living for centuries in a diaspora, not even speaking the same language, were nevertheless considered a nation, by themselves and by others. The term, to be sure, was – and is – evasive. It has had a variety of meanings, especially during the early modern period. Still, its application was a point of departure for any discussion of at least the overall Ashkenazi Jewish world in Central and Eastern Europe. Interestingly, the term first had to be discarded, before it could again be applied to the Jews, and then, no doubt, with a particular intensity in the case of Zionism.

---

[10] The most influential book in this regard was Benedict Anderson, *Imagined Communities*, London, 1983.

Everywhere in the Europe of the pre-modern age, Jews related to their overall continental-wide community, on the one hand, as well as to their immediate local communities, on the other. A small Jewish population in a village or town, in the east or in the west, had its praying house – sometimes very modest – and, depending on its size, a local rabbi and a lay leadership that was – among other things – responsible for contacts with the authorities. A *Melamed*, a teacher of the young, was hired to conduct an improvised beginners' school – a *Cheder*. The community often had its own ritual bathing facilities, as well as a graveyard and – if the community was large enough – a local *Yeshiva*, where more advanced pupils would be studying the Talmud and other religious texts. A kosher butcher was, of course, indispensable.

People knew each other intimately in these communities. A great deal of social control was exercised among them, but also a measure of mutual support and solidarity in troubled times. And, although there were usually no binding rules forcing the widely spread communities to cooperate with each other, such cooperation did normally take place, either within the limits of a certain province, or – very often – beyond its borders. In his path-breaking book, *Tradition and Crisis*, first published in 1968, the historian Jakob Katz wrote that "mutual aid was requested and extended on the basis of a common sense of national unity, and an awareness of a common destiny that linked all the scattered sections of the people."[11] The terms "nation" and "people," so it seems, came quite naturally into the discussion here. In practice, the various Jewish communities cooperated in order to resist religious deviations, worked to achieve compromises in halachic controversies and to share responsibility regarding the poor and in response to various social and economic needs. Marriages were arranged across communal separations, and even across political borders. The poor coming from the outside became the responsibility of a joint local body. The individual could hardly be sustained without his own community, but – significantly – also not outside of the Jewish whole.

We have seen the early disengagement of some Jews from their original national identity, imagined but surely strongly felt during the first half of the nineteenth century. Secularization and migration helped Jews to discard the old identity both before and after the revolutionary years. And, although the process itself occurred at a different tempo in

---

[11] Jacob Katz, *Tradition and Crisis: Jewish Society at the End of the Middle Ages*, New York, 2000, 97. For an emphasis on the inclusion of Sephardic Jews as well, see Jonathan I. Israel, *European Jewry in the Age of Mercantilism, 1550–1750*, Oxford, 1991.

Unification as Rupture

various regions and provinces, everywhere in Central Europe the new self-identification of Jews as Germans proceeded apace. The process clearly required an effort and often the overcoming of painful familial strife, and in the 1860s it was usually bound up with adopting one or another kind of liberal faith. Later on, the sharing of a Kaiserreich patriotism gradually worked to weaken other parameters of one's identity – to a greater or smaller extent.

At the same time, the new political entity under Bismarck's leadership produced a serious rupture, in leaving Austria and its German provinces outside the borders of the new Kaiserreich. As a result, matters of identity became problematic. It was difficult for large segments of the German population within and without the new Reich. It was difficult for Jews on the two sides of the new border as well. There were those – inside Prussia – who could rejoice in its glory, seeing in the Kaiserreich, like Bismarck, no doubt, an extension of their beloved, victorious Prussia. There were even those who saw in the Bismarckian solution the fulfillment of what they had considered Prussian destiny, such as a few prominent historians, who actually invented the story of this destiny themselves. Johann Gustav Droysen, Heinrich von Sybel, and Heinrich von Treitschke first predicted the unification à la Bismarck and then enthusiastically embraced it. Their books and essays provided the educated public with the needed ideological tools for supporting the chancellor, especially during the crucial years between 1866 and 1871, but later on too, as they continued to play an important role in cementing the new German identity.

But there were also many for whom the so-called unification remained painful for a long while and who never accepted it as a satisfactory solution to the German Question. It is true that Austria itself, together with the other German provinces under Habsburg rule, moved steadily away from the mainstream of German developments during much of the nineteenth century – economically, socially, and politically. But, for many, it remained an integral part of Germany, even an important, essential part of it. Its complete expulsion from German affairs was by no means natural or easy to accept. To begin with, unification under Prussian rule turned the Catholics, in and outside of Prussia, into a minority; a large minority, to be sure, but nevertheless a minority. Soon they were officially made into enemies of the state under the *Kulturkampf*, and were for a while seen as outsiders – even dangerous outsiders. In fact, for the south German states, Austria's allies until the war against France, Bismarck's North German Bund was no easy object of identification. They at first stayed outside of it and then joined the presumably united Germany either just before or just after the Prussian victory of 1871. Even then, Bismarck had to yield to many of their demands, and for some time, indeed, feared an act of secession on the part of one or of all of them. Integrating Bavaria was particularly difficult. Finally, when most of the south-western states did join in celebrating Sedan Day after the victory over France, others found themselves excluded and in opposition. The leaders of the Social Democratic Party, for instance, were in jail for treason, having spoken against the violent suppression of the Paris Commune by the Prussian army. They and their followers were soon to become – for decades, in fact, "fellows without a fatherland."

Moreover, the disjunction created in the midst of their cultural nation, so to speak, remained painful for many educated Germans, not to mention those who were now citizens of a multinational Habsburg Empire, defeated by what was suddenly considered Germany, leaving them outside. Here is – yet again – Friedrich Nietzsche's opinion on this matter: "Of all the evil consequences which have followed the recent war with France," he wrote in 1873, "perhaps the worst is a widespread, indeed universal, error: the error, committed by public opinion and by all who express their opinions publicly, that German culture too was victorious in that struggle and must therefore now be loaded with garlands appropriate to such an extraordinary achievement. This delusion is in the highest degree destructive: not because it is a delusion – for there exist very salutary and productive errors – but because it is capable of turning our victory into a defeat: into the defeat, if not the extirpation, of the German spirit for the benefit of the 'German Reich.'"[12]

From the Jewish perspective, ambivalence was likewise deep and often painful. Nationalism, many Jews by then felt, finally carried with it the institutionalization of full equality to all citizens, themselves included. It was meant to bring with it life under a liberal constitution that had failed to be achieved during the revolution and that could be quickly enacted now, even if – unhappily – with the help of Prussian bayonets. Some Germans remained outside the Promised Land, as a result of the so-called unification, and this was also the fate of some Jews.

Naturally, all of Eastern European Jewry, as well as the greater part of its Central European counterpart, remained outside the new Germany. At the time of German unification, there were 500,000 Jews in Galicia, which had been annexed by Austria in 1772, only slightly fewer than the

---

[12] See Friedrich Nietzsche, "David Strauss, the Confessor and the Writer," in Friedrich Nietzsche, *Untimely Meditations*, edited by Daniel Breazeale, Cambridge, 1997, 1–56, quote from page 3.

number of Jews in the new Kaiserreich established in 1871. The Jews across the new border had for generations been an integral part of the overall Jewish settlement in the region and, despite the political rupture caused now by Bismarck's unification, they often remained a palpable part of that community. By the last third of the nineteenth century, most Galician Jews spoke at least some German. Prague Jews – with only few exceptions – spoke German too, and so did Jews in Budapest and even as far east as Chernowitz (now Chernivtsi, Ukraine). Vienna – still hosting only a small Jewish community at the beginning of the nineteenth century, was by the early 1870s a lively Jewish center. Links across the new political border proved enduring and continued to be intensive, above all due to a still meaningful Jewish sense of communality and their mutual need for further cooperation.

Perhaps the most apparent ongoing link between those Jews within and those without was created by the need of the communities for religiously trained personnel. This was now coming all too often from beyond the borders of the Kaiserreich, and, although rabbinical seminaries had been established both in Berlin and in Breslau, later also in Frankfurt am Main, most new rabbis came from abroad: from the neighboring Polish provinces, from Preßburg (now Bratislava) in Slovakia, and from other towns in the old Jewish-Austrian milieu, from Hungary, from Italy, and from Alsace, the latter now actually within the Reich. Jews in Germany, though largely secularized, depended on the supply of religious expertise from the outside.

To some extent, a parallel situation was true for non-Jews as well. For them, to be sure, this was more an issue of culture and cultural exchange. Students continued to move between Berlin and Vienna. Actors and actresses came to Austrian towns and went from there back to Germany. Musicians continued to move from one musical center to another, disregarding political borders. Authors were publishing their works both here and there. In fact, the open border in regard to all cultural affairs enabled the flowering of German culture in the years to come. Paradoxically, it was precisely the educated bourgeoisie, depending on the larger German connection, that was the class that most enthusiastically supported the new Reich and rejoiced in its achievements. So it was easy to forget how deep the rupture had been and how painful, especially for them. A view from the Jewish angle makes the ambivalence and the struggle involved most apparent. Jews, like other Germans, learned to be Kaiserreich patriots, no doubt, but Jews most particularly continued to live within their overall larger European space, sending their sons abroad and bringing over from across the border bridegrooms for their daughters. They depended on the supply of rabbis and accredited religious teachers mostly from the east and could hardly think of their communal whole without the cities of the Habsburg monarchy. Theirs was actually the same pain as that of all other Germans, in having to accept a radical break with the past. And, as we have seen before, the Jewish case brings forth the difficulties, the complexities, and the ambivalence shared by all.

Part III

Living in Germany: 1870–1930

7 Achievements and Unacknowledged Dangers

Beginning January 18, 1871, the map of Europe changed radically. It now included a new nation-state, under the rather elusive name "das deutsche Kaiserreich," or, as it was more simply to be known, Germany. Meanwhile, the Prussian army had again proven its superiority in a war with France, Bismarck had again shown his diplomatic dexterity, achieving unification while preventing a joint European war against the new Germany, and the combined north-German and south-German economy, bolstered by war reparations from France, was thriving, truly booming in fact. To be sure, the borders of this "belated nation-state"[1] did not encompass all Germans, and the Kaiserreich was not a centralized, unified polity, as many had hoped. It was a confederation of princely units of various sizes – large and small – but it seemed to function just as well.

The separate states were responsible for much of the tax administration, for schooling and education, for policing, and for the legal system. Bavaria continued to keep its army and its separate diplomatic core and – like most other states – retained its old symbols of sovereignty, such as its flag and national anthem. The federal state was closely linked to Prussia, which constituted some two-thirds of both its territory and its population. It regularly used many of the Prussian symbols, in addition to sharing Prussia's foreign office and its military establishment. The prolonged tension between Prussia and the south-German states, however, had not yet been resolved; the army still needed reform and modernization, and Bismarck was less adroit in handling the Reichstag (the Parliament) than in maneuvering European diplomacy. Then, late in 1873, the economy suddenly suffered a severe blow with the collapse of the Viennese stock exchange and the onset of a cyclical deflation that slowed down economic growth, caused heavy financial losses, and led to multiple bankruptcies.

The liberals, who had been fighting a lost battle against the chancellor's autocratic tendencies, at first managed to hold on at least to their faith in

---

[1] This phrase was first introduced by Helmuth Plessner, *Die verspätete Nation: Über die politische Verführbarkeit bürgerlichen Geistes*, Stuttgart, 1974.

free trade and to their crumbling political primacy. Towards the end of the decade, however, they were forced to observe Bismarck's swift turn to the right, as he allied himself with the Conservatives and became increasingly dependent upon the Catholics. He then proceeded to introduce protectionist trade policies, in response to the interests of his new coalition partners, and worked energetically to weaken his political adversaries old and new: liberals and socialists.

At the time, the Social Democratic Party had been quickly growing, winning ever more workers' support. It consolidated its forces against both liberals and conservatives, but found itself in the end helpless against Bismarck's tactic. By the fall of 1878, he had managed to get the Anti-Socialist Law through parliament with only feeble liberal opposition and was thereafter determined to exclude the entire organized working class from the political realm – in Prussia as well as in the Reich as a whole. From that point onward, he turned ever more fiercely against the socialists, or rather against the whole working class as such, portraying them as enemies of state and nation.

Pointing out a supposed need to fight internal enemies was Bismarck's preferred way of achieving a measure of cohesion within his newly created national state. But, all his and the general nationalistic verbiage at the time notwithstanding, Germany was still a deeply divided country. Initially, and despite the fact that Bismarck was not in principle against the Catholics, he had readily perceived the benefits of positing himself as their opponent. Together with some conservative Protestants and the majority of the National-Liberals, he had entangled the entire country in what came to be known as the *Kulturkampf,* a "cultural conflict," and, with its subsiding, he worked with even greater energy against the socialists. An assassination attempt against the Kaiser in May 1878 was quickly blamed upon them, enabling the chancellor to direct all kinds of bourgeois dissatisfactions and aristocratic unease into the battle against them.

However, this tactic was bound to become self-destructive. After all, the groups under attack constituted very large segments of the Reich population, and it was not really possible to achieve cohesion, social or political, by excluding them. Surprisingly, Bismarck did not turn against the Jews. They, after all, made up only a small minority and were in any case a familiar scapegoat. Moreover, Bismarck's aversion towards them was well documented, at least since his Landtag speech in 1847, when he had fiercely opposed demands for their emancipation. To be sure, in later years he did engage Gerson Bleichröder, one of Berlin's Jewish bankers, as his private financial and occasionally political adviser, and during the early 1860s allowed himself to even show a measure of respect towards Ferdinand Lassalle, a Jew and an early socialist leader. His repeated fits of rage against Eduard Lasker, were surely fed, partially at least, not only by his basic antipathy to this particular "stranger from the East," but also by his animosity towards his brethren – local and foreign. In any case, the chancellor was above all a calculating man. The growing antisemitism in the Germany of the second half of the 1870s and thereafter was not to his taste. It appeared threatening, bringing with it – perhaps in accordance with his youthful memories – uproar and disorder, possibly even anarchy. The Kaiser mistrusted this movement, too, and was – like many contemporary aristocrats – reluctant to cooperate with what he saw as "the mob."

Despite all that, one could no longer disregard the new wave of anti-Jewish sentiment spreading everywhere throughout the country. The Catholic and then the conservative press took the lead immediately after the economic slump began; former liberals soon joined their ranks. The so-called "founding years" of the Kaiserreich signified the high point of free-trade liberalism, bringing profits to industrialists and better wages to the workers. The liberals had by then reached the peak of their political power and, with the unexpectedly negative turn of the economic fortunes, it was only natural that they would try to avert criticism and seek other culprits. The tone was finally given by one of the typical lower-middle-class journals of the day, the *Gartenlaube*. Between December 1874 and December 1875, Otto Glagau, one of its editors and previously the economic correspondent of the *National-Zeitung* – a liberal daily in Berlin – published a series of articles in which liberalism was attacked both as a doctrine and as a political force. His text, later published in book form, was a mixture of militant anti-Jewish rhetoric and a kind of nostalgic, apolitical conservatism. Glagau adroitly made the case for the identity between antisemitism and the much discussed "Social Question," while somewhat later it was his colleague Wilhelm Marr, who may not have *invented* the term antisemitism, but surely made it popular, that took over this ideological banner and managed to spread its message far and wide.

In 1879, Marr published his own antisemitic best-seller, *The Victory of Judaism over German-ness*.[2] Having previously been a member of the left-wing liberal faction in the legislative body of the free city of Hamburg, occasionally lashing out at the Jews even then, not much of his liberalism remained by the late 1870s. Though something of his anarchic social protest comes through in this piece, antisemitism took center stage now and was becoming ever more robust.

Towards the end of the decade, two additional voices joined this chorus. In the spring of 1878, the court priest Adolf Stöcker began an

---

[2] Wilhelm Marr, *Der Sieg des Judenthums über das Germanenthum – Vom nichtconfessionellen Standpunkt aus betrachtet*, Bern, 1879. See Moshe Zimmermann, *Wilhelm Marr, the Patriarch of Antisemitism*, Oxford, 1987.

election campaign in Berlin, intent on recruiting members of the working class away from the Social Democratic Party and back under the banner of Church and state. Soon, however, it became clear that his true followers were not the industrial workers, but an assortment of lower-middle-class voters, and that the most effective component in his fiery public sermons was not religion, nor the various social reform programs he was advocating, but his anti-Jewish rhetoric. Like Marr and Glagau, Stöcker too – though a man of the Church – tried to distance himself from the old, religiously motivated anti-Jewish discourse. Like his conservative colleague Max Liebermann von Sonnenberg, he too could adopt the latter's maxim, namely that "[f]irst we want to become a political power, then we shall seek the scientific evidence for antisemitism."[3]

Finally, as the antisemites of various hues became ever more vocal and politically organized, obtaining in Berlin as many as 46,000 votes at the election of 1881, additional support came from unexpected quarters. In an article published on November 15, 1879, Heinrich von Treitschke, a highly respected historian, professor at the University of Berlin, by then a National-Liberal Reichstag representative and an outspoken Bismarck supporter, published a longish article in the *Preußische Jahrbücher*. In it he urged for a "true harmony between the Crown and the *Volk*," attacking the endlessly debating parliament and all forms of "weakly philanthropy" – as he put it – as well as what he considered a dangerous "broadminded cosmopolitanism." Instead, Treitschke now favored reliance upon the healthy "instinct of the masses" that had now "correctly identified a serious danger, a critical defect in the new German life," and, lashing out himself against the Jews, whom he now also saw as a danger to German nationality and a threat to German culture, he famously – or rather infamously – announced that "the Jews are our misfortune."[4] Between August 1880 and April 1881, as 250,000 signatures were collected for a petition urging the state to revoke Jewish emancipation – this in fact against Treitschke's expressed opinion – the so-called *Antisemitismusstreit*, namely the controversy about antisemitism, was already well under way far beyond the capital city, everywhere across the country.[5]

---

[3] For the quote and an insightful commentary on the events of these years, see the memoirs of Helmut von Gerlach, *Vom Rechts nach Links*, Zurich, 1937, 112.
[4] This article was reprinted in Heinrich von Treitschke, *Deutsche Kämpfe: Schriften zur Tagespolitik*, Leipzig, 1896, 1–28, and the quotes are from pages 18–23.
[5] It has now become clear that what was known as the *Berliner Antisemitismusstreit* was in fact a nation-wide affair. See Karsten Krieger (ed.), *Der "Berliner Antisemitismusstreit," 1879–1881: Eine Kontroverse um die Zugehörigkeit der deutschen Juden zur Nation. Kommentierte Quellenedition im Auftrag des Zentrums für Antisemitismusforschung*, 2 vols., Munich, 2003.

And despite all this commotion, antisemitism remained of secondary importance for the greater part of the Kaiserreich period, even for Jews. In fact, parallel to this wave of hostility against them, there were early indications of an intensified self-consciousness among the German Jews, expressed, for instance, in the writings of Heinrich Graetz, the eleven volumes of whose *History of the Jews* were being published, one by one during these years. Reading Graetz was, to be sure, only one added source of Treitschke's rage. More importantly, as a result of rapid industrialization, bourgeois society was meanwhile deeply split on many other issues, above all on attitudes to modernity and on matters of equality, manifested by the activities of the working-class movement and in the intensified daily struggle between capital and labor. There were issues at stake between city and countryside, for instance, or between the demands for women's emancipation and a basically patriarchal majority. There were important issues of foreign policy, emerging in clashes with Great Britain and France, and of economic policies involving Russia; in responding to the growth of the Social Democratic Party and in relation to other domestic issues. The unease concerning the Jews was only one among many such conflicting matters, though by then, as a full-fledged ideology, it was itself striving to give meaning and urgency to issues beyond the fate of the Jews.

Many Jews, and surely some non-Jews too, were caught unprepared by the new form of political antisemitism. They were sometimes truly stunned. After all, it was now no longer the "mob" – rural or urban – but elements of the respected bourgeoisie that came out against the Jews; that same bourgeoisie into which these "strangers" had so fervently wished to merge for some 100 years. Opposition to Treitschke came even from some of his colleagues. Seventy-five scholars and scientists added their signatures to what was to be known as the Declaration of Seventy-Five Notables, drawn up by Theodor Mommsen and published in November 1880, repudiating antisemitism. Nevertheless, antisemitism now became *Salonfähig* (acceptable in polite society), to the astonishment of all supporters of emancipation – Jews and non-Jews alike.

Berthold Auerbach, who had devoted a lifetime to reproducing the tales of the south German peasantry and enjoyed some fame in educated circles throughout the land, wrote broken-heartedly in a letter to his cousin Jakob: "In vain have I lived and worked,"[6] and Hermann Cohen, by then an Ordinarius for philosophy at the University of Marburg,

---

[6] Berthold Auerbach, *Briefe an seinen Freund Jakob Auerbach*, Frankfurt am Main, 1884, Vol. II, 438.

composed a detailed public reply to Treitschke, giving voice to his pain. Most touching were his closing sentences: "We, the younger generation," he wrote, "were allowed to hope that we would gradually succeed in joining in with the nation of Kant .... This confidence has now been shattered. The old anxiety is reawakened."[7]

All this happened only a decade since the struggle for legal equality of the Jews had come to a successful conclusion and since they had finally gained what had been considered their legitimate rights. The zigzag course on the road to equality, lasting almost a century, had surely left them somewhat exhausted, but on the whole they were still full of trust and optimism. In fact, even the emancipatory legislation of 1869 was not yet complete, particularly in Prussia, where the government continued to discriminate against Jewish applicants to public office and where they were practically excluded from senior civil service posts and from the much coveted status of reserve officer. Thus surely, despite explicit Imperial legislation announcing their civil equality, many Jews felt hated and excluded. Meanwhile, whether or not in response to Treitschke's warnings against the "host of hustling, pants-peddling youths," coming from Poland and swarming Prussia's cities, the administration decided to tighten its naturalization practices, and in 1885 expelled over 30,000 non-naturalized Poles, mostly Jews. At the same time, antisemitism became rampant in Saxony and in some mixed Catholic–Protestant areas in the Rhineland, being voiced by a variety of social associations and echoed in the press, polluting the atmosphere.

By the late 1870s, participants and onlookers alike realized that something had changed. Both the anti-Jewish rhetoric and its adjacent political activity seemed to be of a different character. One sensed the appearance of a new discourse, the use of a different language, and the application of another terminology. The combination of anti-liberalism with antisemitism clearly was no longer a marginal affair. It was now joined to a vague social reform program, directed at the needs of particular social groups, attacking not only Jewish immigrants or the Jewish poor, but also the successfully integrated Jews living in the midst of bourgeois society. It often played upon envy of Jewish achievement and managed to bring together various themes into a many-sided, well-constructed, and by then apparently much-needed ideology.

"We hate no one," preached pastor Stöcker, "not even the Jews; we respect them as our fellow citizens und love them as the people of the

---

[7] Hermann Cohen, "*Ein Bekenntnis in der Judenfrage*", Berlin, 1880, reprinted with other responses to Treitschke in Walter Boehlich (ed.), *Der Berliner Antisemitismusstreit*, Frankfurt am Main, 1965, 126–150; the quote is from pages 126–127.

prophets and the Apostles, from among whom our Savior emerged." The only objection was to their "spirit of Mammon," he explained, and to their no-longer-concealed desire "to become the masters of Germany."[8] Despite the claim to respect their religion and share their "ancient, holy memories," Treitschke found himself turning and twisting too. He, for one, objected to that "German-Jewish mixed culture," which the Jews apparently wished to substitute for our "thousand-years-old Germanic civilization."[9] Finally, in the so-called Erfurt Program of the Antisemitische Volkspartei (Antisemitic People's Party), led by Otto Böckel, the concrete goal of "the repeal, by legal means, of Jewish emancipation" was openly advocated.[10]

In parallel, Eugen Dühring, an eccentric scholar who since the mid 1860s had been busily publishing philosophical tracts on a variety of topics, came out with a fiercely antisemitic book, entitled *The Jewish Question as a Racial, Moral and Cultural Question*. Here, the terms "people," "nation," and "culture" were used interchangeably and – significantly – together with an added fashionable concept – "race." Racial terminology, rare in previous antisemitic publications, became ever more dominant now, and Dühring's book was apparently not unwelcome even among some social democrats. This is probably why Engels decided to write his famous polemic, known as *Anti-Dühring*, and, later on, August Bebel too was finally convinced to join this half-hidden intra-party strife on the side of the anti-antisemites.

Expectedly, however, it was more often men on the right who willingly added antisemitism to their political propaganda. The Conservative Party added an anti-Jewish paragraph to its "Tivoli" program in 1892, and the *Bund der Landwirte*, its social mouthpiece, was by then using antisemitism regularly in all its campaigns. In the long run, the new ideological formulations shaped by members of what would later be known as the "Bayreuth Circle" were perhaps more important. Under the influence of Richard Wagner's mythical Christianity and Arthur de Gobineau's theoretical racism, Wagner and the group of intellectuals surrounding him gave free reign to their anti-Jewish obsession. They merged "German Christianity, Neo-romanticism, the mystical cult of sacred Aryan blood, and ultra-conservative nationalism," writes Saul Friedländer, and, towards the end of the century, hope for redemption

---

[8] See Adolf Stöcker, *Das moderne Judenthum in Deutschland, besonders in Berlin: Zwei Reden in der christlich-socialen Arbeiterpartei*, 2nd ed., Berlin, 1880, 4–20.
[9] Heinrich von Treitschke, "Unsere Aussichten," in Boehlich (ed.), *Der Antisemitismusstreit*, 7–14, quoted from page 10.
[10] The full text of this program appears in Peter Pulzer, *The Rise of Political Anti-Semitism in Germany and Austria*, Cambridge, MA, 1988, 339–340.

through "elimination" of the Jews – spiritual or even physical – was added to this peculiar mix.[11] Houston Stewart Chamberlain, an Englishman who would become Wagner's son-in-law, delineated the contours of this vision in his magnum opus *The Foundations of the Nineteenth Century*, stressing the deep and critical antagonism between "German-ness and Jewish-ness." Jews in Germany, according to him, could never become true Germans. They had to be somehow removed.

By then antisemitism could no longer be simply talked away. It served an important function in the overall political landscape of the day. What may have been a vague sentiment before, depending on a long tradition of Jew-hating in Christian Europe and reinforced by what some saw as the urgent needs of the new German nation-state, was now a full blown, secular ideology. The old forms of Jew-hating never disappeared, but new layers became ever more important. Together they gave a modern meaning to what could until then be considered merely an obsolete prejudice. Jews were "others," I have elsewhere argued, and attitudes towards them served as a cultural code. Antisemitic positions demarcated a full-blown syndrome, quite powerful at the time, based on a reactionary, anti-modern creed. In parallel, defending Jews turned into a marker for the opposite syndrome, predicated on liberal modernity in all its various forms. By the late nineteenth century, right-wing integral nationalism was clearly counterposed against liberal humanitarianism, and increasingly more vehement in its opposition to social democracy. Antisemitism, or, for that matter, anti-antisemitism, may not have been particularly important as such for the overall scheme of contemporary German politics, but both positions became familiar indicators, strengthening right-wing nationalism of a certain type, on the one hand, and joining liberal or even openly democratic trends, on the other. These two views coexisted within the bourgeois world of the Kaiserreich, and were firmly set against each other in German society, a constitutive element within its political culture.[12]

As indicated before, life for the German Jews, while certainly affected by antisemitism and despite the heartbreak this caused some of them, was not really dependent upon it. In the wake of previous events, under

---

[11] See Saul Friedländer, "Redemptive Anti-Semitism," in Saul Friedländer, *Nazi Germany and the Jews*, Vol. I: *The Years of Persecution, 1933–1939*, New York, 1997, 73–112. The quote is from page 87.

[12] With a somewhat different stress, this interpretation is elucidated in my "Antisemitism as a Cultural Code: Reflections on the History and Historiography of Antisemitism in Imperial Germany," *The Leo Baeck Institute Yearbook*, 23 (1978), 25–45, and now also in Shulamit Volkov, *Interpreting Antisemitism: Studies and Essays on the German Case*, Berlin and Boston, MA, 2023, 61–84.

Bismarck's leadership and through his diplomatic facility, Germany had become a powerful nation-state, gradually but consistently molding its population into a compact nation with wide-ranging imperial ambitions, mightily strengthened in the later years of the Empire. At the same time, the Jewish component of the Reich's population, preserving its uniqueness despite its ongoing integration, was being formed into a coherent – though very small – minority, holding on to its place within society at large. Jews now developed a vigorous self-consciousness, organized their own civil associations, chose a secular communal leadership, and developed a vivid and ever more effective public domain, including a network of newspapers and journals with a unique discourse all their own. Their status within the Reich reflected both this polity's strength and its limitations.

Already during the first half of the century, while many Jews were still deeply traditional, others – more modern and with an actively modernizing agenda – managed to define for themselves a reform type of Judaism that provided even those who were in the process of assimilating with a denominational focus, centered upon vivid communal life. Others, the so-called Neo-Orthodox, likewise had their own synagogues, not to mention their schools and even their rabbinical seminars. New voluntary associations were constantly being organized, replacing the old-style Ashkenazi communality with a new, equally loose but far more effective German-Jewish one. Within the new borders of the Kaiserreich, Vienna, Prague, and Metz were losing much of their old significance, while Berlin, Frankfurt, and Hamburg were replacing them. Similarly, the confessional groupings around the synagogues, led by local rabbinical authorities, were losing much of their significance, while secular associations of regional and even national scope replaced them. There were Jewish professional bodies, some of which published their own scholarly journals; eventually also a statistical bureau, numerous public libraries, and – topping them all – the *Centralverein deutscher Staatsbürger jüdischen Glaubens* (Central Association of German Citizens of the Jewish Faith), known as the CV. This umbrella organization, established in 1892, counted at the peak some 70,000 individual members and 200,000 additional ones, affiliated through membership in other social and cultural associations.

The CV gave voice to this strange but alive-and-kicking creature – a community of Jews of double identity, "hyphenated Jews," the German-Jews. "We are an association of German citizens," it was declared in their name, "we stand firmly on the ground of the German nationality. Our belonging to a community with Jews of other countries is no different from the belonging of German Catholics and Protestants to a community with Catholics and Protestants in other countries."[13] The centuries-old Jewish religious identity seemed to have been well preserved within this context, though its look was no longer directed inwardly, but rather outwardly, towards the surrounding world. On these terms, minority and majority could coexist comparatively peacefully, in relative harmony, despite the insistence on uniqueness by the former and the outspoken nationalism of the latter. Despite the opposition to any kind of pluralism within the life of the nation, even from those who were considered left-wing or of the political center in Germany, Jews managed to maintain a separate, proud existence.

Theodor Mommsen, the famous historian of Rome and Treitschke's main adversary at the University of Berlin, in his "Also a Word about Our Judaism" wrote the following: "The entry into a great nation has its price; the Hanoverians and the Hessians, and we [the citizens] of Schleswig-Holstein are ready to pay it.... Now, no Moses would seem to be leading the Jews back to the promised land; so, whether they sell pants or write books, it is their duty, as much as they can – without acting against their conscience – to detach themselves from their uniqueness and decisively break down the barriers between themselves and the rest of the German citizenry."[14] Jewish difference then, even when described by someone who was on their side, so to speak, clearly opposing antisemitism, was still an irritation. As in a variety of texts from early on in the century, complete assimilation – nothing less – continued to be insisted upon, and to some degree this demand was internalized by the Jews, too. The same Hermann Cohen, whom we have heard from previously, brought forth this German-Jewish dualism in his writings, only for him – theoretically – this ought to have been an easy task, since the two were basically similar and deeply compatible.

In any event, Jews continued to feel that they constituted an integral part of the German society within which they were now living, for better or for worse. For Jews and non-Jews alike, antisemitism often seemed entirely marginal and, as has recently been shown in the literature, Jews as such seemed to have disappeared from the public arena.[15] Success seemed to have compensated for the hostility they sometimes

---

[13] Quoted in Arnold Paucker, "Zur Problematik einer jüdischen Abwehrstrategie in der deutschen Gesellschaft," in Werner E. Mosse (ed.), *Juden in Wilhelminischen Deutschland 1890–1914*, Tübingen, 1976, 479–548; the quote is from page 488.

[14] See Theodor Mommsen, "Auch ein Wort über unser Judenthum," in Walter Boehlich (ed.), *Der Berliner Antisemitismusstreit*, 212–227, quoted from page 227.

[15] For an interesting case study, see Gideon Reuveni, "'Productivist' and 'Consumerist' Narratives of Jews in German History," in Neil Gregor, Nils Roemer, and Mark Roseman (ed.), *German History from the Margins*, Bloomington, IN, 2006, 165–184.

encountered, for occasional public condemnations, and even for some direct personal insults. Surely, there were years in which this hostility made life unpleasant, but then there were times in which Jew-haters lost their significance, while Jews became ever more self-confident and often, at least in some quarters, outstandingly prominent.

In addition, while different Jewish men and women experienced life in the new Germany differently, the mix of discrimination and openness proved fertile for a great many of them. Most learned to live with anti-semitism – either by ignoring it or by resisting it, to the best of their ability. Many suffered under the anti-Jewish sentiment, but would not be discouraged by it. Here is a quote from Walther Rathenau, later Foreign Secretary of the Weimar Republic and one of its early martyrs, a quote in which Rathenau bitterly recalled his time in the military during the early 1890s: "In the early years of every German Jew," he concluded, "there is a painful moment that can never be forgotten, [the moment at which] he becomes aware for the first time that he entered the world as a second-class citizen and that no amount of talent or merit would free him of that status."[16] But, while he never forgot that painful moment, trying in vain to become a cavalry officer in the Prussian reserve troops, this did not stop him from climbing up the social ladder later on, with exceptional ambition and – of course – with the help of plentiful resources provided by his father.

Other Jews may have managed to circumvent such traumatic experiences and then reach topmost positions along other routes. In his memoirs, Gershom Scholem, growing up in Berlin, recalled no antisemitic incidents during his childhood or youth. *He* never tried to become a Prussian cavalry officer and eventually, as a budding scholar and intellectual, few – if any – could challenge his authority. Furthermore, in studying the careers of some of the most successful scientists of Jewish origin in the Kaiserreich, it seems that their achievements often depended, indeed, on that peculiar mix of openness and closedness typical of German society in the earlier years of the nineteenth century and, under somewhat different circumstances later, during the Kaiserreich too. They were allowed into the best universities, but since a career as a full professor was in most cases closed to them, they sought other options, within and outside of the academic world, thus unfolding their creativity and reaching the professional top, each in his own specific route.[17]

---

[16] Walther Rathenau, "Staat und Judentum. Eine Polemik," in Walther Rathenau, *Gesammelte Schriften*, Berlin, 1918, Vol. I, 188–189.
[17] See Shulamit Volkov, "Jewish Scientists in Imperial Germany. Part I: The Social Origins of Success in Science," and "Jewish Scientists in Imperial Germany. Part II: Jews as Scientific 'Mandarins' in Imperial Germany and the Weimar Republic," *Aleph. Historical Studies in Science and Judaism*, 1 (2001), 215–281. These papers were originally published in German; the first in *Historische Zeitschrift*, 245 (1987), 315–342, and the second, ten years later, in *Archiv für Sozialgeschichte*, 37 (1997), 1–18.

Clearly, it was often difficult to evade discrimination, especially in the social sphere. As a result, many Jews often preferred the company of their peers. Scholem, again, reported on the almost exclusively Jewish milieu in his parents' home, and it was not very different at the Rathenaus'. Jews did work with non-Jews, of course. Friendships among them were sometimes made and even long maintained. But regular social contacts took place mostly around the family and within its inner Jewish circle. This theme appears in many written memoirs, in which socializing during Jewish holidays or in specific sites of vacation is described or mentioned. As in the case of non-Jews too, one reads about encounters of relatives young and old, sometimes intended to bring together young couples for marriage purposes, occasionally ending in life-long same-sex friendships, too. Typically, in such protected milieus, success would be cherished despite hostility from the outside, and, under such circumstances, antisemitism could be forgotten, at least for a while.[18]

Moreover, the apparent readiness to adjust to life in a partly antisemitic environment grew, among other things, as a function of Jewish expectations, and these naturally relied on memories of life in earlier generations or on information concerning life elsewhere – in and outside of Europe. Thus, living in the Kaiserreich seemed to most Jews a privilege and, in any case, a considerable improvement. While German Jews had to come to terms with antisemitism à la Treitschke, painful as it was, Jews in Russia, especially in the southern provinces of the Tsarist Empire, were facing violent, bloody pogroms. Reports on these events began to arrive early in the 1870s. They were repeated a decade later and then, with a vengeance, between 1903 and 1905. Later on, the pogroms triggered waves of refugees. Approximately 90,000 East European Jews came to Germany prior to the First World War. Local Jews were not always welcoming, to be sure, but on the whole they did support the newcomers – both financially and socially. Some came of their own accord. Jewish students, for instance, who were unable to enter Russian universities because of the "numerus clausus" there, came willingly and sometimes gladly to Germany. Shmarya Levin, later a leading Zionist, left Russia for Prussia in 1906. In his memoirs he describes the train border-crossing as a moment of liberation, "and if I had not been ashamed," he adds, "I would have embraced and kissed the Prussian gendarme who now boarded the train."[19] Chaim Weizmann, later Israel's first president, was not so ecstatic at first, but he too soon learned to appreciate his years as a student of chemistry at the

---

[18] See Mirjam Zadoff, *Next Year in Marienbad: The Lost World of Jewish Spa Culture*, Philadelphia, 2012.
[19] See Shmarya Levin, *Youth in Revolt*, New York, 1930, 221.

Technical University of Charlottenburg. For many newcomers, both migrants and refugees, Germany was a substitute promised land and in fact, it was for most local Jews too.

Towards the end of the nineteenth century, comparison with France likewise tended to favor Germany. Édouard Drumont's antisemitic book *La France juive*, first published in 1886, won great popularity and gained more serious treatment in well-placed circles than anything produced by the German antisemites at the time. Racial anthropology was at least as influential in France as in Germany and the Ligue antisémitique de France, while not a proper political party, gained a great deal of support both in the home country and in the North African French colonies, especially in Algeria. Moreover, from the early 1880s onwards, antisemitism had been – in France as in Germany – a permanent component of right-wing, integral nationalism. In both countries, it channeled disaffection with and fear of modernity into hostility towards the Jews. Following the financial crash of 1882, when the bank Union Générale suddenly collapsed and the French economy plunged into one of the worst crises of the century, the antisemitic tone heard throughout the Republic was undeniable. German Jews were well aware of all that and, since 1894, during the twelve years of the so-called Dreyfus Affair, they followed events across the Rhine with a mixture of concern, solidarity, and a more or less hidden pride. A scandal of such proportions could not have happened in Germany, they felt. After all, they – unlike the French Jews – lived in a true *Rechtsstaat* (state based on the rule of law), where the mob was restrained by a decent police and a functioning legal system, and opposition against them was being curbed by a powerful, well-balanced monarchical state. During the riots against the Jews in Neustettin (1881), in Xanten (1891), and then during the Konitz blood-libel case (1900), the authorities – both local and national – proved fully reliable, most Jews felt. Public expressions of solidarity with Jews in the context of a ritual murder case in Russia, known as the Beilis Affair, in 1913, were also a source of satisfaction to German Jews. Their own patriotism seemed to be rewarded, and being German continued to be a source of pride and satisfaction for most of them.

Surely, now is the time to introduce the main positive traits of the Kaiserreich era, namely its flourishing cultural life, its internationally successful academic establishment, and its exceptional scientific excellence. These were the years of Wagner's *Ring* cycle, of Nietzsche's philosophy, of Fontana's novels; the time of the young Thomas Mann and Rilke's poetry; of Theodor Mommsen's Roman history and Max Weber's budding sociology; of Hauptmann's theater and some experimental expressionist dramas; of Richard Strauss' operas and Brahms' great symphonies – all prior to the First World War and much of it even before the turn of the century. These were also the years of great scientific discoveries in physics, of breakthroughs in cell biology and physical chemistry, and impressive advances in medicine. Germany was unquestionably at the forefront in these multiple spheres.[20]

The role played by the Jews in this boom is well known. They were among the most outspoken supporters of modernity, as we saw. Thus, despite Wagner's open antisemitism, they were among his most loyal listeners in opera halls up and down the country. They were likewise often to be seen in performances of modern and, in the early twentieth century, expressionist theater, as well. In fact, the tale of Berlin's cultural scene, with its avid Jewish consumers and its numerous creative Jewish contributors, is all too well documented. So is the tale of fin-de-siècle Vienna, outside the Kaiserreich but within the German-language middle-European milieu. It was parading Jacob Wassermann's novels, Arthur Schnitzler's theater plays, Freud's psychoanalysis, and – if one was ready, or willing, to disregard baptism – Gustav Mahler's success as conductor of one of the world's best orchestras, reigning over the musical scene at the capital of the Habsburg monarchy – even if not always to the pleasure of the entire Viennese public. The list of Jewish celebrities in the cultural as well as the scientific scene at the time is long and impressive. Stefan Zweig and his best-selling novellas must surely be included in it. But perhaps it would be more instructive to concentrate here not on Zweig's accomplishments, but on his shortcomings; not upon his individual achievements, but upon his apparent *Weltanschauung* – a prototype for a collective, tragic oversight.

Zweig's memoirs, published posthumously in 1943 under the title *The World of Yesterday*, open with the following statement: "When I try to find a formula for the period in which I grew up, prior to the First World War, I hope that I convey its fullness by calling it the Golden Age of Security." What follows is a description of a perfect social order, a reliable political system, flourishing economy, and glowing culture. "No one thought of wars, of revolutions, or revolts," Zweig concludes, "All that was radical, all violence, seemed impossible in an age of reason."[21]

This is touching. It clearly reflects the sense of well-being typical of the contemporary bourgeoisie – Jewish and non-Jewish alike. But it is also

---

[20] A thoughtful and detailed introduction to the study of these achievements can be found in the last part of Thomas Nipperdey, *Deutsche Geschichte 1866–1918*, Munich, 1990, Vol. I, 602–797.

[21] See the first English translation, Stefan Zweig, *The World of Yesterday: An Autobiography*, New York, 1943, 1–2.

completely mistaken. It hardly describes the situation "in our almost thousand-year-old Austrian monarchy," to use Zweig's own words. Vienna, his beloved home town, was by then a city of immigrants and refugees, with deep class barriers and widespread social strife. In the fall of 1905, following the first, failed revolution in Russia, some 250,000 workers took to the streets along the Ring, demanding equal suffrage, following years of bitter industrial strife near to home and, in fact, everywhere across the continent. But at that time, even closer by, within Zweig's own social milieu, disaffection reached new heights.

To begin with, antisemitism was never far from the surface. Karl Lueger, head of the Christian Social Party and a rabid antisemite, was mayor of Vienna between 1897 and 1910, while still more radical Jew-haters, led by the Pan-German Georg Ritter von Schönerer, stormed its streets. At the same time, bourgeois women, who – according to Zweig's own testimony – were not allowed to disclose more than their ankles in public, were beginning to seek equality, expressing dissatisfaction and causing controversy, sometimes, indeed, bitter conflicts.

Further away, internationally, things were equally unsettled. The Boer War was fought in South Africa between 1899 and 1902; the Russo-Japanese one shortly thereafter in East Asia. And if these were perhaps too far away to disturb Zweig's peace of mind, the countries of the Balkans were, after all, just around the corner, and these were constantly in ferment, most particularly after the Young Turks' revolution of 1908 and then during the bloody struggles of 1912–1913. Grand imperial conflicts elsewhere were raging too, signaling the approach of the First World War. All this uproar was apparently unnoticeable in the elegant salons of the Viennese upper classes and of the well-to-do Jewish educated bourgeoisie.

In an influential small volume, *Jews beyond Judaism*, the historian George Mosse claimed that throughout Central Europe it was the Jews who preserved the liberal tradition of *Bildung*, developed late in the eighteenth century and the early nineteenth, the time of their early entry into German civil society. Upholding this tradition had become, he explained, the main Jewish route to assimilation. Thus, enlightened liberalism, merging with nationalism of a humane and humanistic kind, was – and remained – their creed, even as non-Jews were gradually abandoning it, moving ever more quickly to the right, attaching themselves now to radical conservatism and an anti-modern, outspoken chauvinism.[22] Clearly, among the Jews, too – one must somewhat correct Mosse's thesis – there were those who read Fichte with as much ardor as Kant, Nietzsche instead of Lessing,

---

[22] George L. Mosse, *Jews beyond Judaism*, New York, 1985.

Langbehn as well as Goethe. Many Jews, no doubt, were well aware of the challenge of modernism; some joined the Social Democratic Party or could even be counted among its ideological and political leadership. Others, like Stephan Zweig, remained liberal, and many among them learned to turn a blind eye to the main intellectual – perhaps one may even say spiritual – transformation of the pre-First World War years. They seemed oblivious to the rightward shift even of their trusted liberal allies and the parallel growth of an aggressive, often racially buttressed nationalism, tied to imperial dreams and to self-assertive war-mongering, both in the Kaiserreich and in Austria.

In France, it was in 1906 that the Dreyfus Affair reached its final stage. The French Republic decided through this prolonged and painful affair to choose democracy and the rule of law. It decided, or so it seemed, to move against the excesses of integral, right-wing nationalism. In Germany at that time, there was nothing like the Dreyfus Affair, and no such decision was taken. Instead, by 1906, while the echoes of the Herero catastrophe in South West Africa were still resounding, the colonizers' arrogance together with their military enthusiasm and their willingness to use the utmost force against the native Black rebels signaled the recklessness of which Prussia, indeed Germany as a whole, was by then capable. A couple of years earlier, Lieutenant-General Lothar von Trotha had been sent from Berlin to the colony of South West Africa and then decided to annihilate the rebelling tribes, justifying his policy in explicitly racist messages sent to his commanders in chief at home. It was then that he proceeded first to drive the Hereros into the desert, where they died of thirst and hunger, and then into concentration camps, where they had no chance of survival either.

This atrocious genocide shocked those back home who were prepared to face the facts and reject the attached message, but they were few and far between. The exceptionally appalling behavior of a couple of imperial officers was investigated, and they were finally dishonorably discharged, but not much was done beyond that, on a more general level. After much bureaucratic haggling, the chancellor, Bernhard von Bülow, managed to convince the Kaiser to recall von Trotha to Germany, but for the African population of the colony, this was too late, and at home the general did not stand trial, not even on account of his disciplinary offences, while every effort was made to set the affair aside. At the beginning of 1907, German policies in South West Africa, this time against the Nama tribe, did bring matters to a head again, and they became the focus of a heated parliamentary debate, especially because of the extra budgetary needs of a protracted war that was vehemently opposed by the Social Democratic Party and the Catholic Center Party. Finally, the Reichstag had to be dissolved and new elections – called by some the "Hottentot elections" – were announced. The chauvinistic tone of the following campaign was unmistakable, and antisemitism – always conjoined to the conglomerate of racism, social-Darwinism, and reheated nationalism – was once again very much present in public life. The various splinter antisemitic parties, who had been in retreat, gained an additional ten Reichstag seats, and what had begun as early as the 1890s with the Navy League and the Pan-German movement ended now in a peak of nationalistic fervor and pro-imperialistic crusading.

The history books often stress that cruelty and boundless violence were by no means unique to the German colonialists. Other imperial powers applied equally reckless, racially motivated tactics in treating native populations. The British, the French, and the Belgians were just as brutal. This is doubtless true. However, it may still be legitimate to stay within Germany for the moment, where we cannot refrain from observing that, some two decades before the onset of the First World War, public expressions of militarism-cum-extreme nationalism were loud and clear, and that racism and anti-Jewish propaganda were rampant everywhere. A direct link between racism in Africa and later events in Germany cannot be established. However, it was by then clear that not much remained of the older enlightened patriotism and the promise of a humanistic, tolerant society that Jews had so eagerly embraced in their efforts to assimilate into Germany. To be sure, many Jews supported, sometimes even enthusiastically, the German imperial adventures. The Jewish press repeatedly sought to tell the tales of Jewish heroes fighting in Africa and rarely criticized government policies or the open cruelty of the military. Moreover, like Stefan Zweig, most Jews tended to ignore the signs of danger implicit and occasionally even explicit in the atmosphere of these days. The Kaiserreich was still a land of promise for its Jewish minority, despite the dark omens that were unmistakably there – not only for Jews, but in some ways particularly for Jews.

One exceptional German Jew did comment thoroughly on the events in the African colonies. In the midst of the heated political controversy, in July 1907, Walther Rathenau – whom we quoted above, by then a successful industrialist and financial baron in his own right – joined Bernhard Dernburg, the newly appointed Prussian Colonial Secretary, on a trip to Germany's African territories. Upon returning, he composed two extensive reports to be handed in to both Kaiser and chancellor. In the first, Rathenau described the situation in East Africa, asserting that "on the whole, the work of colonization demands qualities which the Germans possess in rich measure." He also insisted that "education for colonization will eventually open for the German soul a field that corresponds to its earthly mission." However, his comment to the effect that he would have preferred "to achieve submission through exemplary leadership," rather than by the brutal use of force, did indicate the direction of his future critique and later on, indeed, in observing events in South West Africa, he became more outspoken. The handling of the Hereros, Rathenau now stated, involved "the greatest atrocity that has ever been brought about by German military policy." This, he claimed, compared unfavorably with the policies of the British in nearby South Africa and was, in addition, contrary to the true interests of Germany. Still, "through German blood spilt on its fields," Rathenau quickly slipped back into the common discourse of the time, the colony "became part of our homeland, and German land must remain sacrosanct."[23]

This cautious formulation, indicating his willingness to placate his superiors, did not help. Both von Bülow and the Kaiser apparently read Rathenau's second report and simply passed over it in silence. Rathenau's expectation that he would be thanked or even decorated for his services came to naught; critique, even patriotic critique, was clearly not appreciated. And, in any case, Rathenau was in no way representative of German Jewry. He was too rich, too prominent, and too eccentric. Still, in some ways his position was in this case not entirely atypical – neither for German Jews nor for many other bourgeois citizens of Imperial Germany. Rathenau was appalled by the atrocities in Africa, believing that mild censure would would have sufficed. Even he, an independent and influential man, with many personal contacts in the uppermost echelons of the Prussian bureaucracy, was not in a position to face up to the nationalist, imperialist, racially motivated *Weltanschauung* that seemed ever more prevalent in the Germany of his day. Turning a blind eye to the atrocities was no longer possible, but neither was anything even slightly more than meek opposition. Most Jews, like him, did not realize, or did not *want* to realize, that this could possibly mean danger for them, too, even if they could not miss the fact that it was endangering the values they had always stood for.

There were other signs of danger all along. In 1912, in a book carrying the title *If I Were the Kaiser*, Heinrich Claß, leader of the Pan-German League, published a complete political program based on the "Germanic" world view. Claß was indeed famous for his antisemitism,

---

[23] Both memoranda, somewhat shortened, were translated and annotated in Hartmut Pogge von Strandmann (ed.), *Walther Rathenau: Industrialist, Banker, Intellectual, and Politician. Notes and Diaries 1907–1922*, Oxford, 1985, 49–59, 78–92. The first memorandum was first published in Walther Rathenau, *Reflexionen*, Leipzig, 1908, 143–197; the second – posthumously – in his *Nachgelassene Schriften*, Frankfurt am Main, 1928, vol. II, 74–141.

but this was only one part of his ideological baggage. He held firm views on many other issues. His book caused something of a sensation and was widely read. By the beginning of the First World War, some 25,000 copies had been sold – a handsome figure by all accounts. In the book, Claß developed a critique of the German government's foreign policy, rejecting the concept of a "saturated Germany" and the value of a "just peace" by which it should resign itself to a supposedly inferior position on the international arena. He demanded expansion to the east and the acquisition of additional overseas colonies, called for a war of national rejuvenation, and campaigned for a new type of social legislation designed to stop modernization. Above all, Claß was concerned with putting an end to "racial intermingling," a term that was much in use with regard to African affairs, considered a grave danger to the true "German soul," as he claimed. Hatred of the Jews fit only too neatly into this ideological mix. Though it was not always explicit, it was easy to read between the lines. Claß's organization preached militant nationalism, imperial expansion, racism, anti-socialism and militarism, firmly supporting the authoritarian state. With time, it combined anti-Slavism with diatribes against the Poles and expressions of distaste and resentment vis-à-vis the Jews.[24] The book signified a high point in the right-wing nationalistic campaign, but its spirit could surely be felt both earlier and then much later too. However, the Pan-German league and its verbiage was not yet a prominent voice. It was still possible to ignore it and trust in the decency of the *Rechtsstaat*, basking in the sensation of political equality and cultural success.

Across the borders of the Reich, in an atmosphere of national and ethnic strife, some Jews *were* beginning to lose confidence. In fact, the worst year of the Herero war, 1904, was also the year that saw Theodor Herzl's untimely death. A decade earlier, in the wake of the Dreyfus Affair and sensing antisemitism in his Viennese home town, Herzl had begun to delineate an ideology for a separate Jewish national movement, soon to be called Zionism, and managed to establish it internationally, with support coming mainly from Eastern and East-Central European Jewry. Within the context of the Habsburg monarchy, this indicated a realization of the hopelessness of assimilation. Like other nationalities living in this monarchy, Herzl felt that Jews too ought to regain their own nationality and, like others around them, shape it along the model of German nationalism.

It was the old liberal tradition that had been critical for Herzl himself, though some of his colleagues within the movement soon attached themselves to a more aggressive, more right-wing nationalism. Regardless of

---

[24] See Heinrich Claß, *Wenn ich der Kaiser wär': Politische Wahrheiten und Notwendigkeiten*, Leipzig, 1912.

this internal controversy, even among Austrian Jews and more clearly among East European Jewry, the need to weigh the various options confronting the Jews was a topic of great interest. Schnitzler's novel *Der Weg ins Freie* (*The Road into the Open*), written by a man who was no less active a member of the Viennese cultural elite than Herzl himself, discusses these issues in some detail. But all that, though not entirely absent from Jewish life in the Kaiserreich, preoccupied only a small minority north of the Austrian border. By the second decade of the twentieth century, Jews seemed to be confronting antisemitism and other poisonous winds mainly with apathy. When, in March 1912, Moritz Goldstein published in the national-conservative journal *Die Kunstwart* an article under the title "Deutsch-jüdischer Parnaß," it did seem to shake the entire Jewish world, at least for a while. In it, Goldstein seemingly accepted some of the antisemitic claims against the Jews, questioning the logic of assimilation and the premises of its apparent success. But his was a lone voice, and Goldstein was something of an *enfant terrible* even among German Zionists. In the bourgeois milieu within which most Jews lived, anti-Jewish sentiments were not common. One had to acknowledge, perhaps, that among conservatives of all kinds, among aristocrats and some anti-modern *Mittelstand* men and women, and in some cases even among right-wing liberals, integral nationalism bound up with antisemitism was becoming ever stronger. But apparently it was still possible to disregard all of this and trust the positive trends of modernity and democratization, likewise visible and seemingly more influential at the time.[25]

And what was true for the Jews was doubly true for non-Jews. Those who did not themselves share the aggressive nationalism of so many men and women around them did not seem to take too seriously the threat of racism and antisemitism. They usually refused to look danger in the eyes, just like the Jews. Social democrats – themselves constantly a target of right-wing propaganda – were more vigilant than most, no doubt, and Jews who joined the Social Democratic Party were likewise more attentive to signs of danger than other Jews. But, for the bourgeoisie as a whole, Christian and Jewish alike, life was too comfortable, too promising, and too reassuring. Germany was by then a scientific empire; a cultural and academic center of world fame. New forms of art were flourishing. Success seemed easy to achieve. This was an age of great achievements, but, alas, it was also an age of much unwarranted complacency.

---

[25] For the Jewish ways into the bourgeoisie see Simone Lässig, *Jüdische Wege ins Bürgertum: Kulturelles Kapital und sozialer Aufstieg im 19. Jahrhundert*, Göttingen, 2014.

8 Joined and Disjoint in War

This complacency became particularly striking during the summer of 1914, in the days of approaching war. Despite growing tension among the great European powers and the insecurity caused by the various alliances and counter-alliances among them, the bourgeoisie was enjoying its summer vacation as usual. At the end of July 1914, a month after the assassination of the Austro-Hungarian heir to the throne, Archduke Franz Ferdinand, most people still saw no reason to worry. On August 1, 1914, wrote Sebastian Haffner in his posthumously published memoirs, "we had just decided not to take the matter very seriously, and to continue our holidays."[1] A day earlier, Walther Rathenau, surely a well-informed man, with unusually good political contacts and by then also with some actual political experience himself, published an opinion piece in the *Berliner Tageblatt*, in which he rather lightheartedly stated that "[t]he issue of whether or not Austrian representatives would be able to participate in arbitrating Serbian internal affairs is no reason for a world war."[2] This, no doubt, was true enough. However, he too was soon to be proven wrong. On August 4, Germany was at war with Russia, France, and Great Britain; the First World War had begun.

A few days earlier, on July 31, Jean Jaurès, head of the French Socialist Party, had been assassinated in Paris, and immediately afterwards Raymond Poincaré, president of the Republic, who until then had received the news concerning Serbian affairs with complete equanimity, called upon the French people to come together and confirm that much-hoped-for national *union sacrée*, in preparation for the fight to defend their fatherland. They were now expected to act together, setting aside all previous internal discord. The mood in Berlin was – if anything – even more sanguine. Hundreds of thousands filled Unter den Linden, cheering the Kaiser, who promised to see in the future "only Germans," calling for

---

[1] See Sebastian Haffner, *Defying Hitler: A Memoir*, New York, 2000, 12.
[2] The article, entitled "Ein Wort zur Lage," was reprinted in Walther Rathenau, *Gesammelte Schriften*, Berlin, 1918, Vol. I, 306.

brotherly unity within the country in order to stand together against the enemies without. This "emotional smoke," as it was called by the author and politician Ernst Toller, was said to encompass the entire public. Newspapers reported that within a couple of days well over a million men had volunteered to join the army. Famous names were mentioned – poets, novelists, scholars, and artists. Thus, the neo-romantic poet Richard Dehmel insisted on being drafted, even though he was over fifty and had never been a soldier before. Hermann Hesse volunteered, but was immediately refused, and Rainer Maria Rilke, later a proclaimed pacifist, originally felt elated by this "Dionysian experience," while the sociologist Georg Simmel, the art critic Friedrich Gundolf – both of Jewish origins – and the painter Franz Marc, who was killed in action a year and a half later, were equally enthusiastic.

Evidence for the enthusiasm that encompassed groups beyond the educated elite exists, too. We know, for instance, of the innumerable patriotic songs that were written and sung in those days, while private letters from the front were by then also full of patriotic pathos. The general sense emanating from them was that one was living "in great days," to quote one such letter, and that "If justice exists and the hand of God is steering history ... victory must be ours – sooner or later."[3] After years of internal haggling and struggling regarding all foreign and domestic affairs during the Kaiserreich, there was suddenly relief in the air. Many felt that national unity had finally been achieved and that victory would soon follow, though this was and remained contrary to all realistic expectations.

Clearly there were those who remained coolheaded, certainly more than the old historiography allowed for. "Most people in Europe have not expected or greeted the war with enthusiasm," writes the historian Oliver Janz in summarizing the updated research on this topic.[4] In Germany, as well as elsewhere, a wide spectrum of public reactions to the outbreak of war could be documented, ranging between patriotic enthusiasm and indifference, resignation, or even fear and outright opposition. In fact, nowhere in Europe, Janz claims, did so many people take to the streets to protest against the war as in Germany. On July 28, between 100,000 and 200,000 participated in a demonstration in Berlin, probably as many as or more than the numbers assembling on Unter der Linden and in many other urban centers a few days later, for precisely the

---

[3] See Reinhard Rürup, "Der 'Geist von 1914' in Deutschland. Kriegsbegeisterung und Ideologisierung des Krieges im Ersten Weltkrieg," in Bernd-Rüdiger Hüppauf (ed.), *Ansichten vom Krieg: Vergleichende Studien zum Ersten Weltkrieg in Literatur und Gesellschaft*, Hain, 1984, 1–30. The quote is from page 4.

[4] See Oliver Janz, *Der große Krieg*, Frankfurt am Main, 2014, 180.

opposite purpose. The recruitment of volunteers was apparently also never as high as the exaggerated numbers circulated by the press at the time. By the end of the year, the army reported the recruitment of some 300,000 men – no fewer, indeed, but also no more.

Up to this point, even the rather irresponsible past governments of the Reich were trying to contain international competition so as to avoid military conflict. Bismarck, as we saw, had initially opposed active imperialism and changed his mind only gradually, moving ahead slowly and cautiously. Later on, Leo von Caprivi, chancellor between 1890 and 1894, seeking a new alliance with the liberals, was more open to the world, and the atmosphere during his term of office was considerably less belligerent than in the later Bismarck years; even the parliament seemed to be coming into its own at this time. Then, during the years of Prince of Hohenlohe's chancellorship, the pendulum swung again and the government, acting under the pressure of the Junker aristocracy, invested great efforts in the construction of a large navy – commercial and military – thereby finding itself at loggerheads with Britain. Then, under Bernhard von Bülow and the unfortunate intervention of the Kaiser in foreign policy, Germany became hopelessly entangled in imperial strife – this time mainly with France over Morocco – and, in 1914, trust in the military, together with great hopes for finally achieving "a place in the sun" combined to let the army march, in fact, towards inevitable defeat.

Many Jews – the more or less assimilated, liberal and orthodox, mostly living as an inseparable part of the German bourgeoisie – were swept up by the nationalist euphoria, just like their non-Jewish neighbors. Above all else, it was the Kaiser's promise of *Burgfrieden* – that is, civil peace – that fired their imagination. Though this was mainly intended to pacify and recruit the working class, who had been practically excluded from the national community until the war started, Jews – everywhere in Germany – felt it was also meant for them. At last they were to be included in this warm brotherly embrace, called upon – together with others – to join in the approaching, heroic war.

In his memoirs, Arnold Tänzer, rabbi of Göttingen's Jewish community, who soon volunteered to serve as a military rabbi, described the ecstasy he felt as he was suddenly called upon to save the beloved fatherland, attacked by vicious enemies intent on destroying it.[5] The most popular song during these days, reprinted in all newspapers and taught in all classrooms, was the "Haßgesang gegen England" ("Hate-Song

---

[5] See extracts from his memoirs in Monika Richarz (ed.), *Jüdisches Leben in Deutschland: Selbstzeugnisse zur Sozialgeschichte im Kaiserreich*, New York, 1979, 445–448.

against England"), written by the Jewish poet Ernst Lissauer. Eventually, as many as 17% of all German Jews participated as soldiers in the war – only a marginally smaller proportion than the 18.5% of all the non-Jewish Germans. Over three-quarters of them served at the front; some 10% among them fell in action. In fact, since Jews had rarely served in the army before, it was – and still is – difficult to provide a meaningful comparison for their contribution to the military effort. However, their patriotism and their readiness – even willingness – to put their lives on the line could not be doubted.

Finally, as in the case of the proletariat, the fact that Jews could find themselves fighting other Jews – French, Russians, or other East Europeans – played a surprisingly minor role in their own assessment of the situation. At first, and as long as the battle seemed to be directed especially against the Czarist Empire, an enemy much detested by all, the war could be interpreted as aid to their oppressed brethren in the east. Some German and Austrian Jewish organizations even engaged in efforts to convince their co-religionists to act against the approaching Russian troops in revenge for previous acts of discrimination against them and for the recent violent, bloody pogroms. Some Zionists hoped to gain German help for Jewish settlement in Palestine under the new circumstances. But, with the first German setbacks in the fall of 1914, these activities were discontinued. Special Jewish "war aims" were no longer upheld, even while the "spirit of 1914" still seemed to prevail.

At the earlier stage, many Jewish newspapers or newspapers edited by Jews joined in the patriotic excitement; Jewish associations proclaimed their loyalty to the fatherland, and a number of exceptional Jewish figures could be counted among those who were doing their best to secure victory. Walther Rathenau, again, was particularly prominent among them. Being forty-seven years old at the start of the war, he could not join the army, but within days he hurriedly conveyed an excited message to the chancellor, Theobald von Bethmann Hollweg, offering his services, and soon busied himself drafting plans for the import and acquisition of necessary raw materials and the organization of their domestic production. Surprisingly, indeed, the army had had no ready plans in this critical sphere and, following quick consultations, the Prussian War Minister, General Erich von Falkenhayn, met Rathenau and appointed him head of what was to be called the Department of Raw Materials in War – the Kriegsrohstoffabteilung (KRA). For eight months, during which he served in this capacity, Rathenau proved indispensable, though his aggressive intervention in the economy was resented by some other industrialists – his previous friends and sometimes close colleagues.

In any event, his acceptance into the corridors of power, even if done neither graciously nor amicably, indicated a new appointment policy that would be applied from now on by various government agencies. In fact, other influential Jews were soon recruited for other crucial posts. The ship-owner Albert Ballin organized – with some of his colleagues at the necessarily paralyzed HAPAG Company in Hamburg – the so-called Central Company for the Acquisition of Foodstuffs (Zentraleinkaufgesellschaft). The jurist and banker Carl Melchior, like Ballin also from the northern port town, was assigned to negotiate a cereals agreement with Romania early in 1915, while the economist Julius Hirsch ran the Price Controlling Agency and Eduard Arnhold was made head of the Office for Coal Provision. The regular Prussian officers in the bureaucracy and other bureaucrats may not have always felt comfortable with these newcomers, but they were urgently needed at this point and proved vital for the war effort.

Initially, at least, even some antisemites were ready to acknowledge Jewish patriotism. Houston Stewart Chamberlain conceded that Jews "fulfill their duty as Germans in front of the enemy or at home,"[6] and, in Vienna, a former member of Schönerer's antisemitic Pan-German Party, Karl Iro, even stated that any Jew who served at the front "secured his right to be one of us."[7] During these early months of the war, the government fulfilled its part of the bargain by censoring the more outspoken antisemitic publications, and so, on the whole, unity really did seem to be upheld, though – as it turned out – only temporarily.

In fact, a sense of *German* national unity had been considered improper or even dangerous in the eyes of the Prussian leadership during much of the Kaiserreich era. This was the considered opinion of Friedrich Meinecke in his *Cosmopolitanism and the National State*, first published in 1908. In its second, less often read or commented-upon part, Meinecke exposed the inner tensions within the Reich, especially between Prussia and the other German federal states. The gap between a national ideal based upon a common past and a unique culture, typical of the non-Prussian areas of the Reich, had long been contrasted with the centralist, military Prussian nationalism. Despite his admiration for Bismarck, Meinecke saw the Kaiserreich – his major achievement – as an unstable, problematic

---

[6] Quoted from Houston Stewart Chamberlain, *Arische Weltanschauung*, Munich, 1914, in Felicity Rash, *German Images of the Self and the Other: Nationalist, Colonialist and Antisemitic Discourse, 1871–1918*, New York, 2012, 119.
[7] Quoted in Peter Pulzer, "The First World War," in Michael A. Meyer and Michael Brenner (eds.), *German-Jewish History in Modern Times*, Vol. III, *Integration in Dispute, 1871–1918*, New York, 1997, 360–384. The quote is from page 365.

polity. Before the outbreak of war in 1914, Prussia and Germany, according to him, were still far from being joined together. In the early days of the Reich, both left-wing liberals and the admittedly rather few German democrats shied away from its autocratic character. The federal system weakened its unified image, and the existence of a large Catholic minority made internal conflicts ever more acute. In this strange state – neither a unified nation-state, like France or England, nor a multinational empire, like Austro-Hungary or Russia, even nationalism itself was not always a unifying factor.

Surely, of all the inner ruptures within the Kaiserreich, that between the bourgeoisie and the working class was the deepest and most significant. In the past, Bismarck had managed to turn all organized workers into "fellows without a fatherland," constituting an acute and dangerous menace from within. Later on, even as the Social Democratic Party became the largest fraction in the Reichstag following the election of 1912, its members continued to be considered pariahs within it, while in society at large the laboring poor who elected them and sent them to Parliament formed their own complete, separate milieu. They not only had their own journals and newspapers, but also their own associations and interest organizations, their own choirs and theater groups – a full-scale subculture, functioning in parallel with the larger, hegemonic one. In addition, Catholics were posited against Protestants in this polity; Jews, as well as the large Polish minority, were often felt to be outsiders; and finally, by the early twentieth century, the struggle for women's emancipation had caused an additional gap in this male-dominated society.

Inner strife was not unique to Germany, of course. In his book *The Strange Death of Liberal England*, George Dangerfield presents the classical description of the deep divisive lines running through Edwardian society and threatening to break it up. Neither was France during the Dreyfus Affair, between 1894 and 1906, a model of harmony. Still, the two older nation-states could pride themselves on a long joint history, while Germany's imperial past was difficult to turn into a useful, unifying narrative. The Kaiserreich had been merged by a series of wars and by Bismarck's clever politics, operating against long-standing other traditions. It could at best be considered a transitory compromise, requiring much improvement.

The heightened national verbiage overwhelming Germany in 1914, while seemingly intent on providing some meaning for the immediate experience of war, was also expected to define anew German nationalism, profiling the essence of being German in modern times, postulating that longed-for inner unity. It was expected to manifest the uniqueness of the

German nation-state and flesh out its lofty ideals. Thus, for the first time, the generation of 1914 finally experienced a sense of common purpose, though only vis-à-vis its enemies, consolidating "our German-ness" and achieving the "completion of the nation."[8]

The year 1914 brought with it a new "German Uprising," argued Friedrich Meinecke, by then among the outstanding historians in the country, the fourth such "Uprising" since the early nineteenth century. The first was the war of independence fought against Napoleon in 1813; the second came with the revolution of 1848; the third occurred during the wars of unification between 1864 and 1871; and the fourth was now taking place, during the ongoing Great War.[9] One was finally fighting, it was argued, against the arrogant French Republic, the materialistic and selfish English, and the tyrannical backward Russia, added other intellectuals. War, so ran the argument, always served as a consolidating force in German history, bringing with it new expressions of solidarity, reducing inner strife, and fostering unity. Even those who were more skeptical, such as the jurist Otto von Gierke, who, in a lecture on "War and Culture" given on September 18, 1914, reminded his audience that, in fact, inner strife only became bitterer after the War of 1813 and that the wars leading to unification in 1871 likewise did little to foster solidarity, hoped that the present war might, nevertheless, "cure us all," and that Germany would finally be able to secure for itself not only a respectable past but also a hopeful future.[10]

All that, however, was easier said than done. As soon as the army found itself in a static trench war, it became clear that no one – especially none of the acting political figures in Germany – had any clear vision or precise political plan; nor could they even begin to agree among themselves upon the war's final aims. Under these circumstances, it was difficult, indeed, to maintain – not to mention boost – a true unity. By mid 1916, Germany was a society under siege. At the front, casualties were piling up, and exhaustion – physical and psychological – among soldiers was widespread and seemingly infectious. Gradually, tensions between officers and men rose too, as did the rate of desertion, while things were no better on the home front. The population suffered from shortages of food and coal. Attacks on warehouses and shops happened ever more frequently, and, during the so-called turnip winter of 1916–1917, marking the peak of popular unrest, the civil truce in industry finally collapsed and strikes reached new proportions. In an atmosphere of class war, tension

---

[8] Rürup, "Der 'Geist von 1914,'" 13.
[9] See Friedrich Meinecke, *Die deutsche Erhebung von 1914*, Berlin, 1914.
[10] See Otto von Gierke, *Krieg und Kultur*, Berlin, 1914.

increased even *within* the middle class, and it was ever more noticeable on considering relations between town and countryside and those among and between the various regions. Anti-Prussian feelings were rising too – signifying the failure of a joint sense of national harmony. And finally, perhaps the most symptomatic development was the return of antisemitism.

This could have been felt as early as the summer of 1915. In August of that year, complaints reached the Reichstag, leading to a debate about the appointment of presumably too many Jews for posts in the mushrooming "war companies." In December, the military censorship banned a pamphlet written by Hans Liebig, a veteran of the Pan-German League, in which Bethmann Hollweg was called "Chancellor of the German Jews," linking the controversy over war aims to the "fight between German Jewry and the Teutonic Germans."[11] But the censor could not stem the tide. The League was by then clearly at work, exposing its previously concealed antisemitism, and in the army too, old habits of not allowing the promotion of Jews to the officer corps could again be easily documented, while repeated rumors of Jewish dodging of the more dangerous military postings poisoned the atmosphere.

At the outset of war, the Reichshammerbund, which had been established in 1912, ignored the calls for solidarity and urged its members to collect "material" on Jewish behavior at and behind the front. For their part too, Jewish organizations soon established a committee for war statistics and made it responsible for collecting data to counter these allegations. Then, trying to avoid the censor, antisemitic newspapers made it their business to attack Jews living abroad, generalizing from individual cases that presumably voiced anti-German positions to Jews in general – in Germany and not only abroad. Simultaneously, the battles in the east provided antisemites with an opportunity to warn against Jewish refugees and call upon the authorities to close the border against all *Ostjuden* (Jews from Eastern Europe). These, they claimed, threatened to overwhelm the Reich "like a swarm of locusts," a horde of "six million inferior, mongolized people."[12]

---

[11] Quoted in Jacob Rosenthal, *"Die Ehre des jüdischen Soldaten": Die Judenzählung im Ersten Weltkrieg und ihre Folgen*, Frankfurt am Main, 2007, 48. In addition, see the discussion in Ulrich Sieg, *Jüdische Intellektuelle im Ersten Weltkrieg: Kriegserfahrungen, weltauschauliche Debatte und kulturelle Neuentwürfe*, Berlin, 2008, especially the section on reactions to the Jewish census, pages 87–96.

[12] Quoted in Helmut Berding, *Moderner Antisemitismus in Deutschland*, Frankfurt am Main, 1988, 176.

The civil truce was thus clearly being broken by the radical right and the anti-Jewish associations acting on its fringe. These never tired of warning the Kaiser, the chancellor, all heads of state, politicians, and parliamentarians of the imminent Jewish danger. They first turned to radicalizing their own followers and then threatened the government and agitated against it. They aggravated intra-German conflicts, finally calling for the establishment of a military dictatorship in order to suppress them.

Early in October 1916, Mathias Erzberger, head of the Catholic Center Party and expressly *not* known as an antisemite, acting as a member of the Reichstag Budget Committee, requested "a thorough overview of all persons in the war companies according to gender, recruitment age, earnings, and confession."[13] He justified his request by referring to the rumors circulating concerning the over-representation of Jews in these companies, and their presumed dodging of dangerous military postings. An entire gallery of important politicians participated in the following debate, and as a result a list of names was provided, though information on religion was eventually left out of it. But there was no respite. Immediately afterwards, on October 11, 1916, the anti-Jewish lobby scored an even more clear-cut success when it managed to force the Prussian War Ministry to launch what soon came to be known as the "Jewish census," an official set of statistics concerning Jewish participation in the war.

All this caused much irritation among the Jews. It was considered a sign of stark discrimination, unfit for the age of equality and that long fought-for emancipation. Jewish soldiers in particular viewed their "counting" as an insult. At first, some still tried to interpret the statistics either as an unintended blunder or as an honest attempt to *disprove* anti-Jewish claims. But such rationalizations were only rarely taken seriously, and instead the affair was considered by most Jews a significant turning point. Julius Marx, a Jewish sanitary officer from Munich, who kept a diary throughout the war, noted as early as October 1914 signs of antisemitism among his fighting comrades. Now he was simply left to wonder "Whether people would not refuse obedience to the 'counted.'"[14] And Ernst Simon, later known as a prominent thinker and pedagogue, recalled in his memoirs that at this point he finally realized that the "dream of togetherness was over" and that "with one terrible blow the depth has opened before us again, that never closing abyss." Here was the final

---

[13] In Rosenthal, *"Die Ehre des jüdischen Soldaten,"* 54–55.
[14] Quoted in Eva G. Reichmann, "Der Bewußtseinswandel der deutschen Juden," in Werner E. Mosse and Arnold Paucker (eds.), *Deutsches Judentum im Krieg und Revolution 1916–1923*, Tübingen, 1971, 511–612. The quote is from page 518.

proof, he felt, "that we are strangers, that we stand at the margin, especially classified and counted, to be listed and treated."[15]

It was, indeed, difficult to ignore the growing antisemitic mood of the country. "The more Jews fell in this war, the more their opponents would prove that they were all sitting behind the front, making gains by war profiteering," wrote Rathenau to his antisemitic friend Wilhelm Schwaner, in one of his more depressive moods. He himself preferred to disregard the Jewish census, but still felt that, under the circumstances, hatred of the Jews could only be expected to be "doubled or tripled."[16] There was no point in arguing with the antisemites, he pontificated, but it must have all been painful to him, too.

Antisemitism, once again, embittered the life of many Jews, but other issues became more pressing as the war proceeded. Finally, by the winter and spring of 1917, Germans – all Germans – were forced to choose between a program of far-reaching reforms leading to democratization and a government that would strive for peace without annexations, or further loyalty to the old order with its monarchical and military autocracy, including – so it seemed – its rabid antisemitism. This posed a particularly difficult choice for those Jews who were deeply invested in that old order. While Rathenau typically procrastinated at this stage, Albert Ballin kept his optimism and seemed firmer and more self-confident.

Ballin was born in 1857, the youngest of eight siblings, son to Jewish parents with a respectable rabbinical ancestry.[17] At seventeen, he began working in his father's shipping firm, providing passage to mostly Jewish emigrants to England and North America. Moving sometime later to work for the Hamburg America line (HAPAG), he became its general director in 1899 and was instrumental in turning it into the largest shipping company in the world. His was a splendid career, no doubt, and, at the outbreak of war, the shipping tycoon naturally had excellent political contacts as well. In England, these included the prime minister and the foreign minister, and in Germany especially the Kaiser, who was a yearly visitor in his elegant villa near Hamburg, and Bethmann Hollweg – a truly close acquaintance. An entire circle of the highest officials could be added: Gottlieb von Jagow of the Foreign Office and later Arthur Zimmermann; Karl Helfferich – since October 1917 State

---

[15] Cited from Hans Tramer, "Der Beitrag der Juden zu Geist und Kultur," in Mosse and Paucker (eds.), *Deutsches Judentum im Krieg und Revolution*, 317–386. The quote is from page 321.

[16] See Alexander Jaser, Clemens Picht, and Ernst Schulin (eds.), *Walther Rathenau-Gesamtausgabe*, Düsseldorf, 2006, Vols. I and II. The quote is from Vol. II, page 1552.

[17] I rely here on Cecil Lamar, *Albert Ballin: Business and Politics in Imperial Germany 1888–1918*, Princeton, NJ, 1967.

Secretary in the Ministry of Internal Affairs; a number of parliamentary figures, such as Gustav Stresemann, and some influential journalists, including Maximilan Harden. He corresponded with these men when he was staying in Hamburg and met with them frequently when in Berlin. In addition to participating in numerous informal political consultations, he occasionally performed more or less formal diplomatic tasks at the behest of the German government. This influential "Kaiser-Jew" was part and parcel of the autocratic order of the Reich, loyal to the core.

During much of 1916 and then increasingly in early 1917, the central issue being debated among German policy-makers was the application of what was termed "unrestricted U-boat warfare." As early as the first major disaster, involving the sinking of the British *Lusitania* on May 7, 1915, with all its more than 2,000 people aboard, it seemed inevitable that such a tactic would greatly intensify the war against Britain and – even more critically – risk the entry of the United States into the war on the side of the Entente Powers. Thanks to his line of business, Ballin was, unsurprisingly, interested in containing war against England. Nevertheless, he felt that aggressive U-boat warfare was justified, even at the cost of such human disasters. Later on, throughout 1916 and 1917, he tended to vacillate on this issue, sometimes insisting that the future of Germany's economy was in trading with the West and hence relations with it must not be irreparably damaged. Nevertheless, at other times he accepted stalemate on land and justified the intensification of the war at sea despite the apparent risks and his own particular interests. Finally, in 1918, as the convoy system organized by the Americans and the British made this German line of fighting increasingly more dangerous and as it became apparent that there was no way Germany could win the war, while revolution was inevitably approaching, Ballin suffered from deep depression. Under the changed circumstances, he wrote to a friend, "it will no longer be a pleasure to live in this new world."[18]

Immediately thereafter, overcoming his inaction, he traveled to meet the Kaiser, for the last time, as it turned out, and made a last effort to convince him to press for peace. As this came to naught, he returned to his duties in Hamburg, meeting colleagues and co-workers in his HAPAG offices, outwardly as usual. Even upon hearing of the Kaiser's approaching abdication and experiencing the early signs of revolution, he still seemed quite calm, according to witnesses' reports. But, resting at home on that historic November 9, 1918, the day of the revolution, he took on an overdose of sleeping pills and died later the same day in one of the city's private clinics – either directly or perhaps indirectly as a result of

[18] Ibid, 331.

this overdose. For him, in any case, it was a timely death. Like the Germany that he was so deeply attached to and so dearly loved, he had reached a fatal cul-de-sac.

Ballin had an entirely unique place in the landscape of German Jewry, of course. At the same time, Walther Rathenau – never as close to the seats of power as the shipping magnate was, but equally uncharacteristic of other Jews – was in a state of shock, too. At first he publicly and rather inexplicably opposed Ludendorff's offer of unconditional surrender at the end of September 1918, but then quickly changed his mind and turned to offer advice concerning demobilization and the imminent danger of economic collapse. In December 1918, this is how Rathenau concluded one of his "open letters," somewhat theatrically to be sure, but still in a very dark mood: "[M]y life is completed; I hope and fear nothing for me, my country no longer needs me, I believe I would not live long after its downfall."[19] Clearly, men who were – like Ballin and Rathenau – so strongly and deeply attached to the "world of yesterday" were facing dark days.

But most German Jews were much more hopeful at the turn of events. Most of them had supported the opposition in Germany, at least since mid 1916. By then the civilian population was split between hardliners and the ones who wished to see an end to hostilities brought about by German concessions and the introduction of fundamental internal reforms. The latter line was demanded by the socialists, by most liberals, and by the majority of the Catholic Center Party. And after all, Jews – both as individuals and in their organizations and publications – had always belonged in this camp. They were traditionally supporters of the liberal parties even before the establishment of the Kaiserreich, while since 1890 many of them had joined the Social Democratic Party. Since the political right, including the conservatives and the various splinter parties surrounding them, was often openly antisemitic, and even some National Liberals stood not far from the Pan-Germans, most Jews felt they had little choice. As a whole, they were drifting to the left, and since they mostly belonged to the middle class, especially to the lower middle class, they consistently remained within the moderate wing of the socialists.

In war, most Jews joined those who rejected the annexationism propagated by heavy industry, usually maintaining a cautious distance from the supporters of unlimited U-boat warfare, standing for a "peace of

---

[19] This letter can be found in Walther Rathenau, *Gesammelte Schriften*, Berlin, 1929, Vol. VI, 271f.

understanding" and at the same time for reform of the Prussian three-classes voting system and the full democratization of Germany as a whole. In addition to their subscription to central and sometimes also local Jewish newspapers, the educated Jewry in Berlin, for instance, read the liberal *Berliner Tageblatt* or the more moderate *Vossische Zeitung*; in the south they read the *Frankfurter Zeitung*, while a minority sometimes also read Maximilian Harden's *Die Zukunft*. This, more or less, was the tenor of their politics. They were a part, a minute part no doubt, of a discernible block of bourgeois politics during that time. Many Jews were among the active functionaries of the Social Democratic Party (SPD) from its very beginning. Probably not very many Jews were among its regular voters, especially later, in its more radical phase. Their number grew considerably, however, during the war. When in 1917 the SPD split and the USPD (Independent Social Democratic Party) was established, a number of Jews could be found in leading positions in both parties, some even in the radical left-wing Spartacus group. While most Jews were not outright revolutionaries, many had long awaited far-reaching reforms in the political system of the Reich, and, when Germany collapsed before the armies of the Entente, they were among those who looked hopefully to the new Weimar Republic, to quickly reach a permanent peace agreement and introduce a regime of justice and equal rights at home.

And while a significant part of the nation set out energetically to save what could be saved of war-stricken Germany, the other part was left to lick its wounds. The few Jews among them were confused and desperate, as we saw. Of the non-Jews, many of whom were deeply resentful, some found it useful indeed to apply an old tactic; that is, they blamed it all on the Jews.

The historian Werner Jochmann described in a detailed article, published some half a century ago, the spreading of antisemitism during the war.[20] He collected documents and personal memoirs, all showing the significance of this phenomenon. Presenting the various antisemitic accusations coming from within the officer corps and the military administration, he proceeded to prove that their statements were lies and to expose the faulty nature of their claims. All this need not be repeated here. It is important, however, to stress the simple fact that, whereas antisemitism before the war could still be seen by Jews as "irksome ... but by no means dangerous,"[21] – to quote the Zionist leader Richard Lichtheim, it soon became a real and present danger

---

[20] See Werner Jochmann, "Die Ausbreitung des Antisemitismus," in Mosse and Paucker (eds.), *Deutsches Judentum im Krieg und Revolution*, 409–510.
[21] Richard Lichtheim, *Die Geschichte des deutschen Zionismus*, Jerusalem, 1954, 143.

during the war. In the later decades of the nineteenth and the early twentieth century, antisemitism was more of a tool in the hands of the extreme right, a "cultural code" – useful, but not central. It might have still played this role into the First World War, but this function began to be eroded towards its end and surely in its immediate aftermath.

In dealing with this issue, Saul Friedländer stated that "[t]he revival of antisemitism in Germany happened together with the end of the hope for a quick victory of the Central Powers, with the first economic difficulties caused by the blockade of the Entente and quite generally with the end of national solidarity."[22] Clearly, however, antisemitism did not merely *happen* to go together with all these; it now provided a familiar, convenient scapegoat, well tried and efficient, for all those who insisted on upholding their loyalty to the old regime and refused to see the real causes of its collapse. It was not only the Jews but surely the Jews too, perhaps even particularly the Jews, whom one could now blame for all the misery around; not only the Jews but those others – "the traitors," the so-called "alien elements." At this point, antisemitism was no longer a remnant of old prejudices, nor was it a revived hatred needed for self-definition. The Jews were now gradually becoming important in themselves, being held personally responsible, so to speak, for a humiliating military defeat, collapse and the following revolution: for many a real catastrophe.

Whereas, at the start of the war, only a few prominent Jews could be singled out for particular attack, considered draft-dodgers or war profiteers, in its later phase one could assume their collective sinister involvement. The most clearly outspoken opponents of war, especially during 1917 and 1918, were, in addition to Karl Liebknecht, especially Hugo Haase and Rosa Luxemburg – both of Jewish origins. Following the Bolshevik take-over in Russia, where Jews – once again – did in fact occupy a number of central posts, the USPD came particularly under fire, and in it some prominent German Jews, such as Oskar Cohn and the Russian-born Adolf Joffe. From that point onward, the presumed conspiracy of Bolsheviks and Jews was added to the antisemitic agenda. Later on, it enabled the right to resist the new republic, especially the Soviet-style Republic of Councils in Munich, for instance, the peace treaty, and the whole reconstructed post-war Germany.

---

[22] See Saul Friedländer, "Die politischen Veränderungen der Kriegszeit und ihre Auswirkungen auf die Judenfrage," in Mosse and Paucker (eds.), *Deutsches Judentum im Krieg und Revolution*, 26–65. The quote is from page 33.

The "international Jewish conspiracy" would become a major antisemitic trope after the war, together with the publication of the "Protocols of the Elders of Zion" in its German version, in January 1920. Another such trope was constituted by the accusations entailed in the "stab in the back" legend, according to which social democrats, communists, and Jews were to blame for defeat in the war. This was powerfully propagated in post-war revolutionary Munich, where in 1918 three Jews stood at the head of the "Red Republic" in Catholic Bavaria: the Minister-President Kurt Eisner, the utopian anarchist philosopher Gustav Landauer, and the poet Erich Mühsam.[23] Gradually this legend was made into a political tool in the hands of the right everywhere during the early days of the Weimar Republic. The violence experienced by large segments of the population during the revolution was by then added to the shock of military collapse, exacerbated by years of false information about a presumably approaching victory, made ever more painful by the apparent bankruptcy of the entire old elite. On December 10, 1918, Friedrich Ebert welcomed the troops coming back from the war with the words "we gladly welcome you home ... no enemy defeated you!"[24] Inadvertently, so it seems, it was the Social Democratic Party leader who set the tone for a campaign, soon to be led by Hindenburg and Ludendorff, making defeat no longer the responsibility of the army, and laying the blame instead at the feet of the new revolutionary government, seemingly controlled by the Jews. Later on, such half-respectable organizations as the Pan-German League threw to the wind the last traces of their moderation and concentrated on fierce anti-Jewish propaganda. To be sure, they may not have had a very large following at first, but they were then hard at work weaving together an ideology that would be able to save the presumably lost honor of the German *Volk*, publicizing a narrative that would uphold the greatness of the old regime – civil and military – blaming all supporters of the left and Jews most particularly for its devastating end.

Weak as they seemed to be at the time, the right had managed to assemble a powerful toolkit needed for delegitimizing the young republic and undermining its authority, and, while so doing, placing the Jews within their narrative as the main culprits. Shortly thereafter, an anti-Jewish author of some fame at the time, Hans Blüher, summarized the situation thus: "It has, however, already become a fact, running in the

---

[23] For Munich, see Michael Brenner, *Der lange Schatten der Revolution: Juden und Antisemiten in Hitlers München 1918–1923*, Berlin, 2019.

[24] Friedrich Ebert, "Ansprache an die heimkehrenden Truppen," in Friedrich Ebert, *Politische Reden*, ed. Peter Wende, Frankfurt am Main, 1994, Vol. III, 95.

blood of every German: Prussianism and heroism belong together, Jewishness and the spirit of defeat belong together.... No proof is needed for or against, even if a hundred thousand Jews fell for the Fatherland. The German will soon know that the Jewish question is at the root of all political questions."[25] This, despite all hope and expectations, pointed out the dangers ahead. It foretold trouble for the Jews. It foretold – no less – trouble for Germany.

---

[25] Friedländer, "Die politischen Veränderungen der Kriegszeit," in Mosse and Paucker (eds.), *Deutsches Judentum im Krieg und Revolution*, 53.

9 Hopes Shattered

Despite these dark omens, a great many Germans welcomed the new republic, built upon the ashes of war and hazards of revolution. The majority of German Jews were among them. The Republic offered a new beginning to all and, from the Jewish perspective, remembering that the Empire had always been only a "half-fulfilled promise," this new beginning brought with it – once again – great expectations. In the past, the combination of some remaining forms of discrimination with repeated eruptions of antisemitism seemed to have threatened their long-fought-for emancipation. Then, for a brief moment, the war offered a brotherhood of all fighting men, sidetracking Jewish unease. For some of them at least, bitter disappointment came soon thereafter, and with it a painful reawakening. But now, the Republic was expected to finally heal past wounds and fulfill all hopes. It was expected to complete their entry into German society as well as their integration within its culture and politics. Once again, for a short period, and with particular urgency, most of them doubtless felt that they had arrived.

Naturally, not only Jews felt that way. The new Weimar constitution carried with it great hope. It granted all adult women the vote. It abolished the lagging forms of discrimination against the working class – both as a whole and individually – and its comprehensive list of social rights heralded a new age with the promise for a truly humane Germany, topped by a democratic polity of the most complete kind. The constitutional draft prepared by the Jewish political scientist Hugo Preuß and finally approved by the new Reichstag in the summer of 1919 fortified these hopes, despite its not unimportant weaknesses. On the international front, it did *not* convince the Entente Powers to offer Germany better peacetime conditions, as one had expected; on the domestic front, it did *not* pacify the right-wing nationalist opposition. It did provide, however, a clear vision for the future, and it definitely strengthened the peace-loving, progressive forces in the country. These now managed, though with great difficulty, to come together in one great effort for a better, modern and egalitarian Germany.

To be sure, the Republic had an extremely difficult start, and later proved to be extremely short-lived. Had it not likewise proven, despite all this, so critical for future developments, it could have been considered no more than an episode, especially from the historian's bird's-eye view. After all, its first couple of years were eclipsed by a violent revolution and from 1930 onwards the Republic, for all intents and purposes, no longer existed. There was hardly enough time for implementing all the grand plans, instituting all the novel reforms, and achieving all that was hoped for. No sooner had the revolutionary upheaval been calmed down, and before a reasonable measure of orderly routine could be established, the Germans found themselves confronted with suspicious neighbors on all sides and a madly galloping inflation. The latter impovershed large segments of the middle class and eventually brought the entire economy to a halt. Then, as the inflationary crisis was brought under control, attention could not but be directed to the permanent internal political strife, manifested in a series of quickly changing coalitions, soon no longer headed by the Social Democratic Party but instead by the weakened liberal parties supported by the Catholic Center. Historians still debate the nature of the following stage of relative prosperity and stability that characterized the middle years of the republic, between 1924 and 1929. And finally, the so-called Grand Coalition or Great Coalition in 1928, made up of the SPD, the Center Party, and the two liberal parties, namely the Deutsche Demokratische Partei (German Democratic Party, DDP) and the Deutsche Volkspartei (German People's Party), was unable to reach a compromise on some of the burning socio-economic issues at the time, and, in the wake of the world economic crisis, it turned out to be no longer possible to form *any* kind of viable coalition at all. By March 1930, the aged Reichswehr General Paul von Hindenburg, who had been elected president of the republic in 1925, decided to apply the famous – or rather infamous – Article 48 of the Weimar Constitution, allowing him to impose emergency decrees without the consent of Parliament. By this means, he practically – though never quite completely – took over the torn country, first relying on Heinrich Brüning of the Center Party to act as chancellor, and then, for two short periods, on the maneuverings of Franz von Papen and the ever-present General Kurt von Schleicher. On January 30, 1933, though with some obvious apprehension, Hindenburg handed over the post of Reichskanzler to Adolf Hitler.

The inherent weaknesses of the Republic seemed apparent from the very beginning. Much has been made of the effects of the Treaty of Versailles, the reparation agreement, and the fatal link in the minds of so many between the newly constructed German state and the preceding military defeat. Criticism was also directed at the Social Democratic Party for its failure to institutionalize much needed reforms in the early phase of the Republic and its poor showing at the polls as early as 1920. The split within the left, between socialists and communists, was likewise given a great deal of weight, not to mention the by then almost permanent weakness of the bourgeois liberal parties, the greed of the industrialists, and the insistence of the aristocratic landowners, still part of the country's elite, on receiving their share of state support for their failing agricultural enterprises. Prussian militarism was made responsible for the early collapse of the Republic, too, in addition to the lack of a democratic tradition in the country, the feeble character of its liberal spirit, and more. Clearly, the resounding collapse of this promising new state cannot be explained by a single cause. Libraries have been written about it. In the process, perhaps too much emphasis has been placed in much of the historiography on the faults of the Republic and too little attention paid to its achievements. These were surely impressive from the very beginning, in the face of so much disorder and politically motivated violence, and then during the so-called "middle years" – brilliant especially in terms of its culture and its modernizing spirit.[1]

At the same time, significantly, yet another, contradictory aspect of the Republic has too often been neglected. "Violence remained peripheral to most historical work on the German Revolution," writes the historian Mark Jones, and, he claims, it is indispensable for understanding the complexity of this period.[2] For almost four years after its establishment, the new Republic was a scene of bitter civil war, and the deadly clashes were not limited to isolated incidents. They came in clusters. The first, led by the Spartacists, a radical communist splinter group from the Social Democratic Party, occurred in December 1918 and January 1919; the second in March 1919, mainly in Berlin and Saxony; and the third in April, primarily in Munich. A year later, in March 1920, during incessant workers' demonstrations and then as a result of the right-wing Kapp

---

[1] The literature on the Weimar Republic is enormous. Of the older general presentations, I have found especially useful Eberhard Kolb, *Die Weimarer Republik*, Munich and Vienna, 1984; Detlev J. K. Peukert, *Die Weimarer Republik: Krisenjahre der klassischen Moderne*, Frankfurt am Main, 1987; Hans Mommsen, *Die verspielte Freiheit: Der Weg der Republik von Weimar in den Untergang*, Berlin, 1989; and Heinrich August Winkler, *Weimar 1918–1933: Die Geschichte der ersten deutschen Demokratie*, Munich, 1993. Important in taking a more positive look at the Weimar Republic are Anthony D. Kauders, "Weimar Jewry," in Anthony McElligott (ed.), *Weimar Germany*, New York, 2009, 234–259, and Gunther Mai, *Die Weimarer Republik*, Munich, 2018.
[2] See Mark Jones, *Founding Weimar. Violence and the German Revolution of 1918–1919*, New York, 2016, 2.

Putsch, another wave of violence raged up and down the country, while shortly thereafter, in the Ruhr area, some 50,000 armed miners, the so-called Red Ruhr Army, confronted organized military battalions in and around the city of Münster. Each of these clashes ended with *hundreds* of casualties. And then, following a short respite, the year 1923 was again a year of violence, first in response to the French occupation of the Ruhr area and later as a consequence of Hitler's unsuccessful "Beer-Hall Putsch" in Bavaria. From the start, violence came from the radical left as well as from the right, while unprecedented violence by government troops, sent to restore order, considerably increased the number of casualties.

As early as October 1922, a relatively unknown German-Jewish statistician, a left-wing socialist and long-time pacifist, Emil Julius Gumbel, published a book entitled *Four Years of Political Murder*. He had single-handedly investigated hundreds of cases of political assassination, focusing on those in which the precise names and details both of the victims and of the perpetrators were known, excluding random casualties in demonstrations or street fighting. He sought to underline the fact that most of these cases had gone unheeded; they were either never brought to court or, if so, quickly abandoned, ending in one legal fiasco after another.[3]

The numbers are staggering. Gumbel begins in the days of the Spartacist uprising and the story of some anonymous revolutionaries, who stormed the building of the Social Democratic Party daily in Berlin, the *Vorwärts*, and were immediately surrounded and locked in by heavily armed government forces. The besieged then sent out a group of seven publicly known men, mostly former parliamentarians, all unarmed, to negotiate an end to the conflict. These were promptly arrested, taken to one of the army barracks in town, and next morning unceremoniously shot. Even though it was easy to identify the men who shot them and clear on whose orders the execution took place, no one was brought to trial and no one was punished.[4]

The brutal murder of Karl Liebknecht and Rosa Luxemburg happened next. In the prevailing atmosphere of violence, even some of their socialist comrades tended to stress the victims' own responsibility and treated the perpetrators with leniency. On the day following the murder, the prominent SPD politician Philipp Scheidemann declared that they were "victims of their own terror tactics."[5] And finally, though the role of the

---

[3] See Emil Julius Gumbel, *Vier Jahre politischer Mord*, Berlin-Fichtenau, 1922.
[4] Ibid., 9–10.
[5] Quoted by Liebknecht's biographer, Helmut Trotnow, "'... es kam auf einen mehr oder weniger nicht an': Der Mord an Rosa Luxemburg und Karl Liebknecht und die Folgen für die Weimarer Republik," in Hans Widerotter (ed.), *Walther Rathenau 1867–1922: Die Extreme berühren sich*, Berlin, 1994, 209–220. The quote is from page 209.

Garde-Kavallerie Schützendivision (a dismounted cavalry division) in the affair was an open secret, the authorities preferred to look the other way. In the aftermath of this affair, it became evident to all that violence as a political instrument, while not openly condoned, was an option that the authorities themselves learned to disregard or even silently accept; moreover, it was repeatedly used by the authorities themselves.

The list of horrors continued. Gumbel reports on Spartacists who were shot in the woods near Berlin, ostensibly for trying to escape arrest, and prisoners suspected of revolutionary activity shot in prison, randomly on the streets of Berlin, or at various dismal meeting places. Such murders occurred elsewhere too: in the Rhineland, in the Ruhr area, and then especially in Munich. Apparently, fear of revolutionary terror or what one then branded as "Bolshevism" was endemic. During the violent dissolution of the Soviet-style Bavarian Republic of Councils, no fewer than 160 men – and a couple of women – were summarily shot to death. Thereafter, violent murders accompanied the Kapp Putsch in March 1920, mainly but not exclusively in Berlin, continuing almost as a matter of routine into the following two years. Gumbel tells it all with the stress on a number of particular individuals: a city councilor in the Berlin district of Köpenick, a veterinarian in a little town near Erfurt, or a policeman from Düsseldorf.

Most well known, of course, were the assassinations of famous politicians. Aside from Liebknecht and Luxemburg, shot on January 15, 1919, Kurt Eisner was assassinated on February 21, 1919, Mathias Erzberger on 26 August, 1921, and Walther Rathenau – by then the Republic's Foreign Secretary – on 24 June, 1922. He was gunned down in full daylight while riding in his open-roof coupé on the way from his Grunewald Villa to his Wilhelmstraße offices in central Berlin.

A caveat must be added here. Violence characterized other societies in post-war Europe, too. In a 1975 book, the historian Charles Maier dealt with the pains of stabilization in France and Italy, in addition to Germany. A more recent study by Andreas Wirsching, comparing political violence in Paris and Berlin, emphasizes the general chaos in both capitals after the war, though clearly arguing that the attack on the "system" – both from the left and from the right – was far more dangerous in Weimar Germany than in the post-war French Third Republic.[6] Similarities can also be found between the situation in Germany and that in Austria and Hungary, while other cases, particularly from among the countries on the losers' side of the war, could likewise serve to relativize the German

---

[6] See Charles S. Maier, *Recasting Bourgeois Europe: Stabilization in France, Germany, and Italy in the Decade after World War I*, Princeton, NJ, 1975; and Andreas Wirsching, *Vom Weltkrieg zum Bürgerkrieg? Politischer Extremismus in Deutschland und Frankreich 1918– 1933/39: Berlin und Paris im Vergleich*, Munich, 1999.

situation. Still, in contradistinction to some of these, Germany, though not a democracy before the war, was surely an orderly *Rechtsstaat* at that time. Only in the wake of extreme brutalization at the front, the humiliating days of the final capitulation, and a radical, popular revolution that destroyed previous institutions did it become a kind of lawless, violent country. That was an unfamiliar, often frightening and surely a worrying state of affairs.

This must have also been the moment when many Jews began to sense the first pangs of yet another disillusionment. Until then, just like other members of the bourgeoisie, most of them could disregard the constant violent upheaval raging around them. Thus, at the height of the revolution, while life came to an almost complete halt in the poorer sections of the various urban centers in Germany, *their* life seemed relatively undisturbed. It was apparently calm enough in the bourgeois neighborhoods of Berlin, Munich, Frankfurt, and Hamburg. "You could hear the shots almost daily, but you could by no means always figure out their meaning," wrote Sebastian Haffner in his memoirs, and this must have also been the feeling of others, Jews and non-Jews, living in similar situations.[7] In the midst of the Spartacus Uprising, Gerschom Scholem's mother, recovering from four difficult years of war, set out to buy a new rug for her dining room, as she reports in a letter to her son.[8] Life was going on. Moreover, new chances and new opportunities were now available to all, making it easier to disregard signs of danger. Government bureaucracy – in states and cities – practically closed to the employment of Jews during the Kaiserreich, was now wide open to them. Jewish academics that had contributed to their various scientific disciplines previously too, could now realize their potential at the universities, as careers were finally made possible for them. Students of Jewish origins, men *and* women – including many that were coming into Germany from abroad – rushed to the various academic institutions up and down the country, and older Jewish professionals soon proved outstanding, both in numbers and in prestige, in all major German cities. Jewish journalists, critics, and essayists – already prominent during the Kaiserreich – were even more visible and influential in Weimar Germany. And, despite the many crises of the time – affecting everyone – and despite antisemitism – especially affecting the Jews – the twenties were often considered "the golden years."

---

[7] Sebastian Haffner, *Defying Hitler: A Memoir*, trans. Oliver Pretzel, London, 2003, 35.
[8] Betty Scholem and Gerschom Scholem, *Mutter und Sohn im Briefwechsel, 1917–1946*, ed. Itta Shedletzky, Munich, 1989, 39.

As mentioned above, these were years of exceptional cultural blooming. Though most forms of avant-garde art had been developed and often flourished in pre-war Germany, the free atmosphere during the middle years of the Republic enabled their ever more intense thriving, while Jews, both avid consumers and outstanding contributors to these modern trends, continued to enjoy them, sponsored them, and proved vital for their striving. Moreover, in contrast to the situation that had pertained in the Kaiserreich, they were now self-confident enough to argue this point in public. For the first time, books were being written about their success: Arnold Zweig published a book on Jews in the German-speaking theater; others wrote on Jews in music and the arts, in medicine, and in the natural sciences. The publicist Gustav Krojanker elaborated upon this new wave in a book of 1922, and Siegmund Kaznelson sought to summarize it in his *Juden im deutschen Kulturbereich* (*Jews in the German Cultural Sphere*), a book relying on a number of distinguished contributors, published late in 1934, but then – expectedly – confiscated by the Gestapo. It was finally printed and distributed only in 1959.

Achievements in the sciences were best reflected in the often-quoted high percentage of Jews among recipients of Nobel Prizes in pre-Nazi Germany. When the National Socialists came to power, their racial principles made them dismiss 30% of the academic staff in the natural sciences, more than 40% in the medical faculties, and almost 50% of the mathematicians. While there were fewer exceptional Jews in the humanities, some were particularly outstanding – historians, philosophers, and literary critics, whose biographies – beginning before the establishment of the Republic and often ending after its demise – could likewise be told to great acclaim. This was, no doubt, a formidable crowd. Finally, since women were newcomers among Weimar's celebrities – in culture as well as in politics and society – their stories were particularly impressive. Here are three short miniatures. Bertha Pappenheim could be considered a representative of the older generation. Despite her uniqueness, she could still stand for an entire group.[9] A daughter to a well-to-do orthodox family, she was born in Vienna in 1859 and – as has later become known – was treated by Josef Breuer and Sigmund Freud for various nervous symptoms, a treatment that they later described in a case-study report entitled "Anna O." Pappenheim gradually adopted a more liberal life-style, moved from Vienna to Frankfurt, and began a double career as a social activist and an engaged feminist, working for and writing about Jewish women in and outside of Germany. She

---

[9] See Bertha Pappenheim, *Ausgewählte Schriften von Bertha Pappenheim: Erzählungen, Sagen, Drama, Essays und mehr*, Oviedo, FL, 2017, and Elizabeth Lorenz, *Let Me Continue to Speak the Truth: Bertha Pappenheim as Author and Activist*, New York, 2007.

translated Mary Wollstonecraft's *Vindication of the Rights of Women* of 1792 from the English and Glikl's memoirs from the late seventeenth century from the Yiddish. She wrote novellas and various short pieces, some lyrics, and a number of theater plays.

Since the early years of the twentieth century, Pappenheim's social and political activities – first in the Jüdische Frauenbund (League of Jewish Women) and later in the Bund Deutscher Frauenvereine (Federation of German Women's Associations) – seemed to have been the center of her life. Like other women activists of that time, she too attempted to combine the fight for women's rights with extensive social work, caring primarily for women and children in need, occasionally for the generally destitute as well. During the Weimar period, Pappenheim concentrated on combating women-trafficking among Jews, traveling to Galicia to investigate the sources of this trade in humans, publishing her findings, and coordinating the fight against it. She then established an orphanage for Jewish girls in Neu-Isenburg near Frankfurt, providing the inmates with healthcare, basic education, and even some initial occupational training.

These activities ran repeatedly against the Jewish communities' establishment – orthodox and liberal alike; an establishment that often still marginalized women and generally refused to countenance feminist criticism of any kind. Thus, Pappenheim's was a life of struggle against conventions and injustice. At the same time, she was and always remained a German patriot, opposing Jewish exodus from Germany even as existence in that country became practically impossible for Jews. To be sure, she did acknowledge the growing antisemitism in large segments of the German population, especially as the good years of the Republic came to an end in 1929. Still, she could not free herself from the basic assumptions of assimilation that were part and parcel of her upbringing and essential for life in her particular Jewish milieu. Only at the last minute, so to speak, witnessing the enactment of the Nürenberg Laws in the fall of 1935, did she gradually begin to change her mind, cooperating now with the Zionist organization Youth Aliyah, by helping to transfer Jewish youth to safety, particularly to Palestine. In all that, Pappenheim perfectly embodied the story of hope and disappointment that was so characteristic of her generation. Following a short illness, interrupted by an episode of questioning by the Gestapo, Bertha Pappenheim passed away on May 28, 1936.

Käte Frankenthal was thirty years Pappenheim's junior.[10] She too grew up in a well-to-do Jewish home, this time in Kiel, receiving an orderly

---

[10] See her detailed memoirs: Käte Frankenthal, *Der dreifache Fluch: Jüdin, Intellektuelle, Sozialistin. Lebenserinnerungen einer Ärztin in Deutschland und im Exil*, eds. Kathleen M. Pearle and Stephan Leibfried, Frankfurt am Main, 1981.

education leading to her approbation as a medical doctor as early as 1914. She was one of the first women to practice medicine in Germany, and, while there were other Jewish women doctors at the time, *she* was doubly unique in being one of the first *military* women doctors. Since the Prussian army refused to accept women, she eventually served in the Austrian army that was friendlier to Jews in general and, during the war, even to some Jewish women.

Frankenthal joined the Social Democratic Party during the war years, and in the war's wake soon began an energetic career, combining political activity with medical practice. Living now in Berlin, she severed all connections with the Jewish community after her parents' death, and apparently made up her mind to dedicate herself to socialist politics. For her, as for many fully assimilated Germans of Jewish background at that time, working for general causes in the service of the Republic took priority over any other cause, in her case particularly those related to her no-longer-meaningful Jewish identity.

Frankenthal first served on the Berlin City Council, holding the portfolio for public health and social work. Finally, in 1928, she gave up her private medical practice in order to become the municipal physician for the working-class district of Berlin-Neukölln until her election to the Prussian Parliament in 1931. During these years, Frankenthal advocated rescinding the laws against abortion and against homosexuality, and fought for the establishment of marital counselling bureaus that also provided sex education and birth control advice to their clients. At the same time, she was active in both the Federation of Women Physicians and the Association of Socialist Physicians in Germany, leading an active political life with a strong social emphasis. Having joined the new Sozialistische Arbeiterpartei Deutschlands (Socialist Workers' Party of Germany, SAP) late in 1931, Frankenthal failed to be elected – first to the Prussian Parliament and then to the Reichstag – in the two election campaigns of 1932. And it was in any event too late. In March 1932, she left Germany, explaining – though no explanation was needed – that under the circumstances and as she belonged, indeed, to every category detested by the Nazis, being a Jewess, socialist, people's representative, and emancipated woman, she had "nothing more to do in Germany."[11] En route through Prague, Zurich, and Paris, Frankenthal finally landed in New York, where she was later trained as a psychoanalyst and practiced her new profession successfully for many years. This, however, never seemed to her as fulfilling as her

---

[11] Ibid., 190–191.

political and public life in Germany. She died at the age of eighty-seven, in 1976.

Before we move on to our third protagonist, standing for the younger generation of German Jews in Weimar Germany, let us add some comments on the overall situation in the country during the latter years of the Republic. As early as the time of Rathenau's assassination, the entire existence of the Republic seemed to be in imminent danger. But things did not turn out to be as the assassins had hoped. The historian Martin Sabrow has shown that this murder, like the attempt on the life of Philipp Scheidemann, a leading SPD politician, a mere three weeks earlier, or the assassination of Mathias Erzberger, head of the Catholic Center Party, ten months before, was part of a well-calculated strategy intended to create chaos in republican Germany, send the workers to the streets in angry protest, and produce a situation in which the Freikorps (right-wing paramilitary units) would be recalled to impose order and install what they called a "national government," acting according to their political agenda.[12] But, although the masses did march in Berlin and elsewhere, they did so not in protest against the government but in honor of the murdered foreign minister, who had suddenly become their martyr. Over half a million gathered for Rathenau's funeral in Berlin, and mourning masses assembled in many other German cities. At this point, the government managed to pass a Law in Defense of the Republic and, although Bavaria refused to enact it and the year 1923 was still a year of incessant violence elsewhere too, it did eventually seem to put an end to the chaotic situation in the country – at least for a while.

Between 1924 and 1929, the central as well as the states' governments seemed to have regained their monopoly over the use of force. For a short while, Weimar Germany was a magnet for creative people from all over the world. Most Jews felt they were living now in an atmosphere of freedom and equality. They usually enjoyed their integration and felt part and parcel of life in the new Republic. In Austria, too, Jews seemed to have recaptured their prominence, enjoying relative prosperity, mostly in Vienna. There as in many other urban centers, Jewish lawyers and medical doctors often enjoyed an excellent reputation. Importantly, however, some two-thirds of the Jews, even at that time, were occupied in petty commerce. Only a few stood out at the top of large-scale firms. The majority was made up of shopkeepers and small or middle-sized businessmen. The stabilization of the

---

[12] See Martin Sabrow, *Der Rathenaumord: Rekonstruktion einer Verschwörung gegen die Republik von Weimar*, Munich, 1994, and Martin Sabrow, "Märtyrer der Republik. Zu den Hintergründen des Mordanschlags vom 24. Juni 1922," in Widerotter (ed.), *Walther Rathenau 1867–1922*, 221–236.

Mark in 1923 gave them, as it gave the entire population, a new sense of security; a new lease on life, so to speak.

But the good years were quickly over. Following the unexpected onslaught of the world economic crisis in 1929, a second wave of political instability, joined by violent street politics, shook the still unstable Republic. Somewhat less bloody this time, it was in the end, as we know, far more catastrophic. By then, moreover, the overall scene had changed considerably. The years of revolutionary violence in the aftermath of the war were characterized by clashes between marching demonstrators, sometimes relatively peaceful, though occasionally armed and ready for battle, and the so-called forces of order. In the later years, from 1929 onward, violence was staged on both sides by civilians. German society was by then a society in arms. On the far right stood the SA, considered by the National Socialists to be their "self-defense formation," and on the far left the "Red Front Fighters' Association" lined up, equally determined and well-armed. The middle ground was populated by organized paramilitary formations, too. Right of center stood the nationalist Stahlhelm (Steel Helmet), left of center the Social Democratic Party's Reichsbanner Schwarz–Rot–Gold (Black–Red–Gold Banner of the Reich). Clearly, the SA and the communist phalanges were better prepared for civil war and more violent in their daily behavior, but the atmosphere was constantly heated by the fact that political controversy was now almost completely transferred to the arena of daily parades, mass demonstrations, and bloody physical clashes. This became part of everyone's life in Weimar Germany during the early 1930s, though – once again – much less conspicuously in the bourgeois quarters of Berlin-West or the quiet neighborhoods of the well-off and educated in Frankfurt, Hamburg, or Munich.[13]

Meanwhile, unemployment soared and the social state, Weimar's pride and its most notable achievement, crumbled under the burden. Though the time of spectacular assassinations was over, political battles were once more pervasive, while personal threats as a tactic of persuasion became a matter of daily occurrence. Already during 1929, while Germany still upheld at least the formal appearance of an orderly democracy, the police had to intervene in some 580 political meetings that had degenerated into tumultuous scuffles. The fierce escalation of violence was characterized by the shift of focus from the communists to the Nazis, who were

---

[13] In addition to Wirsching, *Vom Weltkrieg zum Bürgerkrieg?*, I have relied on Dirk Schumann, *Politische Gewalt in der Weimarer Republic 1918–1933: Kampf um die Straße und Furcht vor dem Bürgerkrieg*, Essen, 2001.

responsible for hundreds of parades that degenerated into street fighting, constituting – all in all – nothing less than a permanent civil war.

The various branches of government – the cabinets, the judiciary, and the military – could be trusted to act against the left as before, but they displayed sheer incompetence, cowardice, and lack of will-power vis-à-vis the danger from the right. The reasons were many and became increasingly clear with the appointment of the Center Party politician Heinrich Brüning as chancellor at the end of March 1930. During his first year in office, a certain amount of domestic disorder seemed to serve him as an additional tool in trying to put a stop to reparation payments. Strict measures against disorder were usually rejected out of hand by the president as well, anxious to preserve the freedom of action of his supporters in the Stahlhelm on the conservative right. Finally, in March 1931, and then again in July and August of the same year, Hindenburg *did* issue decrees enabling law-enforcement agencies to stop radical violence on both the left and the right, though, in the end, these too were timid and contradictory measures and had hardly any effect. The Nazi shadow was already long, dark, and threatening. The Republic was in its death throes. Its long-beaten supporters, among them many Jews, were beginning to flee.

And under these clouds, Hannah Arendt studied philosophy.[14] In 1929, she handed in her dissertation on Augustine's concept of love, written under the supervision of Karl Jaspers, and intended to continue her studies and prepare for an academic career. Her disposition was, indeed, very different from that of Bertha Pappenheim or Käte Frankenthal. She was at this stage neither a feminist nor a social or political activist. Hers was the *Vita Contemplativa*, shared only by the most accomplished intellectuals of the day. While our information on Bertha Pappenheim and Käte Frankenthal primarily relies on their autobiographical writings, much has been written on this younger and most illustrious of our trio.

Arendt was born in 1906 and thus experienced the Weimar Republic as an adult only in its final stage. It is, however, astonishing to observe how much she absorbed and with what intensity she lived during these years. Arendt spent most of her early youth in Königsberg, where her parents had lived for a short while, and almost all of her relatives on both sides of the family had lived for a long time. There they were part of a vivid Jewish milieu, made up of politically and socially progressive men and women, more or less indifferent to religion, though not without links to the Jewish liberal community and well integrated in the broader German society. Being a precocious pupil, Hannah was ripe for university studies at the

---

[14] In addition to Arendt's many volumes of personal correspondence, see her biography: Elisabeth Young-Brühl, *Hannah Arendt: For Love of the World*, Binghamton, NY, 1982.

age of seventeen, passing through Berlin on her way to the academic centers in south-western Germany. Belonging to the younger generation of German Jews at the time, she turned – like many of her male co-religionists – not to the world of social work or to the professions, but to the arts and humanities. From the mid 1920s onward, Arendt studied classics, German literature, and, above all, theology and philosophy – in Marburg, Freiburg, and Heidelberg. Lately, much attention has been paid to her relationship with Martin Heidegger, whom she greatly admired throughout her life and with whom she had had a brief, passionate affair as a student.

The world surrounding this exclusive intellectual milieu was stormy. Increasingly, antisemitism became ever more noticeable both in the public arena and for individual Jews in their private lives. Increasingly, too, Jews were forced to react. Following a number of years in which a better and calmer atmosphere seemed encouraging, aggressive anti-Jewish propaganda reappeared around 1930, and it was felt everywhere: in politics, in cultural and sport associations, in schools and universities, and – often viciously in fact – on the streets, everywhere throughout the country. The National Socialists, somewhat cautious on this issue prior to the crisis of 1929, now felt able to renew – with a vengeance – their antisemitic attacks. Reports on pogrom-like events came not only from various smaller towns and villages, but also from the best quarters of Berlin, though most particularly from the Scheunenviertel – home to many East European Jewish refugees. The police failed to prevent these actions, just as it failed in cases involving communists and social democrats.

Conscious of this situation, Jews reacted in many different ways. The situation within the Scholem family in Berlin has often been brought forth as an example. Thus, of the four Scholem brothers, only the younger, Gerhard – or, as he would later be known, Gerschom – showed any interest in Judaism. His brother Werner was a member of the Reichstag for the Communist Party (KPD) between 1924 and 1928. Erich Scholem was a member of the liberal DDP, and the oldest brother, Reinhold, a clear-cut German patriot, voted for the Deutsche Volkspartei – still further to the right. Nevertheless and, despite these apparent disparities, a double trend could be perceived during much of the Weimar years. To begin with, some Jews were indeed caught up in what Martin Buber called, perhaps somewhat too ambitiously – a "Jewish Renaissance," personified by Franz Rosenzweig during his short life and later practiced in his Lehrhaus (teaching establishment) in Frankfurt, appealing to those who – like him – sought to reembrace the old faith. Books on Jewish themes were printed, reprinted, and sold. New ones were now written, often finding a willing public. Following a century in which Jews had primarily been preoccupied with becoming German, confronting one's fast forgotten Jewish identity – as meager as it sometimes was – now became ever more appealing. Secondly, as German citizens, Jews were on the whole outspoken supporters of liberal democracy, even when other Germans were losing their faith in the much-beleaguered Republic. For some of them, both trends were relevant.

Hannah Arendt was meanwhile looking for a topic on which to write her second academic work, the *Habilitation*. She was particularly attracted to German Romanticism. But, having had by chance the opportunity to read Rahel Varnhagen's correspondence of almost exactly 100 years before, elucidating the life of that unhappy Berlin Salonnière, struggling in vain to be rid of her Jewishness, Arendt decided to write her biography. Perhaps by then she realized that her chances of becoming a professor, being both Jewish and a woman, were very slim. And meanwhile, being now married to Günther Stern, a fellow philosopher, later known as Anders, she found herself seeking new ways of relating to her Jewishness. Arendt then, rather unexpectedly, renewed her contacts with Kurt Blumenfeld, president of the German Zionist Federation in Germany and a friend of the family. Soon thereafter, with Germany already under Nazi rule and despite the ever growing danger, she was assembling information on antisemitism in the German press at his request. She was promptly arrested by the Gestapo, but luckily released after a short internment, just in time to flee Germany before things got even worse. The finished draft of her work on Rahel – a piece of literature-cum-history, biography-cum-autobiography – was in her hands as she left the country through Prague, Genoa, and Geneva, reaching Paris in July 1933. This chapter in her life, as well as this chapter in the history of German Jewry, came to an end.

Antisemitism was not unknown during the years of the Republic. Walther Rathenau was assassinated for a variety of reasons, no doubt; his Jewishness was surely one of them. In the atmosphere created by the "stab in the back" accusation, other Jewish politicians too – mostly the ones who were affiliated with the socialist parties – repeatedly aroused public indignation. Rosa Luxemburg, a Jewess of Polish origins, who stood at the head of the Spartacist League during the war, was murdered in Berlin, as mentioned above, on January 15, 1919; Kurt Eisner was murdered on February 21 and Gustav Landauer on May 2 – both in Munich. At that early stage of the Republic, antisemitic propaganda was rampant everywhere. It was initiated by conservative circles, financially supporting organizations such as the Pan-German League or the

Deutschvölkischer Schutz- und Trutzbund (German Nationalist Federation for Protection and Defense), who then flooded the market with their poisonous publications. This was, in fact, partially stopped in 1922, when the League was legally banned, but even beyond these extremists' circles, the "Protocols of the Elders of Zion," for instance, and similar antisemitic best-sellers enjoyed startling circulation. In addition, while violence against Jews was not infrequent in the rural areas, it was even more virulent in various urban centers, most especially in areas with a great number of Jewish migrants from Eastern Europe. In Bavaria, physical attacks upon individual Jews, already common enough in the heated atmosphere before Hitler's Beer-Hall Putsch of 1923, brought about the expulsion of the so-called *Ostjuden* from the Free State immediately thereafter, while everywhere Jews were threatened and some were, in fact, taken hostage for a while by Nazi putschists on their one evening of success. The legal system, known for being "blind in the right eye" throughout these years, was even more so in the years after 1929, when disorder and violent behavior resurfaced everywhere across the country, this time led by the SA with its unaffiliated right-wing thugs.

At the time, it could all be considered part of the general lawlessness typical during much of the Weimar period, in and outside of Germany, and for most Jews it could have seemed negligible in comparison with their meteoric success at the time and their continuous upward social mobility. Zionists did feel vindicated in their pessimistic predictions, since for them, after all, repeated manifestations of antisemitism constituted further encouragement to move away from what had previously been – for them, too – a secure sense of belonging to Germany. Even the main liberal organizations of German Jewry showed signs of reconsidering their unquestionable and outspoken patriotism. However, for the majority of German Jews, the experience of these years was not essentially different from what the basic characteristics of their situation in Germany had been for almost a full century: progressive acculturation and social integration, on the one hand; confrontation with open animosity, sometimes even ending in physical assaults, on the other hand. They were accustomed to the combination of acceptance with reservations, exclusion with some cautious openings, success accompanied by envy. Old and new hatred had many facets, but so did friendliness and appreciation. Weimar presented yet another chapter in this prolonged zigzag course, and only gradually did the signs of danger become clearer and ever more concrete.

Finally, what is the added value of the Jewish story to the overall history of the Weimar Republic? After all, it did not yet seem that *their* fate as a religious and ethnic minority would not be the same as that of the

German non-Jewish majority. All democrats were fighting the same battle, and at first only a slight disparity could be detected. However, precisely this initial parting of the ways would prove illuminating, pointing towards the future. To begin with, theirs was a story of diminishing solidarity within the democratic camp. While most of them clung to a particular set of humanistic values, other Germans continued to split among and between the conflicting political factions in the Republic. To be sure, not a small number upheld loyalty to democracy together with most Jews, but, on the whole, the latter's old hopes were soon shattered even more clearly and painfully than before. Weimar completed the formal process of their equalization, and this had been gratifying, no doubt. But especially the late Weimar period seemed to prepare the ground for what was soon to come.

Surely, one ought not to judge the Republic only from its end, but the Jewish point of view, underlining the limitations of sidestepping this perspective altogether, is helpful. After all, contemporaries – Jews, like others – could not know what the future held in store for them. The biographies of the three Jewish women sketched above stand for those who for the first time fully enjoyed and made use of the new opportunities offered by the Republic. One of them dedicated herself to social and literary work; another joined, with great idealism, the working-class movement; and the last plunged into an intellectual adventure with colleagues – by no means only Jews – who shared her hopes and aspirations. All three had to face a sort of bankruptcy at the end. While many Jews, indeed, felt estrangement and the growing gulf between themselves and those who insistently refused to accept them, others retained their optimism, often bravely and not merely by oversight. It was left to the Nazis to finally extinguish even this last measure of hope, taking the course of events towards previously unimaginable extremes.

Part IV

A Lost Homeland: 1930–2000

10 The Abyss

In many ways, as we saw, the fate of Weimar Jewry reflected the fate of the Republic. But, with the access of Hitler to power, it seemed that from one moment to the next the Jews were officially made into enemies of the nation, traitors, dangerous foes – by decree, so to speak; they were no longer a part of German society. Four weeks later, immediately after the burning of the Reichstag on February 27, they also began to be physically hunted. On March 3, only a few days later again, in a speech to his "troops," Hermann Göring, speaking about the presumed Jewish danger, announced: "I am not here to think about justice. I am here to destroy and to exterminate. Nothing less."[1] Against such a threatening, manipulating, ever-present enemy, so he preached, every means was justified. And the Nazis soon began to make good on their promises. First to be achieved was the "immediate imprisonment and judgement of all the communists and Social Democratic party functionaries"; then the "placing of suspicious and intellectual instigators in concentration camps."[2] Afterwards the Nazis were ready to apply the same methods to the Jews. According to what now became their habit, bureaucratic and legal measures were to be followed by widespread violence. In various cities throughout the land, communists and social democrats – leaders as well as the rank and file – were chased, beaten up, and publically humiliated, then dragged into camps which were erected in record time in various localities, ready to receive them. There they were further tormented – men and women, day and night. Soon Jews were treated similarly. Excluding *them* from the *Volksgemeinschaft*, the "Community of the *Volk*", was after all much easier; they had never been fully accepted as legitimate members of this newly defined entity, made up now not of the citizens of Germany but of racially defined Aryans, the source of all sovereignty in the Nazi state.

---

[1] Quoted in Edward Cranshaw, *Gestapo: Instrument of Tyranny*, London, 1956, 48–49.
[2] This plan appeared as early as August 11, 1932 in the *Völkischer Beobachter*. See the English translation in Christian Goeschel and Nikolaus Wachsmann, *The Nazi Concentration Camps 1933–1939: A Documentary History*, Lincoln, 2012, Document no. 2.

The campaign against the Jews took off with zeal and efficiency. After more than 100 years of a fight for equality and over 60 years since all adult male Jews were fully confirmed as German citizens with equal rights and duties, the process of emancipation began to be systematically rolled back. A multitude of orders and legal measures followed each other in quick succession.[3] Then, having abolished all liberal freedoms in the land, banned the communists, and reduced the Social Democratic Party literally to its knees, relying upon the "Enabling Act" that made it possible for them to act without the consent of parliament, the Nazis launched an unprecedented antisemitic campaign.

In fact, the exclusionary measures began exactly where the process of Jewish integration had earlier begun, namely in the various spheres of culture. We have earlier seen how during the second half of the eighteenth century an ever growing number of Jews began visiting German-language theaters, learned to appreciate German literature, acquired a taste for music, and adopted a life-style that had been typical of other educated citizens in their immediate surroundings – all that even prior to the approaching public debate concerning their legal emancipation. Later on, successful acculturation was often made into a precondition for every further step on their road to full equality. It was and indeed always remained the main pillar of their integration into German society. And now – as early as the month of March 1933 – it was the appearances of Otto Klemperer and Bruno Walter, among the most renowned orchestral conductors of the time, that were the first events to be banned. Kurt Weill left Germany on March 21, 1933, and so did, at about the same time, the critic Alfred Kerr and the theater director Max Reinhardt – leading figures in the Weimar's stage life. The actor Fritz Kortner had already left in 1932. Literary figures left, too: Walter Benjamin on March 18, and Lion Feuchtwanger, on a lecture tour in the United States, never came back. It was by then clear that they were no longer wanted; that, in fact, their freedom if not even their lives were in danger in Germany. Albert Einstein, by then the world's most renowned scientist, was in America at the time and, like Feuchtwanger, he too never came back. Other prominent scientists left soon thereafter. Even Fritz Haber, long converted and known for his patriotic services to the fatherland during the First World War, was ordered to dismiss all Jewish colleagues from the Kaiser Wilhelm Institute, of which he was the director, and thereupon handed in his own resignation on April 30, 1933. He left Germany, a broken and bitter man, in August of the same year.

[3] Among the books on this topic, see especially Saul Friedländer, *Nazi Germany and the Jews*, Vol. I: *The Years of Persecution, 1933–1939*, New York, 1997.

Less illustrious Jews likewise faced imminent danger. They stood before closed doors now at every turn. To be sure, the organized anti-Jewish actions on April 1 turned out to be rather unsuccessful, especially in the larger urban centers, and Jewish shop-owners could usually continue to run their business. But, with the law of April 7, "for the reconstitution of the public service," all Jewish civil servants, including a great many university staff members and employees, were unceremoniously dismissed. And, while the absolute number of those actually fired was relatively small, the law added insult to injury by including for the first time an "Aryan paragraph," defining a Jew by using a unique mixture of old and new criteria so as to include persons of whom one parent or even one grandparent was of the Jewish faith. This was a warning signal for things to come. Further regulations aimed at dismissing Jewish physicians from public hospitals, lawyers and judges from posts in the legal establishment, and students as well as faculty members the universities. Finally, all of that was followed by violent mishandling of the Jews. They were being laughed at and abused on the streets, haunted even at their homes up and down the country.[4]

After March 1933, Nazi activists put into effect a variety of additional prohibitions. They managed to ban Jews from sports activities, prohibited the use of Yiddish in marketplaces, and disallowed the official changing of Jewish names. Public signs announced that their entry into public parks and centers of entertainment – most emphatically to public swimming pools – had been prohibited. Jewish children began to be evaded by their schoolmates, while parents were dismissed from various posts in local social associations or forced to leave them by various dubious means. Many found themselves interrogated by the Gestapo and locked up in concentration camps for shorter or longer periods; afterwards they were often forced to flee. Some 37,000 Jews left Germany during 1933; a further 22,000 left in 1934 and similarly again in 1935 – altogether just over 15 percent of the half million Jews living in the country at the start of 1933. The situation of those who remained was properly called by historians "the new ghetto." But, while all that concerned primarily the Jews, it changed the face of Germany altogether, as Sebastian Haffner vividly describes in his memoirs. One could fail to notice the transformation only if one did not look.

After the first 100 days of the new regime, however, some were quick to believe that things were calming down. Surprisingly, the bloody, rather

---

[4] See for the following the many details in Michael Wildt, *Hitler's* Volksgemeinschaft *and the Dynamics of Racial Exclusion: Violence against Jews in Provincial Germany, 1919–1939*, trans. Bernard Heise, New York, 2011.

ferocious "Night of the Long Knives" of June 30, 1934 did not rouse too many – Jews and other Germans – to greater awareness, though in its wake the lawless and violent character of the Nazis could no longer be doubted. Apparently, it could still be considered an internal party matter. Later on, following Hindenburg's death, Hitler was nominated chancellor, and his initial successes in foreign policy together with what was claimed to be the beginning of economic recovery in the land made him ever more popular. At that point, while things seemed to have improved for the general population, the small Jewish minority was ever more isolated and increasingly impoverished. The contrast could not have been more blatant. The Jews were gradually losing their livelihoods just as German unemployment figures were starting to decline. The rearmament program – now less secret than before – gave the government a new power of maneuvering in foreign policy, and, later on, the Olympic Games of 1936 brought with them worldwide prestige. Special programs for children, and social ones for adults, such as *Kraft durch Freude* (power through joy), provided the population with a new sense of well-being. Clearly, while in the past Jews participated in German fortunes, sometimes even reflecting reality in the larger society, none of all this was now shared by them.

Those who were employed by governmental institutions immediately lost their livelihoods, but, as the historian Avraham Barkai convincingly showed, many more were dismissed by large and small private firms. Even business enterprises that were still owned by Jews could no longer hold on to all their Jewish employees. Jews lost their customers or clientele and were expelled from business boards, trade unions, saving banks, and the various cooperative insurance groups. Moreover, many Jewish shop-owners of all sizes began to succumb to an early version of "Aryanization." While the banning of Jewish stores ordered "from above" was discontinued, the process continued "from below." SA men and groups of Hitlerjugend (Hitler Youth) boys were stationed near Jewish shops, scaring potential buyers, painting display windows and mishandling older shop-owners. The latter were now selling their shops for absurd prices, not only to outspoken Nazis but also to small, middle, and even large-scale businessmen, who were quick to exploit the situation. With added threats, informing the Gestapo, or pressing the sellers in various ways, they did, indeed, enjoy fine profits. Somewhat later, "Aryanization" became an official Nazi policy, bringing about the full expropriation of the Jews with the help of multiple rules and regulations; but the actual practice had started before. There was nothing the Jews could do against it.

Meanwhile, persecution became ever more a matter of race. The prohibition of marriage between "Aryans" and "non-Aryans" was not yet anchored in law, but here too, social pressure against "blood relationships" with Jews increased by the day. In general, the anti-Jewish atmosphere was particularly reheated in the second half of 1935 and, on September 15, in a special Reichstag meeting at the end of the annual NSDAP rally, the two so-called Nuremberg Laws were enacted. These were a Law for the Protection of German Blood and Honor and the Reich Citizenship Act. They finally made the discrimination against the Jews according to racial criteria an official matter; in fact, it was now irreversible.

Still, not all Jews lost all hope. Some – including men in what was by then called the Reichsvertretung der Juden in Deutschland, the main Jewish organization allowed by the Nazis, even saw an improvement in the enactment of the Nuremberg Laws, a replacement of arbitrary terror and varied local initiatives by the orderly rule of law. In addition, short intervals of less violent rhetoric by the leadership, caused by Hitler's wish to reduce hostility to his regime outside Germany, were also a source for cautious optimism. This mood is well captured in one of the most touching autobiographies later written by a German Jew, namely that of the distinguished American historian Peter Gay, formerly Fröhlich. The book is entitled *My German Question*, and it focuses on Gay's youth in Berlin of the 1930s.[5]

Gay's father had a successful small business, run together with a friendly non-Jewish associate, and for a long time refused to accept the gravity of the situation. At first, the son too hardly felt the discriminatory policies of the Nazis. In March 1933, he was accepted to the local Goethe-Realgymnasium, apparently not only because of his good grades but also because he was exempt from the Jewish quota restrictions due to the fact that his father had been wounded as a soldier in the First World War. Such exemptions, later made void, were still in force at this early stage. Peter defines the atmosphere in this school as being "almost unpolitical," with only a minority of antisemitic teachers. He describes the pressure on the few Jewish pupils in the school as "selective."[6] Furthermore, he soon learned to replace the normal association with his schoolmates by such youthful preoccupations as stamp collection, the following of sports' events on the radio, etc. In his memoirs, he significantly stresses what he considered the "mixed signals" Jews had then received from the surrounding environment.[7]

---

[5] Peter Gay, *My German Question: Growing up in Nazi Berlin*, New Haven, CT, 1998.
[6] Ibid., 62–63.
[7] "Mixed Signals" is the title of the fourth chapter of *My German Question*, 57–83.

In any event, the family was able to maintain a more or less normal life for an amazingly long time. As a result of the Nuremberg Laws, they lost the services of their "much-liked" Johanna; nothing more.[8] The fact that Jews were no longer German citizens but merely subjects (*Staatsangehörige*) aroused only limited attention, he comments, and legal sanction against mixed marriage or the Law for the Protection of German Blood elicited no more than slight derision. For most of the time, it continued to be possible to separate private from public life, Gay claims. As late as 1936, his father was earning well and apparently even more than before. By the end of 1937, with Göring taking over the Reich's economics ministry and the renewed wave of expropriating Jews together with street violence by the SS that forced many Jews to give up their enterprises altogether, father Gay's business still flourished. "Certainly we never doubted that sooner or later Germany would be no place for us," Gay admits. "Meanwhile, though, however temporarily, it still was."[9]

Indeed, Germany had long been home, and one does not leave home, not even in difficult times. In the meantime, Gay continues, the family took a ten-day-long trip, visiting historic locations in the country, and in 1936 father and son enjoyed watching the Olympic Games, admiring Jesse Owens' victories over his "Nordic" rivals. Only in 1937, as pressure on German Jewry increased again, did a number of sobering incidents convince the father to begin making concrete plans for emigration. Finally, in 1938, news from Nazi-occupied Vienna, reporting on the plundering of Jewish property there and the savage humiliation of the previously so well-established Jewish population in the "city on the blue Danube" brought home the seriousness of the situation. In November 1938, the state-wide pogrom known as the Reichskristallnacht finally made leaving imperative. The Fröhlichs managed to escape and reached – after experiencing a disheartening series of events – the shores of the American continent.

There is a ton of reproach in much of Gay's book, directed at those who, both at the time and in later years, reprimanded German Jews for their presumed blindness. Above all, he explains, it was the insanity, the absolute implausibility of Hitler's plans that made them so utterly unbelievable.[10] It was hard, perhaps impossible, he insists, to read the signals. Indeed, it was only in 1938 and especially after the pogrom that the largest number of Jews left the country. All in all, 40,000 Jews left Germany in 1938 and as many as 78,000 in 1939. Needless to say, emigration was an ordeal for each and every one of them. The bureaucracy heaped piles of paperwork on those wishing to leave, and foreign countries were practically closed to newcomers. However, the fate of

[8] Ibid., 72.   [9] Ibid., 75.   [10] Ibid., 112.

The Abyss

those who did not manage to leave was much worse. They were soon to be swept up by the next and far worse step on that twisted road to the "Final Solution."

And surely, not everyone found the pre-war Nazi state as harmless as the young Gay. The historian Monika Richarz's volume of Jewish recollections from these years opens with Marta Appel's memoirs. Marta had been born in Metz in 1884. She married Dr. Ernst Appel, the Rabbi of Bingen, in 1918 and later moved with him to Duisburg. There, as a mother of two girls, she witnessed the agony of her daughters in the local school, where they were repeatedly excluded from classroom activities and humiliated for their Jewishness. She herself bitterly experienced the growing "gap between us and our '*Mitbürger*' [fellow citizens]."[11] Already before prohibitions to this effect were made into law or proclaimed by the city authorities, Jews had avoided meeting old friends or taking part in public gatherings, she relates. While some friends were at first still willing to meet with Jews, eventually all of them kept their distance. "All our friends – in fact the entire *Volk* – had left us in our need," she felt.[12]

Frau Appel mentions an additional aspect of the developments at the time, namely the departure of rural Jews from their communities for the anonymity of the metropolis, often as a first step leading to emigration. Over a quarter of all German-Jewish communities no longer existed after 1938, and those that remained exhibited an entirely skewed age-structure – in towns as well as in the countryside. After all, particularly urgent was the exit of the young. Parents were eager to send their children away, and, by 1939, some 80 percent of all Jews under twenty-four had left Germany, relocating partly to Palestine, with the help of the Youth Aliyah organization, and partly to England and, if possible, to America. Families were otherwise thrown apart too, and often only old people stayed behind. The entire fabric of Jewish family and community life had been destroyed.

While at first socialists and communists were even more a target of Nazi terror than the Jews, the vicious persecution of the latter gradually became the main preoccupation of the various police forces in the new state. To be sure, Jews were pursued together with groups of Sinti and Roma, other Germans who were considered "asocial," homosexuals, and those deemed "unworthy of life." All Germans were potential targets. But, in fact, the rage of the Nazi fanatics was all too often focused upon the Jews.

Clearly, there were periods during which this issue receded into the background, and there were always some friendly men and women who

---

[11] Monika Richarz (ed.), *Jüdisches Leben in Deutschland: Selbstzeugnisse zur Sozialgeschichte 1918–1945*, New York, 1982, 232.
[12] Ibid., 237.

disregarded Nazi propaganda and were ready to offer help. In fact, historians diagnose three waves of particularly active antisemitism: in 1933, immediately following the Nazi "seizure of power"; in 1935, around the promulgation of the Nuremberg Laws; and in 1938 – before, during, and after the November Pogrom. The themes alternated between a rehash of old stereotypes and frontal attacks on the Jews as the acting power behind Bolshevism or as representatives of a mysterious "World Jewry," presumably controlling Western capitalism and the politics of the United States and Great Britain. Repeatedly, efforts by American and British Jews to persuade their governments to respond more firmly to Hitler's anti-Jewish measures were construed as signs of sinister plans against Germany. Finally, some combination of all three themes was seemingly most expedient, and these were flung at the German public from endless newspaper articles, fiery speeches, and hateful messages in all public media. Hitler and Goebbels set the tone and others followed suit.

To be sure, the overall population continued to be divided among "true believers," usually belonging to the ranks of active National Socialists, most particularly as members of the SA and later the SS and the Gestapo; the more or usually less outspoken opponents of the regime; and a majority of indifferent bystanders. The latter were more often than not ready to comply and sometimes to participate in anti-Jewish activity, while occasionally holding back out of mistrust or indecision. And between episodes of antisemitism or even of anti-Jewish violence, life went on, focused upon other worries that seemed far more pressing at the time. Considering the size of the Jewish population in Germany and its geographical distribution, few members of the "Aryan" population had close relationships with Jews, even if many had *some* professional, commercial, and other kinds of daily contacts with them. With the Nazi ascent to power, the so-called Jewish Question – which had been present before too – now took on a far more central position. Perhaps it was, indeed, that abstract "Jew," known since medieval times for his sinister plotting, that one could see on every street signpost, depicted in caricature on the front pages of the Nazi daily press. Or perhaps it was the "real" Jew, steadily vilified, in obstinate repetition, by all available means. After all, the entire Nazi propaganda machinery – surely, a considerable one – was recruited to present "the Jew" as a personification of ultimate evil. One was taught – no, indeed, indoctrinated – to hate and fear him, even if his true likeness was a familiar person or even a friendly neighbor.

Moreover, the situation was a dynamic one. People were moving among the above-mentioned categories, and in time many passed into the more strictly antisemitic camp. A report of SOPADE – the Social Democratic Party's information center in exile – described how "even people who previously did not even know what a Jew is, today push [the blame for] every evil onto the Jews."[13] The regime, however, remained unsatisfied. People did not break *all* contacts with the Jews, one bureaucrat complained. Peasants continued to do business with Jewish cattle dealers and trade with Jewish merchants, especially in south Germany, another reported. In many towns, large and small Jewish shops continued to be frequented, and the Nazi Party machinery did not always manage to turn occasional anti-Jewish attacks into countrywide campaigns. Even in the aftermath of the November Pogrom, some authorities continued to complain that the "civil population" could not be brought to take part in the *"Aktionen."*[14] There seemed to have still been occasional expressions of sympathy and readiness to help, even as the majority was quick to blame the Jews for everything, reacted positively to the punitive measures against them, and decried the disorder presumably caused by their behavior. Some reports mentioned the unease among church-going people, especially Catholics, at the sight of wrecked synagogues. But little of this opposition was loud enough to be heard in public or have any influence.

Still, Goebbels could not relax. Following the pogrom in 1938, the propaganda ministry began a new anti-Jewish campaign, demanding stricter avoidance of all contacts with Jews, repeating with special venom all the previous accusations against them. This chief antisemite was particularly irked by those who continued to think "that Jews are human too," to use his exact wording.[15] And, in fact, referring to Jews as "subhumanity" that must be exterminated was not uncommon in the Nazi jargon. In an address to high-ranking SS officers a few days before Hitler's famous Reichstag speech in January 1939, Heydrich used this term, too.[16] All this is strangely reminiscent of the eighteenth-century debate at the outset of the controversy concerning Jewish emancipation, more than 150 years before. It was Dohm who, in his book of 1781, had openly proclaimed that "Jews are human too," and it was this statement, radical at the time, that had launched Jewish entry into German society. All this was now over. Dehumanization produced social distancing of hitherto unknown proportions, total estrangement of the Jewish minority, and – very often – moral indifference and a surprising lack of empathy among members of the German majority. It was, no doubt, part of a larger change experienced by this majority, indicative of its transformation into a *Volksgemeinschaft*, devoid of critical reflection; a cheering, ecstatic

---

[13] Quoted in Peter Longerich, *"Davon haben wir nichts gewusst!" Die Deutschen und die Judenverfolgung 1933–1945*, Munich, 2007, 117.
[14] Ibid., 129. [15] Ibid., 142.
[16] See Friedländer, *Nazi Germany and the Jews*, Vol. I, 312.

crowd, with arms raised in the Nazi salute, ready to acquiesce and bend their previously most sacred values to the will of their adored Führer.

By the end of 1938, after the occupation of Austria with its population of some 200,000 additional Jews, antisemitism reached new heights. The extremely abusive handling of the Viennese Jews together with the plundering, intimidation, destruction, expropriation, and physical attacks upon those still living in the Old Reich signaled the high point of the Nazi hate campaign. The German population was meanwhile ready for the next step of the Nazi anti-Jewish policies: their expulsion, making Germany "clean" of Jews, and then – as the Führer prophesized in his speech of January 30, 1939 – their total annihilation.

It is astonishing that the Jews managed to maintain a modicum of normality under these circumstances. In fact, this previously disunited Jewry, split between rich and poor, liberals and Zionists, orthodox and secular Jews developed a new, unexpected solidarity. As early as the summer of 1933, in response to a suggestion coming from a number of previously active Jewish artists, Nazi authorities permitted the operation of a Jüdischer Kulturbund (Jewish Cultural Federation) that soon managed to organize, first in Berlin and later in a number of other urban centers in Germany, theater performances, chamber orchestra concerts, and even occasional opera performances. They even managed to stage some impressive gallery exhibitions – all by Jews and for Jews, but apparently always with an eye on upholding the German humanistic culture. The Kulturbund was placed under strict censorship, of course, yet it still managed to operate in part until well into 1941. At the same time, Jewish religious life went on, too. Synagogues, rabbis' seminars, institutes for adult education – all continued to function at least partly and according to local conditions. Lectures were held, many of them under the leadership of the philosopher and educator Martin Buber as head of the Center for Adult Education, until his emigration in 1938. Here special attention had been given to the remaining Jewish youth in Germany, especially to their spirits and moral. Many Jewish schools remained open too, though often reorganized and with an ever smaller number of pupils. Thus, Jewish children continued to read and be taught the works of Goethe, Schiller, and Hölderlin, but also the more modern texts of Thomas Mann and Hugo von Hofmannsthal. Finally, more than 60 of the previously many more Jewish newspapers and journals continued to appear under National Socialism, with an average combined readership of some 350,000, while a number of Jewish publishing houses persisted in bringing out books with stress on Jewish themes, at least until 1938. This could be seen as resistance on the part of the Jews, a reaction to numerous prohibitions and their general exclusion from almost all social institutions and associations. But it was always also joined to love of German culture and the tradition of *Bildung*, resolutely upheld among German Jews even in these trying times.

Despite all that, they were in fact no longer Germans. Regardless of the precise plans for their "removal," it was clearly decided by the Nazi leadership that they were to become victims and nothing but victims under its rule. Perhaps, indeed, the actual content of this anti-Jewish-project remained unclear for a long time even to Hitler himself. At the time of his last important speech before the war, the Führer still seemed to take into account the international, especially British and American, reactions to any potential anti-Jewish action on his part. In various gatherings, he was throwing around the various available options, according to him, for "solving" the "Jewish Question," such as the expulsion of all European Jews – no longer just the German Jews – to some distant part of the world, maybe to Madagascar or, later on, to the northern shores of Poland or to some desolate steppe of the Soviet Union. The threats may have at first been aimed at blackmailing Jews living in the Western democracies in order to stop what Hitler saw as their "warmongering"; holding them hostage to ensure their co-religionists' "positive behavior towards the Reich."[17] Then, emigration enforced by all possible means was probably the most concrete policy at hand, but the sense that more extreme measures would soon be needed was shared by the entire upper echelon of the Nazi hierarchy quite early on.

It is perhaps not inappropriate to speculate that, apart from the many uncertainties on the international front, the Nazis had to overcome some domestic uncertainties too. Central among them remained the uncertainty concerning the readiness of the "regular Germans" to take part in the future antisemitic project – actively or at least passively – and to endorse the Führer's plans no matter how preposterous they might become. Hitler – like Goebbels – seemed to be uncertain. It was as yet not clear to them how far that strange widespread ethical amnesia, apparently possessing most contemporary Germans, could be trusted. In any case, with the approach of war, all previous plans had to be reshuffled. Hitler was now finally leading the country steadily for what he considered the necessary acquisition of *Lebensraum* (living space) and the repositioning of Germany in world politics, within the overall framework of imperial power competition. These were his large-scale war aims; they did not include a clear or explicit "solution to the Jewish Question." However, victory in the East had always meant the breaking up of that presumed

[17] Ibid., 312.

citadel of "World Jewry" located in Bolshevik Russia. Hitler was now finally leading a racially "purified" Germany to its proper place of greatness, while the meager remnants of German Jewry, shrinking in number and shriveling into poverty, were sinking into temporary insignificance.

By 1939, the Jews in Germany, including many who had been added to this category by the Nazis – those having just one Jewish grandparent, for instance – made up only 0.32 percent of the overall population in the so-called Old Reich. About 250,000 Jews had left the country since 1933, over 100,000 of them after the November Pogrom and before the gates were completely shut in October 1941. By the end of the decade, only a small minority of those who remained were gainfully employed. Whereas in 1935 there were still 75,000 active Jewish firms in Germany, by the summer of 1938 over 60,000 of them no longer existed. The licenses of most of the Jewish doctors who were still practicing had been revoked by then, and only some 170 lawyers, a dismal remnant of a proud and successful professional group, were still allowed to provide services to the few remaining Jewish firms or organizations. All of these were by then impoverished, unable to offer much help to a population that consisted mostly of the elderly and the indigent. Then, what had been "achieved" – so to speak – only gradually within Germany since 1933 became a reality in Nazi-dominated Austria within weeks. About two-thirds of the local Jews left Austria between March 1938 and the outbreak of war, and the remaining 110,000 suffered conditions no better than those of their brethren in the old Reich. In the now so-called Czech "Protectorate" too, after the already-familiar practice of humiliation and swift expropriation, the situation was no different. Everywhere Jews could no longer use public transport, nor own bicycles, radios, telephones, or typewriters. On September 8, 1941, they were ordered to place the *Judenstern* (Jewish star) on their coats and – being deployed as forced laborers – they were hoarded into crowded *Judenhäuser* (Jewish houses) or barracks, dependent on hand-out meals, shoes, and clothing, prey to bouts of cold and hunger.

In Poland, meanwhile, German soldiers moving eastward encountered Polish Jews, who seemed to be living in even worse conditions. They were filthy – the soldiers were quick to report – neglected and helpless. Within days, millions of them were under German occupation, and the "Jewish Question" resurfaced and multiplied. As soon as the fighting came to a temporary halt, "handling" them once more became a major theme, a difficulty to be "solved." Meanwhile, the sporadic killings by the *Einsatzgruppen*, first aimed at the Polish intelligentsia, began, and immediately afterwards, as the Generalgouvernement in southern Poland was set up, tens of thousands of Poles were sent there to be exploited as a work force. Then the Jews were forcibly concentrated in ghettos, "in order to secure better means of control and to remove them at a later date," to quote a circular of the Reichssicherheitshauptamt (Reich Security Central Office, RSHA), issued as early as September 21, 1939.[18] On the way to the ghettos, the mass shootings and executions began.

Deportations of Jews from Germany itself began in October 1940, first in recently annexed Alsace-Lorrain, and then in Baden, the Palatinate, and the Saarland. Further transports, from all the main German cities, brought Jews from Germany to Łódź, Riga, and – after January 1942 – Minsk. In May 1942, it was primarily German Jews who were killed by gas in the process of experimenting with this method near the town of Chełmno. Those brought in from the previous territory of Czechoslovakia or from Vienna were interned, at least for some time, in Theresienstadt, and from January 1943 sent directly to Auschwitz. By then, a few thousand Jews were still living in Germany. Some were meanwhile "protected," being married to non-Jews; others were in hiding with help from friendly Germans, who were sometimes risking their lives to get them food rationings or the bare minimum of other essential needs. Over 4,000 Jews survived the war in Berlin, of them some 800 in the Jewish hospital that curiously continued to operate, and some – even more dreadfully – in the city's Jewish cemetery.

Meanwhile, throughout the rest of the continent, the Holocaust was raging, now well beyond the stages of improvisation. Jews from all over Europe, west and east, north and south, falling into the hands of the Nazi occupiers, were sent to be industrially exterminated – each and every one of them. In fact, killing had started before the idea of mass gassing – which originated from the project of exterminating the mentally ill, known as the T4 project – was put into effect.[19] Already at the end of 1939, three-quarters of the Jewish population of the continent found themselves in countries occupied by the Germans. In Poland, the German occupiers immediately began to expropriate local Jews, deport them, concentrate them in ghettos, and exploit them as forced labor. In Western and Northern Europe, frequently with the help of the local authorities and

---

[18] See Volker R. Berghahn, *Modern Germany: Society, Economy and Politics in the Twentieth Century*, New York, 1982, 162.

[19] The following summary of the extermination is closely based on the relevant chapter in Ulrich Herbert, *Geschichte Deutschlands im 20. Jahrhundert*, Munich, 2014, 467–482. Many of the documents quoted by Herbert are from the collection of Susanne Heim, Ulrich Herbert et al. (eds.), *Die Verfolgung und Ermordung der europäischen Juden durch das Nationalsozialistische Deutschland, 1933–1945*, Berlin and Boston, MA, 2008–2022, especially volumes I–VI and XI. For a full and differentiated description. see also Saul Friedländer, *Nazi Germany and the Jews, 1939–1945*, Vol. II: *The Years of Extermination*, New York, 2007.

local antisemitic activists, Jews were first listed and registered, then forced out of their homes, isolated as much as possible, and exploited in all sorts of ways.

Eventually, with the growing number of Jews under German military control as a result of the army's inroads into the Soviet Union, the option of emigration was becoming absurd. Between June 1941 and March 1942, some 600,000 Jews were shot and murdered by the *Einsatzgruppen*, Waffen-SS, police, and various army units. But by mid October 1941, it was already clear that German victory could not be expected soon, and in December the United States entered the war, more or less exactly at the same time as the beginning of mass deportations to the newly constructed extermination camps in Bełżec, Kulmhof (Chełmno), Sobibór, and Auschwitz. From mid 1942 trains crisscrossed Europe, bringing Jews from all corners of the continent to these and a growing number of other camps. About a third of the Jews were put to work; the rest were executed by gas, often immediately upon arrival, with many dying of disease and hunger later on. The number of murdered Jews by the end of the war according to the latest calculation is 5.7 million, close enough indeed to the by-now proverbial 6 million.

It is well beyond the scope of this single chapter to give a full account of the Holocaust. Since the opening of the archives in the previously occupied areas of the Soviet zone, we know in far greater detail all aspects of the Nazi ruling system and the precise – and horrifying – means by which extermination was carried out. Enough has been said here, however, so that we can now resume our main task, namely accounting for this chapter of German history through a Jewish perspective, attempting to illuminate the whole in this light. But is this still possible? Do we not have here in fact two parallel, interconnected, but fundamentally separate narratives? Is it still possible to weave them together? If the Jews coming from Germany were by then no longer Germans, not even capable of observing their one-time homeland from the margin, could they still reflect the larger German course of events? If, indeed, they were now no longer German Jews, but a segment of European Jewry, destined for destruction – can we still consider them a component of German history?

In slightly different terms, these questions were at the center of some past historiographical debates. To begin with, the German and the Jewish perspective on these occurrences were indeed told separately for much of the immediate post-war period. In fact, until well into the 1960s, the Holocaust played hardly any role in the emerging literature about the Nazi era, as we saw earlier in the Introduction, and this despite the fact that by then a stream of memoir literature had begun to appear and many books on the extermination of the European Jews were beginning to be available. Gerald Reitlinger's *The Final Solution: The Attempt to Exterminate the Jews of Europe*, appeared as early as 1953, and Raul Hilberg's pathbreaking work *The Destruction of the European Jews* was published in London in 1961. Both relied on German archival material, so they were presumably amenable to integration within German historiography. Curiously, while the first was translated into German as early as 1956, the second appeared in that country only in 1982. The peculiar separation of German history from the history of the Holocaust during that time has often been noted since then.

A radical way of joining the two narratives was suggested by Lucy Dawidowicz in her 1975 *The War against the Jews*, published in New York. "The conventional war of conquest was to be waged parallel to, and was also to camouflage, the ideological war against the Jews," she writes in her introduction to that book.[20] Accordingly, in precise contradistinction to the position taken by contemporary West German historians, the main narrative was that of the Holocaust and the secondary one was that of the "conventional war," merely "camouflaging" the major, criminal campaign directed at the Jews. While Dawidowicz's book was at first hardly noticed by German historians, a somewhat earlier book, a small volume by Eberhard Jäckel, *Hitler's Weltanschauung*, of 1969, treating the various aspects of the Nazi ideology, gained much attention. Jäckel, like Dawidowicz, insisted upon the importance of ideology for understanding both the rise of National Socialism and the run of events during its rule, but his stress on antisemitism was not as exclusive as hers. Still, the book clearly ran against conventional wisdom. In the immediate postwar years, it was in fact common among historians to deny the very *existence* of a Nazi ideology. "National Socialism has no political theory of its own," wrote Franz Neumann in exile as early as 1944, "and ... the ideologies it uses or discards are mere *arcana dominationis*, techniques of domination."[21] To be sure, none of the Jewish historians after the war working outside of Germany disregarded ideology; none *could* disregard antisemitism, and at least one influential historian among them never retreated from the line represented by Dawidowicz, namely the leading Israeli historian of the Holocaust, Yehuda Bauer. In articles and lectures, he has insisted that the main, if not the only real reason for launching the Second World War by the Nazis was antisemitism. The context of war, he is convinced, was created in order to achieve the full extermination of the

---

[20] Lucy S. Dawidowicz, *The War against the Jews: 1933–1945*, New York, 1975, xxi.
[21] See Franz Neumann, *Behemoth: The Structure and Practice of National-Socialism, 1933–1944*, New York, 1944, 467.

Jews, in itself a fantasy – or rather a nightmare – not unlike other elements of Nazi ideology.[22] Famously, Daniel Goldhagen too presented a similar version of this thesis.

But is it necessary to reduce the war to this one aim in order to integrate Jewish with German history? Is this the only possible link between the two? It is surely not difficult to imagine that such an insistence on the primacy of the Holocaust in studying the history of the Third Reich, thus leaving aside other aspects of that time, seemed offensive to many. It crassly disregards both the early sense of achievement and success experienced by so many Germans during the latter part of the 1930s and then their sufferings under conditions of war, most significantly the destruction and dislocation experienced by segments of the population in East Prussia during the retreat of the Wehrmacht and the westward advance of the Red Army. In fact, the exclusive stress on the Holocaust brought the two histories – of the war and of the Holocaust – further apart rather than together.

All this and more was in the background of the debate between Martin Broszat and Saul Friedländer in 1988. Friedländer did not share Dawidowicz's and Bauer's focus on the Jewish narrative, but instead insisted on the need to preserve a clear moral stand vis-à-vis the victims and on the centrality of Nazi criminality. These had to be always upheld in studying this time – *all* aspects of this time, he claimed, including the social and economic changes, the modernization issue, and more. Martin Broszat, however, felt that it was time, just over four decades since the end of the war, to "historicize" the treatment of Nazism. In writing about it, he conceded, one had to show "a measure of sympathetic identification with the victims," indeed, but also stress "the achievements and the wrongly invested virtues" that could be uncovered "in this disastrous chapter of German history."[23] Such a perspective, he felt, was needed in order to communicate with a younger generation of Germans and uphold a "German perspective" that could not be documented through the memories of the victims. After all, the latter's "intensive memory," he explained, made it necessary to "roll history backward" in contradistinction to learned scholarship that ought to proceed forwards. The victims' memory, moreover, places "everything else in the shadow," and makes the extermination of the Jews into "the sole criterion for the historical view of this time."[24]

---

[22] See the succinct presentation of his view on this matter in "*Murderous Mutation of Anti-Semitism*," Ha'Aretz, June 24, 2011.

[23] See Martin Broszat and Saul Friedländer, "Um die Historisierung des Nationalsozialismus. Ein Briefwechsel," *Vierteljahrshefte für Zeitgeschichte*, 36 (1988), 339–372. The quotes are from Nicolas Berg, *Der Holocaust und die westdeutschen Histoiriker: Erforschung und Erinnerung*, Göttingen, 2003, 39.

[24] Broszat and Friedländer, "Um die Historisierung des Nationalsozialismus," 352–353.

Unsurprisingly, his position was unacceptable to Friedländer, who was confident of his ability to combine memory and professionalism. He resented the unveiled assumption in Broszat's argument that his own memories as a refugee and victim were more detrimental to the writing of professional history than Broszat's – as a soldier in the Wehrmacht during the last year of the war and, as it later turned out, briefly a member of the NSDAP. In fact, other, equally subjective expressions of identification with those who could be considered "German victims" were also put forward at the time, especially Andreas Hillgruber's extended essay on the collapse of the eastern front in his *Zweierlei Untergang (Two Kinds of Ruin)* of 1986. Dan Diner, a historian then teaching both in Israel and in Germany, claimed shortly afterwards that the historiographical situation in this field could in fact be understood only in terms of court litigation: The "Plaintiff" and the "Defendant" have such conflicting "worlds of experience" that opposing interpretations are "hardly avoidable."[25]

It seemed that the two optional perspectives in studying and analyzing the Nazi era put forwards in this painful debate were irreconcilable. For a long time the historiography was split along lines that could be conceived as "national." Previously, during the protracted and in any event no less crucial debate between "intentionalists" and "functionalists," despite the fact that a number of German historians sided with the "intentionalists," and the "functionalist" interpretation was likewise sometimes adopted by Jewish historians, the split along national lines was still clear enough. Today there is little sense in recapitulating these differences. Within a few years, one could actually observe the emergence of a whole range of compromises between the two positions. Both Bauer and Friedländer eventually saw the merit of some "functionalist" arguments, while an "intentionalist" interpretation became acceptable – perhaps in a milder form – to many German historians. A new generation of researchers was by the 1990s mainly preoccupied with intensive archival work and the debates of a previous decade no longer seemed fruitful or even meaningful to them. And clearly, the historiographical dichotomy has further lost much of its bitterness during the time since then, even if new – and no less significant – controversies continue to emerge.

The perspective of this book is in any case somewhat different. Here we have tried to follow primarily *German* history, on a long-term trajectory, attempting to interweave the story of German Jewry into it, perceiving the

---

[25] See Dan Diner, "Varieties of Interpretations: The Holocaust in Historical Memory," in Igal Halfin (ed.), *Language and Revolution: Making Modern Political Identities*, London, 2002, 379–391. The short quotes are from pages 384–386.

former through the eyes of the latter. The story we presented by no means led simply or inadvertently to Nazism and the Holocaust. For long stretches, Jewish history in Germany could in fact be read as a success story. Despite bouts of antisemitism, often much more impressive and more influential was Jewish successful integration, the economic rise of so many Jews, their share in the country's modernization, and the prominence achieved by so many of them in various spheres of culture, society, and even politics. This was not an unproblematic development, but it allowed us to illuminate many neglected points along the way. With the rise of National Socialism and the exclusion of the Jews from the so-called German *Volksgemeinschaft*, indeed from being Germans at all, it might at first seem that one could no longer use this approach. Jews were made into strangers, even dangerous strangers, despicable and finally dehumanized. Paradoxically, however, their radical exclusion and then the efforts at their extermination together with the majority of their European brethren made Jewry more central for Germany and the Germans than it had ever been before. While they could be considered negligible before, and in fact themselves so often wished to disappear as a minority within the majority, remembering the fate of the Jews during the war, even just vaguely, and realizing the sinister dimension of their tragedy, made it later impossible to dismiss them. Moreover, their narrative made it impossible to disregard Nazi criminality, the complicity of so many German bystanders, and all the guilt and the shame involved.

11 Victims, Witnesses, Plaintiffs

Jews were still being hunted out of their hiding places even during the very last days of the Third Reich. At the end, some 15,000 of them managed to survive in Nazi Germany. Most lived in so-called privileged or non-privileged marriages, according to Nazi terminology, or in some sort of hiding with or without help from German friends and neighbors. Then, soon after the occupation of the main cities in the Western zones of Germany, in Düsseldorf or in Cologne, the scattered survivors came together in order to reestablish their defunct communities. These usually numbered now no more than fifty to eighty members, straining to provide help for the few who managed to return from concentration camps and for refugees from Eastern Europe, who were not yet settled in the displaced persons (DP) camps. Most of these refugees were unable to return to their old domiciles. Sometimes – as in the case of certain Polish towns – they were expelled upon returning, or occasionally even forced to run for their lives. As many as 1,200 Jews were killed in Poland during the immediate post-war years. And now – strangely enough – they, too, found refuge in Germany, of all places.

Thus, despite all their efforts, the Nazis did not manage to achieve a Germany "free of Jews." Instead their country offered shelter now for over 250,000 men, women, and children, exhausted and penniless, living in old or new barracks, especially in the British and the American Zones of Occupation. They made up approximately the same number of Jews as those who had lived in Germany prior to the Second World War. But whereas German Jewry in 1939, decimated as it had by then become, was well rooted in that country and usually still considered it their home, post-war Germany was no more than a temporary asylum for a mixed crowd of Jewish refugees, living under the protection of the Allied occupying powers. And whereas on the eve of the war the Jewish community was mostly made up of old people, since the younger ones had, more often than not, managed to migrate in the nick of time, the majority of the Jewish population in post-war Germany was made up of relatively young people, since the majority of the concentration camp survivors were young. The old, after all, were the first to be sent to the gas chambers. In addition, while many of those who were deported by the Soviet government either to Siberia or to Uzbekistan and Kazakhstan later arrived in Germany with their family members, most concentration-camp survivors lost their relatives there and usually came back alone. Then, immediately after liberation, there were some 200 marriages in the DP camp adjacent to Bergen-Belsen, and in fact, the entire refugee population proved to be a surprisingly active population, considering the ordeal they had had behind them. They soon established an intensive community life, selected committees for a variety of purposes, organized cultural affairs, improvised courts for punishing collaborators, set up educational facilities for children as well as for adults, and more.

Still, while they were doing all that, most of them regarded Germany as a cursed country, the land of the murderers, where life was to be lived *im Zeichen des Banns* (under the sign of the ban).[1] Zionists and the Jewish emissaries from Palestine, helping them to emigrate, surely saw things in this light, but at first even anti-Zionists were equally reluctant to accept a permanent new Jewish settlement in Germany. All considered it now their task to bring as many survivors as possible away, preferably to Jewish Palestine, by then still under the British Mandate or – if and when this route was blocked – by sending them westward, to the United States. Germany was an enemy territory, observed with a mixture of hate and suspicion. Famously, or perhaps notoriously, this went so far that, after the establishment of the state of Israel, Israeli passports carried the stamp "Valid for all countries except Germany."

It was not only Jews who banned Germany. Both Lion Feuchtwanger and Thomas Mann decided to stay in exile – a Jewish and a non-Jewish German. But, with the establishment of the German Democratic Republic (DDR) in the Soviet Occupation Zone, both Arnold Zweig and Berthold Brecht were invited there and chose to come – again a Jewish and a non-Jewish German. Both Adorno and Horkheimer came back to West Germany, as did Ernst Bloch to Leipzig in the DDR. Herbert Marcuse, however, refused to return; and, in a letter to Karl Jaspers, who invited her to join him in setting up a new German language periodical as early as January 1946, Hannah Arendt wrote back in a typically cautious manner: "I trust you won't misunderstand me if I tell you that it is not easy for me to work for a German periodical . . .

---

[1] See Dan Diner, "Im Zeichen des Banns," in Michael Brenner (ed.), *Geschichte der Juden in Deutschland vom 1945 bis zur Gegenwart: Politik, Kultur und Gesellschaft*, Munich, 2012, 15–66, and on the wider context see also Dan Diner, *Rituelle Distanz: Israels deutsche Frage*, Munich, 2015.

As I see it, none of us can come back ... just because people now appear once more to be prepared to recognize Jews as Germans or whatever – but rather only *if we are welcome as Jews.*"[2] However, an invitation of this sort was not forthcoming. A welcoming gesture either to the Jews in particular or even simply to émigrés in general remained "a gesture that was expected and was not made," noted the literary scholar Hans Mayer in a later article.[3] He himself, a "patriot of the German language" in Heine's style, came back to Germany as early as the fall of 1945, a return that he saw as a sort of *Widerruf* (revocation) and repeatedly felt called upon to explain. The actor Fritz Kortner, by then already an American citizen, and other actors exiled in Switzerland came back soon afterwards. Some, like Martin Buber, never came back to settle but did visit Germany repeatedly for shorter or longer periods. Yet others came back at a much later date. The philosopher Hans Jonas, for instance, who left Germany in 1933, first came back as a soldier in the Jewish Brigade of the British army, left to return to Palestine, migrated from there to Canada and later to the United States, and then finally resettled in Munich sometime in the early 1980s.

All of these were well-known figures. On the whole, not many German Jews returned to post-Nazi Germany, and most of the DPs were soon to leave. The number of Jews who decided to stay was finally small, but they continued to be active and insistent. By 1946, there were already some 55 Jewish communities in occupied Germany; the smallest with 12 members in Plauen, the largest with about 5,000 in Berlin. In the Soviet Zone too, a few tiny communities were reestablished, sharing a rabbi, sometimes seeking additional members just in order to constitute a group of ten adult males, a so-called *Minyan*, as needed for a public prayer. Julius Posener, a British officer stationed in northern West Germany at the time and impressed by these unexpected, quick developments, reported them upon returning to London. In his memoirs, he later mentioned Salomon Adler-Rudel's reaction to his report. The latter was a Czernowitz-born Jewish activist, for decades associated with various social-work projects. But now he found no kind word for his co-religionists: "May they wait in their beloved fatherland," he said, "until their throats are slit."[4]

---

[2] See Hannah Arendt and Karl Jaspers, *Briefwechsel*, Munich, 1985, 67 (my emphasis).
[3] Quoted from *Die Zeit* (February 1, 1985) in Frank Stern, *The Whitewashing of the Yellow Badge: Antisemitism and Philosemitism in Postwar Germany*, Oxford, 1992, 210.
[4] Ibid., 67, quoting from Julius Posener, *In Deutschland 1945–1946*, Jerusalem, 1947, 115. From among the early studies on this topic, see Harry Maòr, *Über den Wiederaufbau der jüdischen Gemeinden in Deutschland seit 1945*, Mainz, 1961.

Not everyone was so blunt, but many felt the same. Those Jews who either decided to stay in Germany or were stranded there after years of hardship often had to face not only renewed antisemitism from Germans but also stark incomprehension or even hostility from their fellow Jews. Meanwhile, the Americans began to investigate systematically the attitude of Germans towards democracy in general, and towards the Jews living in their midst again in particular. Following years of anti-Jewish policies and vehement antisemitic propaganda, they unsurprisingly found out that negative attitudes towards the Jews had not disappeared. At the beginning, most people claimed they knew nothing of the mass murder in the East and felt the American reports of what had happened there were exaggerated. And while only a few openly defended Nazi policies against the Jews, most still felt "it was good to break their power."[5] To old antisemitic clichés, new ones were now added, including fear of reprisals and a growing resentment against accusations voiced by individual Jews, by Jewish organizations, and by the occupying Allied forces, often including Jewish officers in their staff.

To be sure, living among ruins and suffering hunger and cold, neither the fate of the Jews nor the loftier questions of shame or guilt with regard to their fate interested most Germans. But these issues seem to have interested their occupiers. Whereas the Soviets practiced a strict policy of extinguishing any Nazi influence in their zone, the Western Allies decided to apply a policy of selective denazification and the punishment of indicted perpetrators. By that time, many of the chief Nazi leaders were dead, and the others were being brought before the International Military Court in Nuremberg. Lesser figures, who did not manage to escape, were soon likewise interned, interrogated, and placed before one sort of court or another, while the efforts at general denazification continued for some time, with only limited success. It did, however, arouse a great deal of resentment. In many cases legal proceedings merely brought about the easy whitewashing of the Nazi stigma for minor offenders, and later, in any case, most imprisoned Nazis were gradually freed and some were even allowed to reassume their bureaucratic posts, their roles in the justice system, or their place in politics. Clearly, the occupying forces were determined to introduce a new moral standard into the ongoing public discourse in their respective zones, but the opposition was equally ubiquitous and insistent. Thus, surviving Jews were often faced not only with a sort of barely concealed antisemitism, but also with the sight of old Nazis and their supporters being accepted and re-integrated into West

---

[5] Office of the US Military Government, report (November 19, 1945), quoted in Stern, *The Whitewashing of the Yellow Badge*, 88.

German society. Surely, Jews too were mainly busy with issues of more immediate existential importance at this time. But, especially for those who were originally German, this must have been bitter, no doubt.

In the meantime, some newspaper articles, dealing with what they continued to call "the Jewish Question," began to note the emergence of a new side to the relationships between Jews and Germans. These now became "a touchstone for the sincerity of democratic convictions" in post-war society, some claimed, a kind of litmus test.[6] It was, indeed, repeatedly applied by the American occupation authorities – first the military and then, after 1949, the civilian too. In the summer of 1949, the US High Commissioner, John McCloy, a guest speaker at the first inter-regional meeting of representatives of the new Jewish communities in Germany, used almost precisely the same language: "The fundamental reason that prompted me to come here," he said, "is the world significance of the relationships of the new Germany to the Jews and of the Jews to the new German community." "It will, in my judgment, be one of the real touchstones and the test of Germany's progress toward the light," he added poetically.[7]

At that time, it did not yet seem that Germany could, in fact, honorably stand this test. Since 1945, the overall situation in the country had, of course, changed considerably. The division of Germany into sectors had by then been replaced by the establishment of two states, at first only partly independent and not fully sovereign, namely the West German Federal Republic and the East German Democratic Republic. While the need to weaken Germany for the foreseeable future at first united the wartime Allies, the growing rift between them brought forward new and more urgent priorities. Both Allied sides, originally mistrusting the Germans, were now eager to have them as part of their geopolitical coalitions. The communist leadership in East Germany, considering itself the only authentic representative of German anti-fascism, accepted no responsibility for the mass murder of the Jews and did not allow this matter to play any apparent role in its politics. Following a short anti-Jewish campaign, initiated by Moscow and conducted throughout the Soviet bloc during the early 1950s, the small contingent of Jews in the country lived there in a partly protected and partly privileged status. They constituted

---

[6] See Stern, *The Whitewashing of the Yellow Badge*, 83.
[7] Quoted in Stern, *The Whitewashing of the Yellow Badge*, 297–298. This meeting and McCloy's speech are discussed also, for instance, by Atina Grossmann and Tamar Lewinsky, "Erster Teil: 1945–1949. Zwischenstation," in Michael Brenner (ed.), *Geschichte der Juden in Deutschland vom 1945 bis zur Gegenwart*, 67–152, see especially pages 146–147.

a segment of the so-called "Victims of Fascism," among whom the politically persecuted comrades made up by far the larger, particularly privileged group. At the same time, attitudes towards the Jews in West Germany, at first a measure of disengagement from Nazism, gradually received another and quite different dimension.

As soon as the matter of restitution and compensation had been raised, West Germany found itself faced with three Jewish collectives: first, the not too many Jews who were settled or sometimes resettled in the Bundesrepublik (West Germany); secondly, the organized American Jews, together with the refugees who found shelter there or elsewhere in the now so-called "Western World"; and thirdly, those who now lived in the newly established State of Israel. Demands for compensation came from all three, forming a front of witnesses and plaintiffs that could not be ignored. In fact, discussion of retribution had begun during the war and was then continued during the years of the Allied occupation of Germany. Legal demands for compensation were drafted and began to be applied first to individual cases and later on to collectivities as well. Immediately thereafter, these demands ended the quiet and consensual stage regarding these matters and caused passionate and heated debate, especially in Israel and in West Germany.

The two countries achieved independence at almost the same time, and both faced gigantic projects of reconstruction as they worked to join the family of nations. Paying some sort of reparation to the Jews was indeed critical within this context, but, at first, any official negotiation between the two sides seemed impossible. The prime ministers of the two countries, Konrad Adenauer and David Ben-Gurion, faced unrelenting opposition to any such move, not only from their political adversaries but also within their own ranks. Both needed their entire political prowess and all their rhetorical skills in order to overcome this internal resistance. Finally, diplomatic dexterity was needed too in trying to achieve a compromise between them. Clearly, Adenauer appreciated the importance of such a compromise, while simultaneously recognizing the extent of opposition in wide strata of the German population and among some of his closest advisors. Ben-Gurion, in turn, insisted on what he saw as necessary financial support for his country, which was at that time struggling to "absorb" – to use the language of the time – hundreds of thousands of refugees. However, he too realized that it all had to be done without too much open interaction with the German side. It was for both leaders an extremely delicate situation.

In fact, Ben-Gurion had the advantage of being able to avail himself of the services of a number of German Jews who were by then high-level bureaucrats in the Israeli Foreign Office. They were sent to carry on the early tentative negotiations with their German counterparts, far away from the public eye. Meanwhile, he took it upon himself to counter the deep unease felt by many Israelis, both his friends and his foes, with regard to the forthcoming agreement with Germany, only a few years after the end of the war. Thus, in addition to his pragmatic arguments, explaining Israel's urgent economic needs, Ben-Gurion tried to introduce a new narrative concerning Germany into the raging, emotionally loaded debate. Germany had become "another country," he insisted, a country with which it was now not only possible but even desirable to have open relations. He may have been oblivious of the widespread anti-Jewish feelings among contemporary Germans and perhaps also of the fact that, precisely at this time, public opinion was expressing demands for full amnesty for Nazi criminals, and that these were soon to be completely integrated within the new state, even within its uppermost administrative echelons. But despite all that, and despite the fiery opposition in Israel, in and outside of parliament, led by Menachem Begin in a highly demagogical fashion, direct negotiations with representatives of the West German government were officially begun on March 21, 1952, in the Dutch town of Wassenaar, and then agreements were signed on September 10 of the same year in Luxembourg.

Adenauer faced no lesser problems in this regard. To begin with, he himself had been less than eager to accept Jewish demands. It was John McCloy and his staff at the American headquarters that urged him first to make public his opposition to antisemitism and then to accept joint responsibility – if not collective guilt – for the fate of the Jews under the Nazi rule and for Jewish needs in the following years. Interesting, and in the end most important, was the fact that the negotiations with the Israeli representatives, joined by spokesmen for the so-called Claims Conference headed by Nahum Goldman, representing the Jews outside of Israel, ran parallel to other negotiations, this time in London, attempting to settle German debts to Western firms and governmental agencies. Completing both agreements was a precondition for Germany's integration into the Western Alliance and the reestablishment of its full sovereignty. McCloy himself had to vouch for Germany's capacity to respond to Jewish demands as well as to the claims of its international creditors. Without the American pressure, therefore, the minority of those who openly supported reparations in Germany could not have gained the upper hand, as historian Ulrich Herbert explains.[8] Likewise essential was the unequivocal support of the Social Democratic Party

---

[8] Ulrich Herbert, *Geschichte Deutschlands im 20. Jahrhundert*, Munich, 2014, 670–676.

from the opposition benches and, finally, Adenauer's reawakened personal commitment to this matter.

Thus, by mid 1952, West German relations with Jews in Israel and in some of the Western countries seemed to be – at least officially and in any case for the moment – practically settled. The Bundesrepublik took upon itself the responsibility for what would now be called the *Wiedergutmachung* (reparation), both vis-à-vis individual German Jews, regardless of their present domicile, and vis-à-vis the state of Israel.[9]

Within West Germany, things seemed to settle down, too, and, despite opposition from worldwide Jewish public opinion, some Jews were now making Germany their permanent home. On July 19, 1950, the Zentralrat der Juden in Deutschland (Central Council of Jews in Germany) was established. It had a bumpy start, but eventually, led by its energetic general secretary Hendrik George Van Dam, it became the public voice of these Jews. To be sure, Van Dam had begun by concentrating – like Ben-Gurion in Israel and Nahum Goldman in the United States – on matters of financial reparations. But, shortly afterwards, he was already able to put forward his main credo for the task of politically representing the new German Jewry, resettled in Germany in the aftermath of war and the Holocaust.

Even Leo Baeck, the old rabbi of Berlin, a survivor of Theresienstadt and a man famous for staying in Germany with the members of his community to the very bitter end, was now voicing cautious optimism. Immediately after liberation, still in 1945, Baeck announced that "the epoch of the Jews in Germany is finished once and for all."[10] But, as early as 1951, he was already able to admit, perhaps even prophesize, that, despite everything, "there will be Jews in Germany for a long time."[11] And, indeed, this minimal prognosis has soon proven correct.

By then, of course, not only the Jews were rehabilitating their life, but the entire country was in the process of being rebuilt – first, in the most basic, material sense and then in ever more complex social, economic, institutional, and political terms. New foundations had clearly been established. The National Socialists and their army had been vanquished; Prussia, its

---

[9] There are a few works on the West German–Israeli relationship during this time. Among them, see especially Yeshayahu A. Jelinek, *Deutschland und Israel 1945–1965: Ein neurotisches Verhältnis*, Munich, 2004, and Michael Borchard, *Eine unmögliche Freundschaft: David Ben-Gurion und Konrad Adenauer*, Freiburg im Breisgau, 2019.

[10] Quoted in Nachum T. Gidal, *Die Juden in Deutschland von der Römerzeit bis zur Weimarer Republik*, Hagen, 1997, 426.

[11] Michael Brenner and Norbert Frei, "Zweiter Teil: 1950–1967. Konsolidierung," in Michael Brenner (ed.), *Geschichte der Juden in Deutschland vom 1945 bis zur Gegenwart*, 153–293. The quote is from page 214.

Junker aristocracy, and its military tradition were not going to be reinstated. In the eastern sector, a communist state controlled by the Russians had been established, and in the west a new federal democracy was being constructed with generous financial help from the Americans and according to their anti-communist political agenda. As early as the summer of 1948, a monetary reform enabled the introduction of a free-market economy in West Germany, and all were joining hands in launching what would soon be known as the *Wirtschaftswunder* (economic miracle). At the same time, the party system was being reshaped, the main democratic institutions were being set to work, and the Grundgesetz (Basic Law) – significantly not called a constitution, in view of the German division, which was considered temporary at the time – was being drafted and put into effect.

The first years of the new Bundesrepublik were characterized by the quick and all-encompassing economic recovery, on the one hand, and the ever growing enmity between West and East, on the other hand. The latter represented not only the struggle between two world powers but also the competition between two over-arching ideologies. Within this context, while much of the foreign politics of the two German states was being dictated by the immediate interests of the two superpowers, both were left to concentrate on their internal affairs. The communist dictatorship in East Germany built up its coercive structure, run by its powerful secret police, that extended into all spheres of life. Meanwhile, the Soviet Union, unable to execute its economic recovery plans, insisted upon enormous war reparations from East Germany and transferred most of the large-scale local heavy industry eastward to Russia. The DDR was gradually drained of most of its resources, while at the same time large segments of the non-communist elite, together with disillusioned socialists and the majority of the Jewish refugees from the East, left for the West. The country had therefore neither the needed capital nor the requisite labor power for achieving lasting economic recovery. Finally, in 1961, in order to prevent further drainage of brains and labor power, the government decided to hermetically close its borders to the West and build the so-called "Berlin Wall."

Meanwhile, the West enjoyed unprecedented economic growth and a measure of political stability under the leadership of Konrad Adenauer. Despite the fact that he was not averse to readmitting previous Nazis or Nazi-supporters into his administration – the most extreme case was surely the appointment of Hans Globke, among those that provided the legal props for the National Socialist ruling system, as Chief of Staff in his own Chancellery – the foundations of a stable democracy were gradually being laid and it was seemingly acceptable to the majority of the citizenry. At the end of 1954, West Germany even became a member of NATO, strengthening its standing within the Western alliance. By then, it had its own small army, and later seemed to have gradually gained international recognition and at least partial sovereignty. Although the Americans insisted on the upholding of a strictly capitalist economic system in the new Bundesrepublik and prevented all attempts at socializing major industries, the first decade of its existence saw the introduction of a *social* market economy, a combination of capitalism, indeed, with a strong intervening state. This was a part of an overall European trend, and in West Germany, indeed, the extreme poverty and high unemployment that characterized the immediate post-war years were thus overcome. The household income in West Germany grew between 1950 and 1960 by as much as 400 percent. Soon, the outlines of the educational and healthcare systems were being drafted too, and the principles of a welfare state were applied – these too, like in many other European countries at the same time. Somewhat later, the ruined cities and the devastated countryside were quickly rebuilt, reconstructed and receiving their modern present form. Germany became an economic giant, although not yet a major political force.

What did the Jews see in that new Germany? As in the past, of course, not everyone saw the same thing, and different Jews had different perspectives. In Israel, many felt that their trust in German renewal had been reaffirmed in the existence of a renewed Germany, soon to be revitalized by a youthful generation. Formal diplomatic relationships between Israel and the Bundesrepublik were established in May 1965, but informal contacts were frequent and, in fact, all-inclusive as early as the summer of 1953. By that time, German merchandise began to be sent to Israel as part of the reparation agreement, and Israeli oranges were sent to Germany as partial return. Journalists reported on political events in the two countries. Tourism in both directions thrived, and scientific cooperation was outstanding in its depth and breadth. Surely, the migration of some Israelis *back* to Germany was disturbing for others, but even that was considered a minor matter in the face of such an ongoing rapprochement. In 1956, Germany and Israel found themselves on the same side of the Suez Canal conflict, and immediately afterwards, with the direct intervention of the influential Defense Minister in Bonn, Franz Josef Strauss, Israel began to receive military aid from Germany. Even in 1959, when news of antisemitic incidents in Germany reached Israel, Ben-Gurion was as sure as ever of the true "other Germany," as he used to put it. But shortly afterwards, when Adolf Eichmann – responsible for transferring Jews from throughout Europe to extermination camps in the East – was forcefully brought from Argentina to stand trial in Israel, old wounds were reopened.

Even before, the Jews living in Germany again, were increasingly worried about the wave of antisemitic acts late in 1959 and at the beginning of 1960; the German government apparently was too. On January 16, 1960, Adenauer gave a speech, broadcast on all radio and television stations throughout Germany, expressing his deeply felt indignation vis-à-vis the persistent scribbling of Nazi slogans and swastika signs on Jewish graves and on the synagogue walls in Cologne and in Düsseldorf. To be sure, he was particularly worried about the effect of these events on foreign public opinion. Still, many government officials, mostly members of the conservative Christian Democratic Union (CDU), publicly expressed their concern, too. The old elite, despite its own mingling with the Nazis in and outside of government, was generally apprehensive.

Voices expressing similar unease came from some American Jewish organizations, stressing the requirement for better historical enlightenment of the youth in Germany and for acting against educational misguidance by parents and older school teachers. And this same tone of reproach against forgetting and in favor of the need for more historical instruction of the public – old and young – came finally from Israel in the days of the Eichmann trial as well. Thereafter, the so-called Auschwitz Trials in Frankfurt am Main between 1963 and 1965 were, indeed, visited by thousands of school classes – teachers and pupils – and the General State Prosecutor in Hessen, Fritz Bauer, openly and decisively stood behind this pedagogical project.

It was, in fact, Fritz Bauer, from his office in Frankfurt am Main, who had contacted the Israeli Mossad and provided it with details of Eichmann's whereabouts in Argentina. And, while Bauer's biography is by no means typical of the fate or of the behavior of German Jews prior to, during, or after Nazism, it may well stand for the role of the Jews in postwar German society. It was all too often they who pointed out, and were even expected to point out, Nazi perpetrators who were living and acting undisturbed within this society. Jews were indeed standing witnesses of their crimes, even if the best witnesses had been murdered in the concentration camps and the actual witnesses in the planned trials against the perpetrators were more often than not brought from abroad. Living Jews in Germany were sometimes also the plaintiffs – in trying the perpetrators – rarely in actual fact, but always symbolically.

Fritz Bauer was born in 1903 to a highly assimilated Jewish family in Stuttgart.[12] As was often the case, such an apparently secular bourgeois

---

[12] For the biographical details, I have relied primarily on the full and detailed biography by Irmtrud Wojak, *Fritz Bauer 1903–1968: Eine Biographie*, Munich, 2011. See also Ronen Steinke, *Fritz Bauer oder Auschwitz vor Gericht*, Munich, 2015, who pays particular attention to Bauer's Jewish origins and his protagonist's behavior in regard to his

life, typical of his family, was only one generation away from the religiously orthodox lifestyle of the grandparents; in Fritz's case, especially so on his mother's side. Surely, his Jewish roots were deeper than he himself realized or was willing to admit. Bauer once told a touching story of an intimate discussion with his mother, who answered his question "Mummy, what is God?" by quoting a well-known saying that she had probably learned from her father in its Jewish version, namely "That which is hateful to you do not do unto another." "This is the entire Torah," continues the saying of Rabbi Hillel the Elder in the Babylonian Talmud. But, while there seems to have been some Jewishness in his parents' home, it was a few childhood memories, together with incidents of antisemitism at school, that eventually brought home to the young Fritz the meaning of being different. As we have seen in previous chapters, the milieu of assimilated Jews included outspoken German patriotism with a great deal of Goethe, Schiller, and Lessing; love of the fatherland was combined with social concerns, partly grown out of one's own vulnerable status.

Bauer studied law and political science, joined the Social Democratic Party, and soon took an active leadership role in the local Reichsbanner Schwarz–Rot–Gold – the self-defense organization of the Social Democratic Party of Germany (SPD). For some time, he fought for the Weimar democracy, while taking his first steps as a jurist in the legal administration of Württemberg, where he eventually served as a junior judge. He was an energetic and talented man, taking the first steps in what ought to have developed into a brilliant career. But all this abruptly ended on January 30, 1933. As a Social Democratic Party activist and an outspoken anti-Nazi, Bauer was soon imprisoned and sent to a concentration camp, but then, at the end of the same year, suddenly – and for no apparent reason – released. After having been dismissed from his legal post – this time probably because he was a Jew – he still hesitated before deciding to leave Germany for Denmark, where his married sister lived. It was only on the first day of 1940, at the very last moment, that their parents could join them, and shortly thereafter the entire family managed to escape, together with the majority of the Danish Jewry, landing on the shores of Sweden. Just like previously in Denmark, Fritz, together with other exiled social democrats, cooperated with Willy Brandt in publishing their own journal and later on returned to Germany in the spring of 1949.

Jewishness. See especially Chapter 2, pages 28–52, and the first section of Chapter 10, pages 243–252.

Throughout this time, Bauer clearly considered himself a loyal German patriot. He had repeatedly expressed his eagerness to take part in rebuilding a new democratic Germany that would rely upon its liberal tradition despite all that had happened under the Nazis. But, being a Jew, he still found it difficult to get a proper job in the legal administration of the newly constituted country, where his presence seemed "inopportune" even to the Allies' regime. Then, as soon as he took up his first post in the State Prosecutor's office of Braunschweig, he found himself surrounded by some ex-Nazis in the legal administration and was forced to act – directly and indirectly – against them. Throughout this time, Bauer – though he had never made a secret of his Jewishness – was rather careful about presenting himself as a Jew. Surely he always remained one in the eyes of his detractors as well as most of his friends.

It may have been, then, a matter of chance that Bauer could take upon himself the role of *Generalstaatsanwalt* (chief prosecutor) in the so-called "Remer case." At this point, the former General Major Otto Ernst Remer had been charged with publicly – and repeatedly – insulting the men who had planned Hitler's assassination on July 20, 1944. But, in handling his case, Baer immediately set out to go beyond this individual case and bring about the overall rehabilitation of these aristocratic anti-Nazi conspirators. In a passionate courtroom plea, Bauer managed to convince the court, or perhaps only to bring about its concurrence with his claim that resistance to what he then termed an *Unrechtsstaat* (unlawful state) was not only morally required, but also legally permissible. Although the court deliberations lasted no more than a week, they were widely reported in all the West German media and aroused a heated debate. In fact, the Remer trial was the first case against Nazi sympathizers in the early years of the Bundesrepublik processed not by the occupiers, but by a strictly German court, and it involved – even if indirectly – questions regarding the entire role of the military under Hitler's rule. Bauer was treading on dangerous terrain.

At first, unexpectedly, this brought about relative success. The energetic prosecutor continued his campaign of holding Nazi criminals to account and of informing the German public of their crimes when he moved from Braunschweig to Frankfurt am Main in 1956, invited by his SPD comrade Georg-August Zinn, the Hessian Prime Minister at that time. There he was soon caught up in the attempts to bring to trial a triad of major Nazi figures: Eichmann, Bormann, and Mengele.

The story of bringing Eichmann to trial, in Jerusalem to be sure and not in Germany, has been told many times, including the secret involvement of the Frankfurt *Generalstaatsanwalt* in it. From the start, apparently,

Bauer doubted his ability, most particularly his ability as a Jew, to bring about the extradition of Eichmann. By then, he was well aware of the oppositional stand of most German legal officials in matters of bringing Nazis to trial and, in addition, mistrusted the sincerity of the German diplomatic staff in Buenos Aires, as elsewhere. Nevertheless, having failed to conclude the Bormann case and in bringing Mengele to court, Eichmann's prosecution became all the more crucial to him, and he then decided to share the information that came his way regarding the latter's whereabouts in Argentina not with the German authorities, but with the head of the Israeli Delegation in Cologne, Felix Shin'ar. Upon *his* advice, Bauer later contacted the Israeli Mossad, claiming only in retropspect that he had sought Eichmann's extradition from Israel and that the Justice Ministry, upon direct instructions from Bonn, declined to act upon it. Bauer had in the meantime flown to Israel, in fact more than once. There he met his counterpart in the Israeli Justice Ministry, Haim Cohn, born in Lübeck and a former student at the Goethe University in Frankfurt. The two could easily find a common language, though throughout this episode Bauer was apparently known to Ben-Gurion himself only as "a German Jew."[13] Interestingly, the trial in Jerusalem ran along legal principles similar to the ones decided upon by Bauer in the so-called Auschwitz Trial a couple of years later, and Ben-Gurion did in fact use Eichmann's trial in Jerusalem for public educational purposes, just as Bauer later hoped to do in Frankfurt am Main. The Eichmann trial was reported daily for months in all the media, both in Israel and in Germany, and had an enormous effect. For the first time, the fate of the Jews in what came to be called the Holocaust was publicly and openly exposed, by living witnesses and in some detail.

During this period, Bauer continued to look for signs of life for Bormann and for the precise location of Mengele, but all his efforts came to naught. It was at this point that he began preparations for the so-called first Auschwitz Trial, prosecuting a group of twenty-two concentration-camp functionaries, guards, and SS officers. In the slowly changing atmosphere of the Germany of those days, and because the accused were relatively small fish, he could hope to proceed without too much public or administrative obstruction. And then, when the trial began, it immediately aroused much interest and – as could be expected – a great deal of antagonism, too. It surely did not escape the attention of his challengers that their main adversary was a Jew. Bauer was continuously criticized in the press, threatened, and harassed; his apartment house was repeatedly smeared with Nazi insignia.

[13] Wojak, *Fritz Bauer*, 301.

Moreover, he himself was becoming keenly aware of the dilemmas before him. The outcome of this large-scale trial could turn out to be counter-productive, he knew. It could inadvertently strengthen the ever-present antisemitism in the Bundesrepublik. It could produce empathy with the accused, and in the end present them in a false light. It could also jeopardize his own personal position, perhaps even endanger his life. But, by then, Bauer must have felt that here lay his mission in life. He was acting in memory of the victims, no doubt, but above all in order to fortify the young German democracy. Over 200 witnesses appeared in the trial, mostly Jews brought over from various countries, asked to tell their personal stories of agony and survival. Many private individuals and organized groups, especially school classes, came over to listen. The media reported from the court room, and the public effect was considerable. In the end, however, the final verdicts and the individual punishments seemed minimal, though even these absurdly meager results were often criticized as excessive, and the agitation against Bauer continued.

He gained some support, too. For a while the young rebels at the University of Frankfurt, with not a few Jews among them, were captivated both by Bauer's legal efforts and by his personality. He himself continued to lecture, give interviews, and write on all relevant matters, repeatedly meeting with students' groups. At the same time, he was becoming ever more despondent. The Auschwitz Trials now seemed to him to be a failure, after all. To the Israeli journalist Amos Elon, he once said that "the educational effect of these trials was minimal, if indeed they have had any effect at all."[14] And his further attempts to bring to justice Nazi jurists and medical doctors who had served in the so-called euthanasia project T4 were – according to his biographer – "truly catastrophic."[15] It was during these days that Bauer also stated that "when I leave my office, I walk into a foreign land."[16] He sometimes even considered emigrating again and, in a discussion with Danish newspapers in later years, painted a dark picture of the Bundesrepublik – antisemitic and resistant to every true reform. In an undated letter from the end of 1967, complaining of exhaustion, he wrote of the permanent opposition to all his legal decisions. This is how he concluded: "It is horrible to see how these allow the

---

[14] Quoted in Amos Elon, *In einem heimgesuchten Land: Reise eines israelischen Journalisten in beide deutsche Staaten*, Munich, 1966, 376.
[15] See Wojak, *Fritz Bauer*, 396. See also Erardo C. Rautenberg, "Die Bedeutung des Generalstaatsanwalts Dr. Fritz Bauer für die Auseinandersetzung mit dem NS-Unrecht," *Forschungsjournal Soziale Bewegungen*, 28(4) (2015), 162–196.
[16] This has often been quoted. See the extended article in *Der Spiegel*, Nr. 31, July 31, 1995.

'Browns' in this country to unite in organizing a witch-hunt. The Jew shall be burnt."[17]

Fritz Bauer died suddenly on June 30, 1968, probably from a heart attack, bronchitis, and a mixture of sleeping pills with alcohol. He wished to be cremated, strictly against Jewish custom – distancing himself one last time from all things Jewish. Certainly, however, his appraisal of his own achievements was wrong. He did set important new standards in his life-long "search for justice," especially regarding the "duty to disobey," and in his insistence on bringing National-Socialist criminals to trial. Socially, his legacy was a significant contribution to the beginning of what the historian Norbert Frei saw as a long-lasting "fight over memory," which would be conducted intensively in Germany during the following decades.[18]

However, it was still during his lifetime that the important controversy over the limitation period for crimes in general and most particularly for Nazi crimes and acts of inhumanity was publicly raging in Germany, in the press as well as among jurists and politicians. It served as a bitter finale to Bauer's previous legal battles. Apparently, most Germans were against this prolongation or – more precisely – against the further prosecution of Nazi perpetrators, and, unsurprisingly, almost all politicians chose to be led rather than to lead in this matter. Some pressure from foreign governments and international Jewish organizations came from abroad, but it was the critique coming from the Israeli side that received particular attention. "We cannot allow ourselves to be put under pressure from Israel in a matter that is a strictly legal one for us," countered the Free Democratic Party (FDP) Minister of Justice in the Bundestag. And, indeed, the general feeling of the majority was that Jews – in and outside of Germany – ought to stop pressing Germany to bring Nazi perpetrators to trial. They ought no longer to appear as plaintiffs in that imagined court room, artificially constructed within the German public sphere. Franz Josef Strauss, head of the Bavarian Christian Social Union (CSU), brought the matter to a head. It ought no longer to appear, he insisted, as if "only the Germans had committed war crimes."[19]

Beyond legalities, participants in the debate were interested above all in reviving what was considered a "healthy national self-esteem," in Germany and among the Germans. In order to achieve this end, many felt that a *Schlußstrich* (final line) ought to be drawn, and crimes of the past

[17] Wojak, Fritz Bauer, 442.
[18] See Norbert Frei, "Erinnerungskampf: Zur Legitimitationsproblematik des 20. Juli 1944 im Nachkriegsdeutschland," *Gewerkschaftliche Monatshefte*, 46(11) (1995), 669–676.
[19] All quotes are from Herbert, *Geschichte Deutschlands*, 776.

should no longer be considered relevant. The new chancellor, replacing Adenauer in 1963, Ludwig Erhard, was eager to see Germany "step out of the post-war period," as he put it.[20] But, by then, his and all similar hopes were being expressed against the background of a powerful contrary trend, especially felt among the youth, who were now showing growing interest precisely in that past which was all too often being repressed by their elders. In their case, significantly, the stress was no longer on the issue of legal prosecution. This way of dealing with the past was slowly losing its political allure. In effect, it was merely leading to "personalization and psychologization of the criminal character of National Socialism," as the sociologist M. Rainer Lepsius explained in a later article, and to possible disregard of the moral implications of their crimes for the further development of the Bundesrepublik.[21] To be sure, even if the rebellious students themselves played the role of the plaintiffs now vis-à-vis their elders – symbolically, if not always concretely – this whole approach soon reached a dead end. Confrontation with one's parents was in the final analysis a personal act, even if it was multiplied many times over. And, important as this was, the students themselves were aiming higher. They now sought a move that would be meaningful for their project of changing their entire social and political milieu, for the near and distant future.

Thus, it was no longer the Jews that were leading the struggle, but instead a younger generation of German political activists. Some of them, talented young men – and a growing number of young women, too – entered immediately thereafter both the hitherto strictly hierarchical academic establishment and the new research departments of the defunct concentration camps turned memorial sites as well as a number of other institutions, dedicated to the study of National Socialism and the Holocaust. With time, important too were the young individuals who became active in towns and villages – large and small, up and down the country – researching their communities' past on their own initiative, often with their own meager means and against the strict opposition of older local inhabitants.

By the summer of 1968, the students' movement, of which these youths were usually a part, was sweeping the country. It was composed of various

---

[20] Ibid., 777.
[21] See M. Rainer Lepsius, "Das Erbe des Nationalsozialismus und die politische Kultur der Nachfolgestaaten des 'Großdeutschen Reiches,'" in Max Haller, Hans-Joachim Hoffmann-Nowotny, and Wolfgang Zapf (eds.), *Kultur und Gesellschaft: Verhandlungen des 24. Deutschen Soziologentags, des 11. Österreichischen Soziologentags und des 8. Kongresses der Schweizerischen Gesellschaft für Soziologie in Zürich 1988*, Zurich, 1988, 247–264. The quote is from page 260.

groups, some more radical than others, having a variety of political and social goals. A strong Marxist strand was typical of many who targeted the alliance between conservative politicians and capitalist entrepreneurs, which had been dominant in the Bundesrepublik ever since its inception, to the detriment of its poorer and weaker elements, as they argued. Others concentrated on what they saw as the anachronistic structure of the West German universities, protesting against an academic establishment that had cooperated with the ruling political one in the not so distant past and was still doing so in the present. A reawakened womens' rights movement joined in with a great deal of energy, and this complex, explosive mix was spurred to ever more radical action by the opposition to the war in Vietnam and by a sense of solidarity with oppositional students' movements elsewhere in the world – mainly in France, Great Britain, and the United States. The activists enjoyed an exhilarating sense of renewal at that time, while their opponents were often plagued by stifled rage and indignation that were to remain with them very long thereafter.

By then Germany was undergoing other important transformations. In October 1966, the SPD entered a coalition government with the ruling CDU party, and Willy Brandt became first vice-chancellor and foreign minister and then, in 1969, the chancellor. The atmosphere in the country was changing. Brandt introduced a large number of social reforms, financing more generously social welfare, pensions, housing, and educational projects. Thereafter, in a series of bold moves, he strove to normalize relationships with the Soviet Bloc, signing a number of international agreements in which West Germany accepted existing borders in the East. Next came a path-breaking treaty with the DDR, legitimizing the status quo between the two Germanies, and, capping this so-called *Ostpolitik*, his falling to his knees before the Ghetto Heroes' Monument in Warsaw, on December 7, 1970. This was a memorable, even touching scene that carried – and continues to carry – much symbolic value for the overall moral standing of contemporary Germany.

Thus, despite the fact that the government was all too often called upon to act against radical or even violent left-wing demonstrators and against the terrorists of the Red Army Fraction (RAF), this was a time of growing optimism, whose peak was reached with the Olympic Games of 1972. West Germany seemed to be at the height of its international prestige, an open and forward-looking country, a model democracy. Unfortunately, it was precisely during these carefully planned Olympic Games that one of the worst acts of terror in post-war Germany occurred, this time directed at the Israeli athletes in their accommodation at the Olympic Village.

The tragic failure of the security forces to free the nine hostages captured by the Palestinian terrorists made things even worse. Still, writes the historian Ulrich Herbert, "in memory, the Games in Munich remained a symbol of a modern, purified Germany, of which the Germans could be proud again."[22]

German Jews were perhaps somewhat less sanguine. Many of them were preoccupied with quite another matter, one that was probably less central for non-Jews, namely with the fate of Israel. While anxiety in this respect had been somewhat calmed down in the aftermath of the reparation agreement of 1952, fears resurfaced on the eve of the Six-Day War in June 1967, first during the tense weeks before the war and then during the subsequent fierce fighting. Finally, the experience of the quick Israeli victory turned out to be formative for many Jews outside of Israel, strengthening their ties with that country as well as their collective Jewish solidarity. At first, in fact, both Jews and non-Jews shared this enthusiasm. However, this was only a short-term phase, a kind of intermission.

Soon, the next war was being fought, namely the Yom Kippur War of 1973, when "a praying and fasting people were suddenly attacked," as Hans Mayer sympathetically, perhaps even somewhat sentimentally, later wrote. In its aftermath, as he added, "the attitude in the West, and especially in Germany, became considerably cooler."[23] Israel was now being harshly criticized for its policies against the population in the occupied territories, and for many – including at least some of the left-wing Jewish students within the students' movement – it now stood for colonialist behavior to be criticized, repudiated and renounced. Efforts undertaken by a number of intellectuals to steer a balance between their critique of Israel and the tendency within their ranks to equate Israeli practices not only with the French in Algeria, but even with the Nazis, did not manage to solve the dilemma.

Israel was a "bold experiment," Mayer stated, taking this expression from an earlier book by Friedrich Dürrenmatt. As a result, Jews in Germany, setting such high moral standards for their own country, found that the situation became awkward, indeed. "In a land almost without Jews," he adds, "in discussing foreigners, refugees, and other strangers, the non-existent Jews were always included." The Jews, always different to some extent, were standing for the difference of all others, among them the various newcomers to the Bundesrepublik from Turkey

---

[22] Herbert, *Geschichte Deutschlands*, 882.
[23] See the text of his speech given in Cologne on the Israeli Day of Independence 1996, Hans Mayer, "Deutsche und Juden am Ende des Jahrhunderts," in Hans Mayer, *Reisen nach Jerusalem*, Frankfurt am Main, 1997, 151–173; the quotes are from pages 169–170.

and from some of the countries in Southern Europe. At that early stage, and in the eyes of all others, they were still the paradigmatic victims, demanding justice for all. As for themselves, however, following their years of ordeal, German Jews concentrated now ever more intensely on rebuilding their communities and rehabilitating their private lives. The confrontation with the National Socialist past had by then been taken over by the 1968ers and, with the passage of time, by a new generation of investigators and historians too, all working outside of and beyond the memories of the survivors.

12 Strangers at Home

Beginning in the mid 1970s, Germany became a land of emigration. Government spokesmen repeatedly tried to deny this fact, but to no avail. From 1955 until the first oil crisis of 1973, a gigantic demand for labor, produced by the quick economic recovery of Germany, meant that some fourteen million workers immigrated into West Germany, at first coming on a short-term basis, from Italy, Spain, and Portugal, and particularly from Turkey. Owing to the quickly reduced demand once the recession of 1966–1967 was felt everywhere, some eleven million returned to their homelands. Nevertheless, by 1980 there were still as many as 4.4 million foreign workers in Germany, many of them striving to stay permanently after having brought over their families to live with them in the new country.

Jews were never the only minority in Germany, but now, under the new circumstances, they were a particularly small one. To be sure, among the incoming workers from various countries there was also a contingent of Soviet Jews who preferred Germany to Israel and managed to filter in, always in small numbers. It was later that a larger wave came over, during the 1990s, but even accounting for them, Jews remained a smaller minority than they had ever been in pre-Nazi Germany. Following the Munich debacle in 1972 and then the bomb attacks on synagogues, together with the smearing and destruction of gravestones – old and new – they required permanent protection now, while at the same time they were closing in upon themselves, mainly preoccupied with their own private and intra-group affairs.

From the outset it was the atmosphere in the city of Frankfurt am Main that served as a measurement for the new status of the Jews in Germany, and it was, indeed, particularly unrestful there during much of the 1970s. By then, radical students were attempting to prevent the renovation of some buildings in the old Westend of the city, seeing in it a battle against the dislocation of the poor for the purpose of enriching the rich, or – differently put – against exploitative capitalism. The fact that Jews were among the owners of some of these buildings and resisted the students' action, together with others, heated the situation, and the fight was further inflamed as the young rebels tried to prevent the destruction of a few archeological remains of the old Judengasse (the former Jewish ghetto), likewise part of the old city's renovation. Later still, in 1984, spirits were roused by the insistence of the City Theater on staging the world premiere of Rainer Werner Fassbinder's play *Der Müll, die Stadt, und der Tod (Garbage, the City and Death)*, which was seen by many as blatantly antisemitic. At this point, it was the conservative Jewish community heads that took the lead, preventing the event by an act of civil disobedience, occupying the theater's stage. If, in fact, this incident signaled the end of the "protection period" for the Jews in the Bundesrepublik, it also indicated the end of their shadow-like existence, most particularly that of their institutional leadership. Individual leaders were now beginning to step out into the open, no longer relying on covered-up contacts with politicians and on half-secret arrangements with government officials. Security – personal and communal – until then the main purpose of Jewish organizations, both the Zentralrat (Central Council) and the local community heads, was now being replaced by demands for civil recognition and proper respect. And this shift, expectedly, brought about new confrontations, sometimes more tension and more open strife.

The worst confrontation occurred during the joint visit of Chancellor Kohl and President Reagan in May 1985 to the military cemetery in the township of Bitburg, not far from Trier, where not only Wehrmacht soldiers but also Waffen-SS men were buried side by side. The choreography of the two heads of state honoring the fallen in this way turned out to be an international scandal. Even their common visit to the remnants of the Bergen-Belsen concentration camp did not succeed in calming the indignation. A couple of years later, there was an equally embarrassing public uproar in reaction to a speech given by the President of the Bundestag, Philipp Jenninger, on November 10, 1988. The occasion was planned as the central item in commemorating the fiftieth anniversary of the November Pogrom in 1938, but, although the intentions were good, the wording chosen by the speaker was scandalous. Jenninger tried to explain the attraction of National Socialism to contemporary Germans, thus openly creating a distinction between Germans and Jews, between "we" and "they" – apparently irritating and insulting all. Germany was, no doubt, seeking ways to respectfully commemorate its victims, but it seemed that Jews in Germany, often Holocaust survivors, could not stand side by side with non-Jewish Germans in performing this task. On the other hand, at least some of them *could* stand together in acknowledging the more general lessons of the past. On May 8, 1985, in a festive speech on the occasion of the fortieth anniversary to the end of the Second World War, President Richard von Weizsäcker openly declared that this was "a day of liberation," not merely the closing day of the war. While rejecting collective guilt, he stressed the need to remember and face up to the past, "looking truth straight in the eye – without embellishment and without distortion," as he put it.[1] This speech, which gained a great deal of approval – though it was met with some opposition, too – could be considered a turning point.

Efforts to rethink the nature of National Socialism and the magnitude of its crimes in post-war Germany began earlier, of course. They were noticed and commented upon in an insightful little volume, published by Saul Friedländer, first in French and immediately afterwards, as early as 1982, in German and in English. In this book, the respected Israeli historian, who survived the Shoah as a youngster, contemplated the handling of Nazism and the Holocaust in contemporary European – not only German – popular culture. The book appeared in English under the title *Reflections of Nazism: An Essay on Kitsch and Death*, but in the German edition its thesis was still more strongly stressed by cleverly reversing the order of title and subtitle on its front page.[2] Apparently, even during the mid 1950s, it was possible to notice the approaching "Hitler wave" of the 1960s and later on the writings of counter-histories of the so-called Third Reich, glorifying the soldiers of the Wehrmacht on the eastern front, conveniently leaving out other events, or what Friedländer later, in the second volume of his memoirs, called the "criminal side of the coin."[3] Meanwhile, it was the Holocaust that moved to the center of public attention. The NBC television series under this title was screened in Germany in January 1979, combining effectively what Friedländer diagnosed as "syrup mentality" with scenes of extreme violence. Coming apparently at the right moment, this mini-series had a considerable effect, seemingly deepening public interest in the extermination of the Jews, and sharpening even the contemporary academic discourse on the relevant issues.

Many years later, Friedländer goes into the details of his relevant past experiences. On the whole, as he began to visit Germany more often in the

---

[1] For the full text of this speech, see Richard von Weizsäcker, "Zum 40. Jahrestag der Beendigung des Krieges in Europa und der nationalsozialistischen Gewaltherrschaft," in Richard von Weizsäcker, *Reden und Interviews*, Vol. I: *1. Juli 1984–30. Juni 1985*, Bonn, 1986, 279–310.
[2] Saul Friedländer, *Kitsch und Tod: Der Widerschein des Nazismus*, Frankfurt am Main, 1982; English version *Reflections of Nazism: An Essay on Kitsch and Death*, New York, 1982.
[3] Saul Friedländer, *Where Memory Leads: My Life*, New York, 2016, 192.

early 1980s, the Bundesrepublik was perceptibly moving to the right and, in the fall of 1982, Helmut Kohl, until then head of the CDU fraction in the parliament, was voted chancellor, to be later handsomely confirmed in this post by the early elections of 1983. He was to remain chancellor until 1998. Neoliberal winds, likewise pushing German society to the right since the 1980s, were directing the economy away from the social democratic welfare state, seeking means to combat recession, the slowing down of economic growth, and the general disappointment with the grand hopes of a previous era. Meanwhile, the Cold War, somewhat relaxed during the previous decade, was entering – as it turned out – its last stage, and an insistence on a prouder, more positively trimmed national consciousness in Germany seemed now to have emerged through various channels. Clearly, a particularly important one was the contemporary discourse of historians, as once more observed and recorded by Friedländer.

January 1983 brought with it memorial ceremonies and historical conferences to commemorate fifty years since the coming to power of the Nazis. In May 1984, a large-scale international conference on the Holocaust was convened in Stuttgart. Martin Broszat, among the outstanding historians at the time, did not give a lecture, but his sporadic remarks sufficed to cause an immediate controversy with Friedländer, which later led first to the publication of Broszat's article in the widely read *Merkur* entitled "A Plea for the Historicization of National Socialism," dated May 1985,[4] and then to that exchange of letters between the two, previously mentioned in this book.[5] Ernst Nolte's little-noticed piece "The Third Reich Seen from the Perspective of the 1980s" was meanwhile published in a volume of collected papers in England and served as a prelude to his much better-known piece, the opening chord for the publicly staged *Historikerstreit*, "Vergangenheit, die nicht vergehen will" (The Past That Will Not Pass). This appeared in the *Frankfurter Allgemeine Zeitung* of June 6, 1986.

The philosopher Jürgen Habermas and a gallery of distinguished historians soon joined this debate, while matters quickly became particularly heated in the wake of the publication of Andreas Hillgruber's book *Zweierlei Untergang: Die Zerschlagung des Deutschen Reiches und das Ende des europäischen Judentums* (*Two Kinds of Ruin: The Fall of the German*

---

[4] Martin Broszat, "Plädoyer für eine Historisierung des Nationalsozialismus," *Merkur*, 435 (1985), 373–385.
[5] For the details of this encounter, see Friedländer, *Where Memory Leads*, 224–225. See also Martin Broszat and Saul Friedländer, "Um die 'Historisierung des Nationalsozialismus.' Ein Briefwechsel," *Vierteljahrshefte für Zeitgeschichte*, 36(2) (1986), 339–372; English translation *Yad Vashem Studies*, 19 (1988), and Chapter 10 above.

Reich and the End of European Jewry) late in 1986. Hillgruber rhapsodized in its first part on the glory of the Wehrmacht in defending the eastern Prussian provinces and mourned the tragic loss of this "middle-European balancing state," namely Prussia, at the hands of the Red Army. In the second part of his book, he then dryly and concisely described the extermination of the Jews by the Nazis, implicitly – or so it seemed – comparing the two "projects." The book aroused irritation among British and American scholars as well as many German historians, turning the controversy into an ideological as well as a methodological one, all with obvious political implications.[6] It seems that the efforts of the three historians Broszat, Nolte, and Hillgruber to save at least some aspects of Nazism for a presumably more balanced history and by doing so provide Germany with that sought-for national narrative, needed for building up a solid and unperturbed identity, reached a dead end. Broszat had done it by stressing the line separating Nazis from other Germans, emphasizing daily life and resistance to Nazism on the smallest scale. Nolte, originally known as a highly respected expert on European fascism, strove to relativize National Socialism by comparing it with Bolshevism, showing the first, in fact, to be a mere copy of the second. And Hillgruber proceeded to save the honor of old Prussia and underline the suffering of its conquered population, even as he compared it with the agony of the Jews in the Holocaust. All three were finally held back mostly by their German colleagues, and as the controversy came to its end, it seemed that an honest balance had finally been achieved.

At this stage it was not Friedländer who achieved this balance; in fact, he did not even participate in the debate. Instead, it was Dan Diner, himself a German Jew, who in his book *Zivilisationsbruch: Denken nach Auschwitz* (*Rupture in Civilization: Thinking after Auschwitz*), published early in 1988, managed to turn the discussion away from issues of war and peace and back to the preeminence of the Holocaust. Friedländer's single handed effort to save the legitimacy of a Jewish perspective on German history came only a decade later, with his two volumes *Nazi Germany and the Jews*, appearing in 1997 and 2007. The last word was again left to Richard von Weizsäcker, who was invited to the West German Historians' Congress of 1988 and in his speech reaffirmed the uniqueness of the Holocaust and the need to tell its history and commemorate its victims. His audience seemed to agree. The decency of the West German Republic was confirmed, and the importance of facing

---

[6] The best critical English presentation of the debate and its historiographical background is Richard J. Evans, "The New Nationalism and the Old History: Perspectives on the West German *Historikerstreit*," *The Journal of Modern History*, 59(4) (1987), 761–797.

the past with all its horrors was generally reasserted. It was just in time, indeed, since a new and unexpected drama was now brewing, this time truly on the world's stage.

On November 9, 1989 – strangely, no doubt, yet again on this same date – the gates of the Berlin Wall were opened and soon it was completely dismantled, together with the state that had erected it almost three decades earlier. Within less than a year, the two Germanies were united. This came after months of demonstrations, especially in East Berlin and in Leipzig, in which thousands of DDR citizens demanded reforms and exerted mass pressure on their government. Others simply wished to leave for the West and were finally doing so, in fact, through Hungary and across the Austrian border. In the meantime, various political groups were hastily formed, at first unanimously demanding the democratization of the DDR under the slogan "We are *the Volk*" and later allowing this slogan to almost imperceptibly turn and read "We are *one Volk*," demanding union with the Bundesrepublik.

Even in the recent days of the Historians' Debate, such a union had not been deemed feasible. In the West, most observers agreed that a German nation-state, more or less within the Bismarckian borders, was forever lost and that one had to accept the Bundesrepublik as a proper substitute, a fatherland in its own right, worthy of loyalty even for those who criticized it. It was, after all, a successful capitalist-style country in prosperous and less prosperous times, enjoying a measure of prestige on the international stage and a great deal of influence in Europe. In fact, an overall European identity was gradually replacing the national one, some believed, and a limited Federal Republic with its present constitution well fitted within it. A majority of German intellectuals no longer relied upon the validity of ethnic collectivities and preferred the democratic order through which their post-national stable political existence had finally been achieved.

Now, suddenly, a quick reorientation was urgently needed on both sides of the German–German border, while speedy decision-making and effective international diplomacy were the order of the day. In addition, each Germany had to find ways of coordinating its policies with its own allies. In the East, most significantly, it soon became clear that the USSR, which in the past had prevented every attempt at reform by sending in its tanks, was no longer in a position to do so. The Soviet Union was itself in a process of disintegration. The pressure of keeping up an armaments race with the United States had brought its economy into total disarray. The entire federation was shaken. On October 6 and 7, 1989, moreover, Mikhail Gorbachev, Chair of the Communist Party himself urged the leadership of the Sozialistische Einheitspartei Deutschlands

(Socialist Unity Party of Germany, SED), still ruling uncontested, to take the path of reform. And then, on the next Monday, October 9, some 70,000 marched peacefully in Leipzig, demanding, indeed, the introduction of radical reforms. The communist state was now fighting for its life.

Among its last efforts, the overwhelmed state leadership of the DDR tried a new tactic on issues related to the Jews, not unlike Adenauer's prior move during the 1950s, and in both cases – no doubt – a hidden reliance on old antisemitic clichés seems to have been involved. Erich Honecker first met with Siegmund Rotstein, president of the Verband der Jüdischen Gemeinden in der DDR (Association of the Jewish Communities in the DDR) early in 1988 and thereafter with the Chairman of the West German Zentralrat, Heinz Galinski, who came for a visit from West Berlin. In preparation for a commemoration of the November Pogrom of 1938, conspicuously planned now for the first time ever in the DDR, the government even invited guests from Israel – which had long been a target of hostile propaganda in East Germany that had occasionally even supported terrorist activities against the Jewish state.[7] Now, the Israeli Minister of Internal Affairs, Dresden-born Joseph Burg, was invited together with the by then Chairman of the Yad Vashem Memorial Institution in Jerusalem, Yitzhak Arad. These were the first official Israeli guests to the DDR since its establishment and, as it turned out, also the last. In discussions with Edgar Bronfman, President of the Jewish World Congress, clearly aimed at indirectly reaching better relationships with the United States, Honecker finally expressed readiness to negotiate reparations for Jews living outside the DDR, though these were last-minute concessions that apparently had no practical consequences.

Up to this point, the National Socialist past and the Nazi crimes had always been handled by the DDR in the context of its declared anti-fascism. The communist leadership of this country, a member of the Warsaw Pact and part of the European Soviet bloc, had indeed belonged to the resistance and spent much of the Nazi period in exile, mostly in Russia. Thus, in that additional process of "universalization," to use Rainer Lepsius' fitting phrase again, issues of guilt and the need to confront and commemorate Nazi crimes played a different role in the political culture of the DDR than they did in that of the Bundesrepublik.[8]

---

[7] For details, see Jeffrey Herf, *Unerklärte Kriege gegen Israel: Die DDR und die westdeutsche radikale Linke, 1967–1989*, Göttingen, 2019.
[8] See M. Rainer Lepsius, "Das Erbe des Nationalsozialismus und die politische Kultur der Nachfolgestaaten des 'Großdeutschen Reiches,'" in Max Haller, Hans-Joachim Hoffmann-Nowotny, and Wolfgang Zapf (eds.), *Kultur und Gesellschaft: Verhandlungen des 24. Deutschen Soziologentags, des 11. Österreichischen Soziologentags und des 8. Kongresses der Schweizerischen Gesellschaft für Soziologie in Zürich 1988*, Zurich, 1988, 247–264.

The few hundred openly Jewish citizens in East Germany, defined as "victims of National Socialism," were awarded some social and financial advantages from the start, but they were at no point considered as critical in constructing a view of the past as the heroic communist opponents of the regime and the triumphant Soviet army that had in the end successfully fought against it. Most related policies in the DDR were in any case dictated by the Russian occupiers, who were supposed to be regarded not only as liberators, but also as "beloved friends" and brethern. Now, by the late 1980s, another approach was required, both towards the Soviets and towards the Jews.

There followed days of indecision until the unexpected fall of the wall, marking the end of the Cold War, the collapse of the Iron Curtain, and then of communism as such, even in the Soviet Union. These were affairs of world-historical significance and a moment of critical change in the so-called German–German affairs. But, even at that later date, forty-five years after the end of the war, the quickly evolving transformations apparently involved issues related to the Jews. In the East, a new democratically elected Volkskammer (Parliament) was established, and perhaps its single most significant act was the declaration of April 14, which in four detailed paragraphs accepted joint responsibility for the German past and specifically for the National Socialists' crimes against the Jews. It then asked forgiveness from the hitherto hated state of Israel, promising restitutions as well as the generous maintenance of the small Jewish community in the country.[9] In the end, this new awareness brought about only two practical moves: the undertaking of a costly project to renovate the Oranienburgerstraße synagogue in Berlin, and – surely of much greater significance – the opening of the East German borders for Jewish migrants from the Soviet Union – a policy later continued, though not without some restrictions, by the united Germany.

Finally, it was the continuing stream of Germans from the East to the West and then the application of a common currency to the two Germanies on July 1, 1990 that made the further existence of the DDR no longer feasible, and, with the signing of all the requisite documents, unification became a political fact on October 3, 1990. While Chancellor Kohl was directing the process with unerring resolve, Willy Brandt too, at the time honorary chairman of the SPD, was in favor of quick unification, airing his nicely ringing and memorable slogan: "now what belongs together will grow [back] together."[10]

[9] See the full text in the *Süddeutsche Zeitung*, April 14–16, 1990.
[10] For the exact place and date of this utterance, see Bernd Rother, "Gilt das gesprochene Wort? Wann und wo sagte Willy Brandt 'Jetzt wächst zusammen, was zusammengehört?,'" *Deutschland Archiv*, 30(1) (2000), 90–93.

The unification, to be sure, was not inevitable. After all, Germany's existence as a nation-state had lasted only seventy-five years, or – if one excludes the Nazi era, in which it acted as a multinational empire – even less.[11] This short-lived polity, moreover, had mainly been based on the aggressive policy of Bismarck, who intended to achieve an enlarged Prussia, free of its centuries-old subservience to, and later its cumbersome confederative ties with, Austria. Thus, the option of two – or rather three, counting Austria – German-speaking states in Central Europe or under the umbrella of the European Union was historically as legitimate as the option that was by then so clearly preferred by the majority of contemporary Germans, on both sides of the border, namely the unification of East and West into a single Germany. To be sure, this did not happen without opposition. Not a few citizens of the defunct DDR rejected the *Anschluß* (annexation-like) character of the emerging agreement between the two states and the rude way in which many agreed-upon arrangements dismissed the communist experience lock, stock, and barrel. Voices of disapproval were heard in the West as well. Among politicians, Oskar Lafontaine, the Social Democratic Party's candidate for chancellor, warned against the growing nationalism in the process of unification, while Jürgen Habermas, in what became a famous article, criticized the total dismantling of the DDR and urged the Germans on both sides of the prior divide to give up their nationalist dreams and uphold loyalty to the "universalist principles of citizenship" over all other forms of identity.[12] No less impressive was Günther Grass' appeal, articulating the views of at least some on the West German left by criticizing what he too saw as the discarding of the achievements of the democratic movement in the DDR, trusting that "the German forgetfulness will take care of it" and declaring "my fatherland needs to be many-sided, more colorful, friendlier with its neighbors, wiser the hard way, more compatible with Europe." For him, the right solution was a German federation rather than a complete unification, based on the history of Germany as a cultural nation, not on economic power games and political aggression.[13]

Significantly, both of these authors brought Auschwitz into their arguments, as if no change in Germany could be made without coming to terms with that aspect of its history. "Whoever now thinks and seeks

---

[11] At that time, I argued in the same vein. See my "Die deutsche Einheit ist kein Imperativ der Geschichte," *Süddeutsche Zeitung*, February 8, 1990.

[12] See Jürgen Habermas, "Yet Again German Identity: A Unified Nation of Angry DM-Burghers?," *New German Critique*, 52 (1991), 84–101. For an earlier and sharper, though in essence similar text see Jürgen Habermas, "Der DM-Nationalismus," *Die Zeit*, March 30, 1990.

[13] See Günther Grass, "Kurze Rede eines vaterlandslosen Gesellen," *Die Zeit*, February 9, 1990.

answers for the 'German Question' must also think of Auschwitz," wrote Grass, while Habermas stated that Auschwitz must remind the Germans that "they can no longer rely on the continuity of their own history," and must now constitute their identity on the basis of something other than their joint past and culture. They could no longer depend on an old-style nation-state à la Bismarck.[14] Both apparently felt called upon to use Auschwitz, so to speak, in order to strengthen their respective arguments, sealing them with this final, irrefutable imprimatur.

Opposition to unification was more widespread and perhaps also more heartfelt abroad. At the very outset of the process, both Margaret Thatcher and François Mitterrand were more than reluctant to see a united Germany in Central Europe. They were at first truly alarmed. The Americans, on the other hand, while insisting on adding their own conditions to the deal, were in principle ready to accept it; and the Russians, who at first strictly opposed unification, eventually came round, preoccupied as they were with their own affairs. Soon, while everyone else accepted the run of events, only one country persisted somewhat longer in expressing reservations, even fear, vis-à-vis a united Germany, though clearly it could do nothing to prevent it – namely, Israel.

The news agency AP summarized the views in Israel in the days following the fall of the Berlin Wall: "Happiness at the Falling of the Wall. Suspicion over Reunification of Germany," ran the headline of the major evening paper in the country, it reported. Shimon Peres, vice-premier in those days, not a man known for being delusional, asked rhetorically in a television interview: "When we hear of a united Germany, we must ask what kind of Germany will it be? A Germany with or without an army? A militarized or demilitarized Germany?"[15] And some were even more outspoken, expressing fear of rising fascism and even of yet another world war.

In an article published by *New German Critique* in winter 1991, German-born Israeli and later Austrian historian Frank Stern expressed his concerns and reservations. "It remains a decisive question for the future," he wrote, "as to whether the date November 9th will be principally associated in German historical consciousness with the fall of the wall or with the 1938 pogrom." And later, more explicitly, he adds that "it is my suspicion that the process of German unification and its aftermath can be dangerously fertile ground for new antisemitic sentiments infused with older content." Stern feared that a German majority would now tend

---

[14] Ibid. and Habermas, "Yet again German Identity," 98.
[15] Quoted from a journalist's report in AP, November 13, 1989.

to develop "aversions" towards alien minorities – "Jews, foreigners, seekers of asylum,"[16] while Dan Diner, for his part, explained, in a lecture delivered before formal reunification had occurred, that, whereas for the Bundesrepublik since 1949 even the mere existence of Jews provided the needed legitimacy, for a later Germany, their "active agreement" had now become necessary. In a resigned mood he then finally concluded that "[I]t appears to make little sense to oppose people who at any, really any, price are determined to be happy."[17] There were, indeed, many happy people in the streets of the newly united Germany. In those early days, only a few could foresee how difficult unification would turn out to be.

In fact, most of the gloomy prophesies voiced at the time remained unfulfilled. To the surprise of many, some turned out to be entirely off the mark. For instance, interest in the Nazi past or in the Holocaust did not decrease, but rather grew explosively. The sales of books on these topics increased exponentially.[18] The opening of the archives in Eastern Europe enabled historians to provide detailed descriptions of events under German occupation during the Second World War, and the German public was eager to learn about it. This interest has been proven several times over with the appearance of Daniel Goldhagen's book *Hitler's Willing Executioners: Ordinary Germans and the Holocaust* in 1996. The young Jewish-American author concentrated on the actual practice of extermination and provided some previously unknown details, especially about the horrors of the "death marches" in the summer and early autumn of 1944, during which approximately a quarter of a million camp prisoners died, either by exhaustion or at the hands of their camp guards. All this capped a prolonged introductory part, in which Goldhagen expressed his main thesis, considering the Holocaust a "national project of the Germans," based on centuries of unremitting "eliminatory antisemitism."[19] Despite the harsh critique it elicited from many respectable historians, the book in its German translation sold upon publication some 80,000 copies and gave rise to a heated

---

[16] See Frank Stern, "The 'Jewish Question' in the 'German Question,' 1945–1990: Reflections in Light of November 9th, 1989," *New German Critique*, 52 (1991), 155–172. The quotes are from pages 166–169.
[17] See Dan Diner, "Zwischen Bundesrepublik und Deutschland. Ein Vortrag," in Hajo Funke (ed.), *Von der Gnade der geschenkten Nation: Zur politischen Moral der Bonner Republik*, Berlin, 1988, 188–199. The quotes are from pages 197–198.
[18] For exact figures, see Herbert, *Geschichte Deutschlands*, 1193.
[19] See Daniel Jonah Goldhagen, *Hitler's Willing Executioners: Ordinary Germans and the Holocaust*, New York, 1996; German edition *Hitlers willige Vollstrecker: Ganz gewöhnliche Deutsche und der Holocaust*, Berlin, 1996. For the quotes and a short summary of the so-called Goldhagen controversy, see Herbert, *Geschichte Deutschlands*, 1194–1195.

public discussion. The historian Fritz Stern, for instance, attacked Goldhagen above all for his methodology, for arguing out of context, and for his intention to present all Germans as potential murderers, a claim that was, according to Stern – "deeply unhistorical."[20] Nevertheless, Goldhagen's straightforward one-dimensional explanation and his uncompromising thesis readily circulated among his readers, and it was perhaps his later insistence that he did not mean to apply the accusation of collective guilt to the present generation of Germans that made his book into a best-seller. It apparently provided a kind of societal catharsis, after which some relaxation could be achieved.

In fact, no such relaxation was felt, and related issues did not cease to preoccupy the public. First among them was the role of the Wehrmacht in the extermination of the Jews and in the killing of Polish and Russian civilians on the eastern front. An exhibition on these themes, set up by the Institute for Social Research in Hamburg, opened its gates early in 1995, leading to a fierce public debate. On March 1, 1997, some 5,000 people marched in protest through the streets of Munich – seemingly the largest neo-Nazi demonstration since 1945. Finally, the heated controversy gradually subsided after a dramatic meeting of the Bundestag, during which some members of parliament defended the "clean" army that presumably stood for "the entire population of the war era" and others defended the presented documentation as it stood. A touching personal rejoinder by Otto Schily, originally of the Green Party and by then speaker for the SPD, seemed to close the matter.[21] Despite the fact that the exhibition included a number of wrongly attributed photos, it went on to be displayed in 33 cities throughout Germany and was attended by an estimated 800,000 visitors.

Meanwhile, whereas some Germans, though by no means all, now finally felt forced to confront the extent of the Nazi crimes, others were already moving beyond that, seeking ways of publicly commemorating the victims. In 1995, Günther Demnig, an artist from the city of Cologne, managed to convince the local authorities to insert cobblestone-size memorials for individual Jewish victims into the public pavements in front of their former homes. The idea of these *Stolpersteine* (stumbling stones) was quickly taken up by numerous other cities, where this project was seen as a way of bringing home the memory of real victims to everyone, everywhere, and on a daily basis. As could have been expected, this, once again, was not

---

[20] See Fritz Stern, "Die Goldhagen-Debatte," in Fritz Stern, *Der Traum von Frieden und die Versuchung der Macht*, Berlin, 1999, 292–308. The quote is from page 294.
[21] See Herbert, *Geschichte Deutschlands*, 1199–1200.

acceptable to all; some Jewish personalities, for instance the President of the Jewish Community in Munich, Charlotte Knobloch, saw in it a desecration of the deceased. Elsewhere, however, minute memorials of this kind became widespread, usually much appreciated by relatives of the deceased, their former neighbors, and their few surviving friends. At the same time, a large-scale memorial in the center of Berlin was being contemplated and then actually planned, likewise arousing an intense controversy well beyond the boundaries of the capital.

To be sure, most people may not have been aware of the general content and certainly not of the details of this or that ongoing debate. The arguments were mainly conducted on the pages of the national press, and not always on the front pages even there. For the educated elite and the intellectuals, they were often crucial, and most Jews must have followed them as closely as possible. But then, the high point of it all was reached in an entirely unexpected form.

On a Sunday morning, October 11, 1998, novelist Martin Walser was to receive the prestigious Friedenspreis des Deutschen Buchhandels (Peace Prize of the German Book Trade) in the Paulskirche in Frankfurt. The entire intellectual and political elite of the country, a few hundred people, were invited to the ceremony. As it turned out, Walser decided to use this opportunity to express his irritation with the way Germany was handling the rituals of commemorating Nazi victims and, more generally, confronting the past, before and during the Second World War. He opened in a surprisingly bitter tone of complaint, implicitly presenting himself and all other Germans as the victims of a false *Erinnerungskultur* (memory culture), having to face day in and day out their own *Schande* – a term he used repeatedly – namely, their own, deep-seated disgrace. This permanent exhortation, he claimed, was being carried out not for the purpose of "memorizing and enlightening," but with the intention of "accusing", accusing all Germans, making use of their disgrace for "present purposes," finally "monumentalizing" it with "a nightmare the size of a football pitch." As his audience must have immediately realized, he was referring to the planned Berlin memorial. Auschwitz, he went on to complain, as if oblivious to the force of his words, was being held against "us" by an army of self-appointed "conscience guardians," used against us as a *Moralkeule*, a moral club.[22]

This must have been Walser's privately held opinion for some time. However, it could have hardly been expected that he would think it appropriate to share it with the entire nation on this festive occasion,

---

[22] All the quotes are from Frank Schirrmacher (ed.), *Die Walser–Bubis-Debatte: Eine Dokumentation*, Frankfurt am Main, 1999, 12f.

giving it widespread legitimacy and making it, in fact, *Salonfähig*. The dangerous implications of such a public confession, especially its effect on the younger generation, who were now being taught about the horrors they did not personally experience, and its boost for neo-Nazis and their like on the extreme right were either consciously willed by him or at least considered insignificant in comparison with his need to give vent to his frustration.

In the end, the reactions to his speech were even more unsettling. When, precisely 120 years earlier, the historian Heinrich von Treitschke publicly announced his support of antisemitism, the first response came from the equally prestigious professor of Roman history Theodor Mommsen, energetically repudiating his colleague's position. Somewhat later, a joint petition signed by other notable scholars, arguing against antisemitism, had been published and a stream of counter-arguments by Jews and non-Jews alike could be read in the pages of the national and local press everywhere in the Germany of that day.[23] Towards the close of the twentieth century, the crowd in the Paulskirche responded to Walser's performance with a standing ovation. At that moment, the only adverse reaction came from the president of the Zentralrat der Juden, Ignaz Bubis, who was present in the hall and conspicuously did not applaud. Immediately after the ceremony, he criticized the speech as "spiritual arson," and later on denounced it as propagating a dangerous "intellectual nationalism."[24] Moreover, in the immediate aftermath of this event, the press published practically only positive responses to Walser's speech, some of which included in addition more or less open attacks on Bubis' critique. These responses became all the more vehement after Bubis reformulated and perhaps also reinforced his position on November 9 – the fiftieth anniversary of the so-called Kristallnacht – in a speech given at the Rykestraße synagogue in Berlin. At this point, self-righteous responses came from Klaus von Dohnanyi, the one-time SPD mayor of Hamburg, whose father Hans had been a member of the resistance group associated with the attempt on Hitler's life in summer 1944. Even sharper and more unambiguous were the words used by Rudolf Augstein, editor *of Der Spiegel*. Clearly, support for Walser did not come only from the far right or from the margins of society. It was being expressed by more or less prominent voices from the center or even, directly and indirectly, from the so-called

---

[23] See Chapter 7, pages 114–116.
[24] The quotes here and later in this chapter are from Hans-Joachim Hahn, "Die Rolle von Ignaz Bubis in der Walser–Bubis Debatte," in Fritz Backhaus, Raphael Gross, and Michael Lenarz (eds.), *Ignaz Bubis: Ein jüdisches Leben in Deutschland*, Frankfurt am Main, 2007, 149–155.

establishment. Particularly unsettling was the fact that the debate created a confrontation between Germans and German-Jews, or simply between Germans and Jews, as Henryk Broder later wrote, arguing "about the topic that must divide them most deeply, the Holocaust and the ways by which one ought to come to terms with it today."[25] Despite the efforts to close the gap that had been opened here again, a return to the intimacy of previous generations, limited as it had sometimes been, was now impossible.

Bubis could well serve as an example for those who had always insisted on the need to bridge this gap and on the possibility of closing it. Born in Breslau to parents of Polish-Jewish origins, Ignaz – eight years old – was forced to leave Germany with his family in 1935.[26] The family later came under Nazi occupation in Poland and he, after living for a time in the local ghetto, was transported to a labor camp. Though his father and two of his siblings were murdered, he himself managed to survive the war. Having then immediately begun a career as a businessman, dealing with jewelry and precious metals, Bubis eventually moved from Dresden to Frankfurt in 1956 and became a real-estate entrepreneur as well. He was soon to be involved in the struggle over the renovation of the old city center, being attacked as a heartless speculator, worse still as a "*Jewish* speculator" by the student opposition in town. Indeed, Bubis remained a highly controversial figure, all the more so since in the mid 1980s he surprised his critics on the left by leading an act of civil disobedience in an effort to prevent the staging of a play by Fassbinder, as mentioned before. By the 1980s, Bubis was clearly an outstanding, well-known public figure, even on the national stage – an unusual position for a German Jew in contemporary Germany. He was a member of the FDP, a locally elected representative of the Frankfurt City Government, and Chairman of the Zentralrat until his death on August 13, 1999.

Bubis was an exception. Whereas previous presidents of the Zentralrat had seen themselves as representing only Jewish interests and preferred to act behind the scenes, he was a political man, involved in a variety of issues that preoccupied the general public, not only and sometimes even not particularly the Jews. Thus, he was a supporter of liberal asylum legislation, acting in favor of the rights of migrants in general, Turkish and others, a clear voice for tolerant living together. Seeing himself – at least initially – as a "German citizen of the Jewish faith," he was

---

[25] Henryk Broder, "Ein befreiender Streit?," *Der Spiegel*, December 7, 1998.
[26] For Bubis' biography, I have profitably used the various articles in Backhaus, Gross, and Lenarz (eds.), *Ignaz Bubis*.

a combatant for the right of Jews to be treated equally both in private life and in public affairs. At the time, this may have been self-evident legally, but it was by no means universally accepted socially. In his later memoirs, Bubis recalled being asked, apparently more than once, for his credentials as a German, thus being treated as if his were a temporary stay in a foreign country and as if he were incapable of understanding non-Jewish Germans. Israel was his homeland, it was insinuated. On such occasions, this surprisingly sensitive man seemed easily insulted, often having a sharp answer ready at hand. Finally, the debate with Martin Walser and with his defenders turned out to be the crucial experience of his later life. As a self-conscious, even proud German Jew, he felt it was his duty and not only his right to express his anger and disappointment, arguing not only for the memory of the dead but also for the respect due to the living. Eventually, this speculator of the mid 1970s became an important moral voice in Germany, by no means merely in matters related to Jews or on issues relevant to them.

It all ended tragically. Shortly before he died, in an interview given to *Stern*, Bubis recalled his efforts to close the gap between Germans and Jewish-Germans, but in the end insisted that he had achieved "nothing or almost nothing."[27] And even more telling was his request to be buried in Israel. No doubt he feared the desecration of graves in Germany, especially after the earlier bomb attack on the grave of Heinz Galinski, his predecessor at the head of the Zentralrat. But it remained a powerful symbolic act, a sign of his despair, rather uncharacteristic of this previously so hopeful and confident man.[28]

Bubis' despair was understandable, but, in the longer run, was it justified? Clearly, by the end of the twentieth century the older generation, including many one-time Nazis, was no longer active. The middle generation, often still finding it difficult to accept Jews as equals, particularly within the newly united nation-state, seems to have made its last appearance in the Walser–Bubis debate. The stage was now clear for a new generation and for a new chapter in German–Jewish relations. With the coming of the twenty-first century, the controversies on memory and history lost much of their explosive nature, sometimes even their relevance. In fact, during the 1990s too, most Germans were still mainly busy with other issues, above all with completing the unification of their country and with strengthening European ties while further calming international fears vis-à-vis the newly united, powerful Germany.

[27] The interview appeared in *Stern*, July 29, 1999.
[28] On this, see Dan Diner, "Das Grab in Tel Aviv," in Backhaus, Gross, and Lenarz (eds.), *Ignaz Bubis*, 156–158.

Then there was the 1991 Iraq War and a large protest movement against it in numerous German towns. This brought up again the old dilemma of the left, which found itself supporting Israel's enemies, while they were threatening to attack it with German-made weaponry. And when war suddenly broke out in Yugoslavia, bringing with it violent interethnic conflicts and horrors of genocidal cruelty, the like of which had not been seen in Europe since the end of the Second World War, Germany participated only hesitantly in responding to these challenges. The public was continuously unsettled by the disturbing news, and, finally, a fierce controversy erupted when the involvement of some Bundeswehr units in Kosovo was justified by the Green Party Foreign Minister, Joschka Fischer. In a speech of May 1999, his resounding maxim "No more Auschwitz" seemed to stand in contradiction to his "No more war" exhortation. It caused indignation even among his party colleagues. In Israel, the danger of making political use of the Holocaust had already become clear before; it was now apparent in Germany, as well.

Meanwhile, nothing worried the public more than the waves of immigrants, first especially from Eastern Europe and from Russia, seemingly flooding Germany. In the wake of this inrush of approximately half a million immigrants, coming into Germany between 1989 and 1992, the most worrying items of news, no doubt, were reports on the hostility aroused by the newcomers in the hearts and minds of many Germans, particularly in the area that had previously belonged to the DDR. The large Turkish minority in a number of cities in the western part of the country had already worried the ex-citizens of the communist state, who were not accustomed to life with so many "outsiders." Now, opposition was directed at the incoming East Europeans and later against other asylum-seekers from countries yet farther away, among them many Muslims. These were often seen as illegitimate invaders and dangerous competitors, so that violent attacks on their temporary housing became a not-uncommon event. The case Walser mentioned in his Paulskirche speech occurred towards the end of August 1992 in Rostock and included mob attacks on Vietnamese living there in temporary barracks, who finally had to be evacuated by the police, to the glee of the watching crowd. Similar events occurred before and after this incident, some involving actual arson and murder. And, while these caused much consternation among many Germans – both in the east and in the west of the country – the anti-foreigner movement everywhere strengthened existing right-wing groups in Germany as a whole. These were suddenly given new nourishment, beyond and above their prior anachronistic Nazi or neo-Nazi content. When, shortly afterwards, new legislation helped reduce the number of immigrants, the matter lost some of its urgency, but the Jewish community in Germany was deeply unsettled. After all, antisemitism was never far behind racism in general, and hatred of Jews all too often followed the hatred of the various newly incoming foreigners. There *was* cause for alarm.

Thus, once again, Germany was sending its Jews a double message. Incidences of antisemitism and expressions of racism were causing fear, or at least unease and irritation. At the same time, the successful German state, of which these Jews were now full citizens, was, after all, a functioning modern democracy, relying upon an open, pluralistic civil society and what seemed like a long, painful process of learning from the past. It gave its Jewish citizens a keen sense of security despite their fears; even a measure of optimism. Bubis' dream of full integration would probably remain unachievable, most of them now realized, but Leo Baeck's reconciliation with reality some fifty years earlier, a reality of Jews simply "living in Germany," proved quite accurate. For some, it is surely less than they had hoped for; for others, it seems only fitting. In a new Germany, they too were capable of living their lives while preserving their own culture or otherwise, as they saw fit, living side by side with non-Jewish Germans and together with the various minority groups in the country. Moreover, Jews seemed to no longer have a special role to play – as Jews – in the enlarged Bundesrepublik. Clearly, it is the non-Jewish Germans that by the early twenty-first century took upon themselves full responsibility for remembering the past and commemorating the victims. For the time being, this finally seemed to have been accepted by the majority of Germans as the indispensable moral groundwork of present-day Germany.

Epilogue: Berlin is not Weimar

The building of that large, much contested "Memorial for the Murdered Jews" in the heart of Berlin has been completed. It was festively inaugurated on May 10, 2005, symbolizing what Aleida Assmann later called "the reorientation from forgetting to remembrance," or, even more fittingly, the turn away from the model of a *Schlußstrich* (final line) to the model of a *Trennungsstrich* (separation line).[1] The work of professional historians was at this point urgently required, and, in parallel to the various historiographical controversies – just before and just after unification – many of them were busy outlining the details of the Nazi system and the precise means by which its supporters implemented the so-called "Final Solution." Old and new documents were now collected and presented to the public in printed books, in small and large exhibitions, and in new documentary centers. The "topography of terror," built upon the former SS Headquarters on the borderline between the two no longer extant Germanies in the unified Berlin, as well as numerous memorials in previous concentration camps, became sites of pilgrimage, part of that ever more pronounced German *Erinnerungskultur* (memory or remembrance culture). If major and minor monuments, memorial signposts, and *Stolpersteine* (stumbling stones) are being added, Germany could paradoxically be proud, so to speak, of the fact that "in no other country is there such a thick representation of one's own offences."[2] In the worst cases, to be sure, this could lead to a kind of perverted *Erinnerungsstolz* (remembrance smugness), usable for various political purposes, and in

---

[1] See Aleida Assmann, *Der europäische Traum: Vier Lehren aus der Geschichte*, Munich, 2018, 47 and 53.

[2] This and the following quotes in this paragraph are reformulations of statements in Aleida Assmann, *Der lange Schatten der Vergangenheit: Erinnerungskultur und Geschichtspolitik*, Munich, 2006 (English-language edition *Shadows of Trauma: Memory and the Politics of Postwar Identity*, trans. Sarah Clift, New York, 2015), by Konrad Jarausch, *Selbstkritik als Erinnerungskultur: Grundlagen moralischer Politik in Deutschland?*, Oranienburg, 2017, 12. See also Assmann, *Der europäische Traum*, 54.

the better cases it constitutes part of an ongoing enlightening project, possibly leading to "learning, reflecting, and reconciliation."

At the same time a parallel German-*Jewish Erinnerungskultur* has likewise evolved. Museums, especially the one in Berlin – renovated, enlarged, and redesigned by the architect Daniel Liebeskind – but also much smaller and less spectacular ones elsewhere throughout the country, reveal centuries of Jewish life in Germany, well beyond its tragic, murderous end. They attract millions of visitors, Germans and tourists from all over the world, as they simultaneously tell the tale of the past and portray Jewish life in Germany in the present. New or renewed synagogues have been built – in Munich and Dresden, in Mainz and Regensburg. They are usually centrally located and architecturally distinct. To be sure, they must be always securely guarded and are often – unlike most churches – closed to unannounced visitors. Nevertheless, they arouse a measure of interest. No less important is the growing interest in German-Jewish history among students and the public at large. During the intellectual upheaval of the late 1960s, only a few pioneering historians dedicated their work to Jewish themes. This field has now grown to be a full-fledged academic discipline with its own professorial chairs and institutions, providing a thick description of German-Jewish history, going many centuries back in time.

Although the Jewish presence in present-day Germany will probably never be as brilliant and outstanding as it was during the Weimar Republic or in the later years of the Kaiserreich, the fact that Jews join in now as equal citizens and, despite bouts of antisemitism, usually manage to live in a decent polity, together with non-Jewish Germans and with migrants from many other countries, is in itself a cause for gratification – modest but genuine. In addition, the long post-war era, in which the Jews in Germany have fulfilled – sometimes intentionally, but more often despite themselves – a number of important roles, has come to an end. Only a few surviving witnesses of past crimes are still alive and able to tell their story; neither are there too many remaining Nazi perpetrators that ought to be prosecuted and punished in Germany or elsewhere. Finally, most issues related to the National-Socialist past have been either settled or – more often – set aside.

Jews in the enlarged Bundesrepublik constitute a minority of no more than 0.4 percent. Nearly 100,000 are members of the various religious congregations, and the estimated number of additional, non-registered Jews is between 50,000 and 100,000, including some 20,000 Israelis, living mainly in Berlin. Only a few of these Jews take part in politics and – as in the past – more than a few are physicians, lawyers, scholars, and scientists. With the emigration of some 100,000 Jews from the lands of the former Soviet Union, Germany gained a number of outstanding musicians and some original prose authors. But, on the whole, Jews in Germany are usually inconspicuous. It seems they are quietly respected and their "collective opinion" is occasionally sought and then civilly listened to – no more, but also no less.

In any case, as mentioned above, present-day Germany has been acutely preoccupied not with the small Jewish community living in its midst but with the large wave of refugees from afar – since 2015 primarily from Syria, Afghanistan, and North Africa – all trying to reach its border. It is now a much-coveted "promised land." In parallel, it is equally preoccupied with the rise of the right, particularly in the eastern part of the country, that seems to have suddenly been multiplying in response to this wave of incoming migrants. The resentment still alive in eastern Germany long after unification, felt even among men and women who are too young to have ever experienced life in the DDR, is now joined to the not-yet-extinguished xenophobia in both east and west, as well as to a widespread fear of economic competition and to the permanent undercurrent of racism in a more or less constant and perhaps now growing segment of the population. Some 12 percent of voters had aligned themselves with the newly established party Alternativ für Deutschland (Alternative for Germany, AfD) by 2016, a proportion considered "normal" or even "minimal" for the far right in most Western countries, but the AfD's support had increased to 22 percent by September 2023, and the party suddenly became the second-largest one in Germany. Naturally, this has aroused wide concern, not least among Jews. While hostility from the right is more often than not directed at Muslims, occasional terror attacks against Jews, such as the one directed at the synagogue in the city of Halle on Yom Kippur 2019, deeply unsettled Jews and non-Jews alike. It has brought to light the fact that Jews, despite all promises, are still not sufficiently protected, but, more importantly, it has deeply shaken the confidence of Jews and many German non-Jews in the stability of the Bundesrepublik and in the strength of its democracy.

Then, in the aftermath of the terror attack on Israel on October 7, 2023 and as the Israeli retaliatory operation in the Gaza Strip quickly evolved into a full-scale war, pro-Palestinian demonstrations in Germany as well as in France, Great Britain, and the United States often also manifested implied or sometimes explicit antisemitism. These demonstrations may have been organized by Arab or Moslem associations, surely strengthened numerically by recent immigrants from the Middle East, but they have attracted a large supporting crowd. In the past, similar conflicts in the region drew members of the so-called new or extreme left onto the streets.

This time, apparently, a considerable segment of the established middle, so to speak, joined these demonstrations, despite their tendency to spill over into antisemitic provocations, verbal and even physical. Israel – the state that had initially been expected to guarantee Jewish life – has now become a source of new unease among diaspora Jews. In Berlin, a Jewish student was brutally beaten. Throughout Germany, Jewish schoolchildren have been harassed and public lectures or cultural events have been disrupted because of aggressive anti-Israeli but sometimes also anti-Jewish interference and protests. In Germany, at least, this has not yet brought about any change in the official stand of the country, with the government clearly placing itself on Israel's side, but it has greatly shaken both Jews and non-Jews out of their previous comfort zone.

In fact, controversies regarding Israel's policies in its occupied territories, especially in the West Bank, had sometimes been hotly debated in Germany before too, but they usually aroused only limited interest. Even the call by Israeli and Jewish-American intellectuals to allow more critical discussion of Israel and its policies towards the Palestinians and exclude such critique from the definition of antisemitism remained rather marginal. The official stand towards Israel has in fact become so routinized that it has remained unchanged throughout. The president of the republic or its foreign ministers occasionally censure the Jewish state, stressing Germany's commitment to human rights, but Israel continued to receive German official support in various international bodies and – significantly – continued to receive armaments for its defense, including the most modern submarines, even though negotiations leading to their purchase were often carried out in an atmosphere of reciprocal suspicion. The security of Israel, declared Angela Merkel, the German ex-chancellor, on a number of occasions, is inseparable from the *Staatsraison* (political legitimacy) of the Bundesrepublik. The imperative of remembrance dictated this policy in the past and will probably continue to dictate it, while domestically the obligation to preserve and protect the Jewish community *in* Germany is still self-evident, even today. After all, Germany is expected to be particularly watchful in this respect. Memory of its past, though no longer so acutely present as before, still sets higher standards for this country.

On the whole, and by any sort of comparison, present-day Germany can still be considered a stable, well-functioning democracy. Berlin is not Weimar, goes the saying. But, in the end, Berlin has been more promising than Weimar – partly at least – because of the insights gained from the study of the past. Whether or not these lessons have truly been internalized and whether this internalization will prove sufficient to withstand new tides of Jew-hating in the future remains an open question. The historian Michael Brenner has reminded us that "one always recognizes danger too late," and the new situation is clearly a cause for particular watchfulness.[3]

This book attempts to contribute insights regarding the German past. Many of its themes are still with us. The nature of integration, for instance, presented and analyzed here in the early chapters of the book, together with arguments concerning the failure to accept pluralism even among German liberals may serve as an example, and the prolonged fight for equality, yet another major theme of this book, is particularly relevant in a world in which inequality has reached gigantic proportions. Finally, the ambivalence created by the mixture of inclusion and exclusion, promises and disappointments, so typical of the life of the Jews in Germany for generations, perhaps even today, is surely characteristic not only of them.

From a Jewish perspective, ran the argument above, German history in the modern age receives new contours. The eighteenth-century enlightenment is here criticized especially for its unabashed intolerance, while political liberalism is seen in a critical light even as early as the beginning of the nineteenth century. Its high point, during the revolution of 1848, is here presented in its stark duality – being modern and traditional, egalitarian and exclusionary at one and the same time. Then, a different light is thrown on the nature of early industrialization and the role of the Jews both in it and more generally in the later stages of modernization, too. Even the great achievement of the first German unification is relativized by observing the rupture it then created within the traditional European Jewry, though – again – by no means only within it. Jews in the Kaiserreich, enjoying a sense of belonging to a beloved fatherland while at the same time suffering painful rejection during waves of organized antisemitism, demonstrate again the tension between success and failure typical of the entire tale told in this book. Tragically a painful awakening from the dream of sharing German identity, which had always been fragile, was brought about by the National Socialists' takeover in 1933, and at this point, in fact, German Jews as such no longer existed. They were completely excluded, sent to be exterminated together with and just like all other Jews in occupied Europe, alongside Sinti and Roma, the mentally ill, and those deemed "unworthy of life." The bond that had been so carefully interwoven was violently torn apart; forever, it seemed. The link between Germans and Jews that had been so close and so exceptionally productive was severed with the most unimaginable crimes,

---

[3] Michael Brenner, "Die Gefahr erkennt man immer zu spät," *Der Spiegel*, January 20, 2020.

on the one hand, and the most painful loss, on the other. However, against all odds, even this complete rupture, separating perpetrators from victims, proved repairable. In a defeated Germany, liberated from Nazi rule, Jews and Jewish life in Germany received a new meaning. While Jews never sought a special role for themselves in post-war Germany, surely not at the horrific price that had had to be paid for it, neither could they free themselves of the responsibility associated with their re-entry into it. Finally, in times of international crises, particularly linked to Israel and the complexities of the Middle East conflict, some unexpected worries have reemerged. That measure of optimism, drawn from what has just seemed to be Jewish successful integration and their peaceful re-entry into modern German society, became questionable again. At such times, perhaps a long-term view of the past, such as the one offered here, may at least provide a needed compass; a view - this time - through Jewish eyes.

Index

academic careers
  entry of Jews into, 152
  exclusion of Jews from, 56
Adenauer, Konrad, 188, 189–190, 191, 193, 210
Adler-Rudel, Salomon, 185
Adorno, Theodor, 15, 16, 184
Afghanistan, refugees from, 223
Africa, refugees from, 223
agriculture, Jews in, 81–82
Alliance Israélite Universelle, 95
Alternativ für Deutschland (AfD), 223
Aly, Götz, 82
Antisemitic People's Party, 117
antisemitism
  adjustment of Jews to, 121–123, 129–130
  Allied occupation, persistence of antisemitism during, 186
  in Austria, 125, 174
  in Bundesrepublik, 193
  Catholics and, 113, 173
  Conservative Party and, 113, 117
  in contemporary Germany, 223
  ethnography and, 3
  in First World War, 135, 138–142
  Gaza terror attack and response to, 223–224
  Heine on, 51
  Holocaust and, 179–180 (*see also* Holocaust)
  in Kaiserreich, 113–118
  liberalism and, 51, 113, 118
  nationalism and, 117–118, 123
  in Nazi Germany, 159, 165–169, 171–172
  non-Jews ignoring, 130
  in post-Congress of Vienna period, 48–51
  propaganda, 52
  in Prussia, 28
  race and, 117–118, 128–129
  in Revolution of 1848–1849, 67–68
  with social reform, 116–117
  students and, 51
  Treitschke and, 114, 115, 117, 122
  violence (*see* violence)
  at Wartburg festival, 51
  in Weimar Republic, 159, 160–161
  Zionism and, 161
Anti-Socialists Law (Kaiserreich), 112
Appel, Ernst, 171
Appel, Marta, 171
Arad, Yitzhak, 209
Arendt, Hannah, 158–159, 160, 184–185
Arnheim–Eskeles circle, 35
Arnhold, Eduard, 135
Arnstein, Nathan Adam Freiherr von, 35
Aryanization, 168
Ascher, Saul, 48, 51
Assmann, Aleida, 221
Auerbach, Berthold, 115–116
Augstein, Rudolf, 216
Auschwitz Trials, 196–198, 206
Auspitz, Lazar, 36
Austria
  antisemitism in, 125, 174
  Bismarck and, 97
  Christian Social Party, 125
  condition of Jews in, 176
  culture in, 124–125
  delegation to Congress of Vienna, 35, 36–37
  emancipation of Jews in, 95
  flight of Jews from, 176
  inter-war violence in, 151–152
  Jewish equality under French occupation, 33
  lack of reforms in, 44
  liberalism, lack of, 42
  Nazi occupation of, 174
  Pan-German Antisemitic Party, 135
  Prussia and, 77, 94
  Revolution of 1848–1849 in, 73
  rupture with Germany, 103, 105–108
  unification (1871) and, 96–97
Austro-Prussian War, 94, 97

227

Baden
  anti-Jewish riots in, 51
  emancipation of Jews in, 95
  Jewish equality under French occupation, 31
  Revolution of 1848–1849 in, 67, 70–71
  uneven development of reforms in, 45
Baeck, Leo, 190, 220
Ballin, Albert, 135, 140–142
Bamberg, anti-Jewish riots in, 51
Barkai, Avraham, 82–83, 88, 99, 168
Baron, Salo, 37
Baruch, Jacob, 34
Bauer, Fritz
  Auschwitz Trials and, 196–198, 206
  death of, 198
  Eichmann case and, 193, 195–196
  legacy of, 198
  life of, 193–194
  as prosecutor, 195
  Remer case and, 195
Bauer, Yehuda, 179–180, 181
Bauman, Zygmunt, 16
Bavaria
  attacks on Jews in, 161
  delegation to Congress of Vienna, 37
  emancipation of Jews in, 95
  Jewish equality under French occupation, 31, 33
  in Kaiserreich, 111
  Matrikel, 95
  migration of Jews from, 99
  reforms in, 67
  Republic of Councils, 144, 145, 151
  Revolution of 1848–1849 in, 67, 71
  uneven development of reforms in, 45
Bayreuth, anti-Jewish riots in, 51
Bayreuth circle, 117–118
Bebel, August, 117
"Beer-Hall Putsch" (1923), 150
Begin, Menachem, 189
Beilis Affair (1913), 123
Belgium, colonialism and, 127
Ben-Gurion, David, 188–189, 191, 192, 196
Ben-Israel, Menasse, 24
Benjamin, Walter, 166
Bergen-Belsen concentration camp, 204
Berlin
  commemoration of Holocaust victims in, 215, 221
  cultural associations in, 55
  growing significance of, 119
  industrialization in, 83
  Memorial for the Murdered Jews, 221
  "topography of terror," 221

Berlin Olympic Games (1936), 168, 170
Berlin Wall, 191, 208
Bethmann Hollweg, Theobald von, 134, 140
Bildung
  culture and, 88
  education and, 38, 88
  Enlightenment and, 15, 19, 20, 53
  Haskalah and, 17
  Jews and, 75, 125, 175
  women and, 89
Bismarck, Otto von
  Austria and, 97
  on capital punishment, 102
  Catholics and, 111–112
  Center Party and, 102, 112
  Conservative Party and, 102, 111–112
  domestic politics and, 111
  imperialism and, 133
  Jews and, 98, 112–113
  Kulturkampf, 112
  Lasker versus, 101–103, 112–113
  liberals and, 98
  Social Democratic Party and, 112
  south German states and, 105–106
  trade policies, 111–112
  unification (1871) and, 94, 95, 105, 106–107, 111, 136
  war and, 94
  working class and, 136
Bitburg, visit of Kohl and Reagan to, 204
Bleichröder, Gerson, 83, 112
Blüher, Hans, 145–146
Blumenfeld, Kurt, 160
Böckel, Otto, 117
Boer War, 125
Bohemia, Revolution of 1848–1849 in, 67
Bolshevism, 144
Bonnet, Charles, 23, 24
Bormann, Martin, 195–196
Börne, Ludwig, 34, 65
Bracher, Karl Dietrich, 5, 178
Brahms, Johannes, 123–124
Brandt, Willy, 194, 200, 210
Brecht, Berthold, 184
Bremen
  Jewish equality under French occupation, 31–32
  Jews at time of Congress of Vienna in, 41
Brenner, Michael, 225
Breslau, anti-Jewish riots in, 51
Breuer, Josef, 153
Broder, Henryk, 217
Bronfman, Edgar, 209
Broszat, Martin, 180–181, 206

Index

Brüning, Heinrich, 148, 158
Buber, Martin, 159, 174, 185
Bubis, Ignaz, 216, 217–218, 220
Buchholz, Carl August, 34
Budapest, German-speaking Jews in, 107
Bülow, Bernhard von, 126, 128, 133
Bundeswehr, 219
Burg, Joseph, 209

capitalism, 79
capital punishment, 102
Caprivi, Leo von, 133
Carlsbad Decrees (1819), 47
Cassirer, Ernst, 15
Catholics
  antisemitism and, 113, 173
  Bismarck and, 111–112
  Center Party and, 98–99, 112
  Jews compared, 119–120
  Protestants versus, 90, 91–92, 136
  secularization and, 98–99
  unification (1871), impact of, 105
Center Party
  Bismarck and, 102, 112
  Catholics and, 98–99, 112
  coalitions and, 148
  colonialism and, 126
  First World War and, 142
Centralverein deutscher Staatsbürger jüdischen Glaubens (Central Association of German Citizens of the Jewish Faith), 119
Chamberlain, Houston Stewart, 118, 135
Cheder schools, 86, 104
child mortality, 80
Christian Democratic Union (CDU), 200
civil service
  entry of Jews into, 152
  exclusion of Jews from, 56, 167
civil society, 49
Clark, Christopher, 17
Claß, Heinrich, 128–129
class conflict, 136
Clermont-Tonnerre, Comte, 30
Cobban, Alfred, 14–15
Cohen, Hermann, 115–116, 120
Cohn, Chaim, 196
Cohn, Oskar, 144
Cold War, 206
colonialism, 126–128
commemoration of Holocaust victims, 214–217, 221–222
communists
  Nazi suppression of, 165, 171
  split within left and, 149

concentration camps, 167, 204
Congress of Berlin (1878), 95
Congress of Vienna (1815)
  civil rights and, 39–40
  failure to protect Jewish rights, 41–43
  German Confederation and, 35
  growing hostility towards Jews following, 45
  Humboldt at, 36, 37–39
  Jewish interests at, 34, 35–36
  Jewish representatives at, 34, 95
  liberalism and, 39–40
  Metternich at, 34, 35, 38, 40–41
  religious freedom and, 38–39
  Revolution of 1848–1849 compared, 77
Conservative Party
  antisemitism and, 113, 117
  Bismarck and, 102, 111–112
  First World War and, 142
  Jews and, 96
Constitution, Article 48 (Weimar Republic), 148
constitutionalism, 47–48
conversion
  Heine and, 57
  Humboldt on, 64–65
  as necessary for certain employment, 56
  in Prussia, 65
  sham conversions, 46–47
Cranz, August, 26, 27
Crimean War, 2
cultural associations, 55
culture
  in Austria, 124–125
  Bildung and, 88
  entry of Jews into cultural life, 53–54
  in Kaiserreich, 123–124
  Nazi Germany, cultural figures fleeing, 166
  in Vienna, 124–125
  in Weimar Republic, 153
Czech Protectorate, condition of Jews in, 176

Dangerfield, George, 136
Danzig, anti-Jewish riots in, 51
Darnton, Robert, 15
Dawidowicz, Lucy, 179
Declaration of Seventy-Five Notables (1880), 115
Dehmel, Richard, 132
Demnig, Günther, 214–215
democracy
  in Bundesrepublik, 191
  in Weimar Republic, 147–148

denazification, 186–187
Dernburg, Bernhard, 127
Deutsche Demokratische Partei, 148
Deutsche Volkspartei, 148
Deutschvölkischer Schutz- und Trutzbund (German Nationalist Federation for Protection and Defense), 160–161
Diner, Dan, 8, 181, 207, 213
displaced persons' camps, 183, 184
Dohm, Christian Wilhelm, 20, 24, 25, 29, 173
Dohnanyi, Klaus von, 216
Dresden, synagogues in, 222
Dreyfus Affair (1894–1906), 123, 126, 136
Droysen, Johann Gustav, 105
Drumont, Édouard, 123
Dubnow, Simon, 21, 74
Dühring, Eugen, 117
Dürrenmatt, Friedrich, 201

East Berlin, protests against DDR in, 208
Ebert, Friedrich, 148
economic growth
  role of Jews in, 83–84, 93
  Wirtschaftswunder (economic miracle), 191
Edict of Nantes (1598), 26
Edicts of Toleration (Austria 1781), 29
education
  Bildung and, 38, 88
  Cheder schools, 86, 104
  Free Schools, 86–87
  of girls, 88–89
  Gymnasium, 87–88
  high schools, 87–88
  modernity and, 86
  Yeshivas, 104
Eichmann, Adolf, 192, 193, 195–196
Einsatzgruppen, 178
Einstein, Albert, 166
Eisner, Kurt, 145, 160
Elon, Amos, 197
Elstätter, Moritz, 96
emancipation of Jews
  barriers to in Prussia, 66–67
  Heine on, 64
  liberalism and, 66
emergency decrees, 148
employment of Jews
  conversion as necessary for, 56
  Nazi Germany, loss of employment in, 168
Enabling Act (Nazi Germany), 166
Engels, Friedrich, 117
Enlightenment

entry of Jews into bourgeois culture, 17–18
French Enlightenment, 14–15
German Enlightenment, 14
Haskalah (Jewish Enlightenment), 17, 21, 22
intolerance in, 25–27
Judaism, compatibility with, 26
legal rights in, 25
Mendelssohn and, 19–21, 26, 45–46
modern history, as starting point for, 13–16
modern Jewish history, as starting point for, 16–17, 21–22
Erfurt program, 117
Erhard, Ludwig, 199
Erinnerungskultur (remembrance culture), 221–222
Erzberger, Mathias, 139, 151, 156
Eskeles, Bernhard, 35
ethnography
  antisemitism and, 3
  Jews and, 2–4
Ettlinger, Jacob, 70
Euchel, Isaac Abraham, 22
exclusion of Jews
  from academic careers, 56
  from civil service, 56
  in Nazi Germany, 167
extermination camps, 178

Falkenhayn, Erich von, 134
Fassbinder, Rainer Werner, 204
Federation of Women Physicians, 155
Feiner, Shmuel, 23
Ferdinand (Austria), 73
Fest, Joachim, 178
Feuchtwanger, Lion, 166, 184
Fichte, Johann Gottlieb, 48–49, 125–126
First World War
  antisemitism in, 135, 138–142
  censorship in, 138
  Center Party and, 142
  commencement of, 131
  Conservative Party and, 142
  costs of, 137–138
  enthusiasm for, 131–132
  "Jewish census," 139
  Jewish support for, 133–135
  Jews blamed for defeat in, 143–144, 145–146
  nationalism and, 136–137
  protests against, 132–133
  SPD and, 142
  surrender in, 142

Index   231

U-boats in, 141–142
Zionists and, 134
Fischer, Joschka, 219
flight of Jews
    from Austria, 176
    from Nazi Germany, 166, 167, 170–171, 176
Fontane, Theodor, 123–124
Fortschrittspartei, 101
Foucault, Michel, 21
France
    colonialism and, 127
    Dreyfus Affair, 123, 126, 136
    First World War and, 131
    French Enlightenment, 14–15
    French Revolution, 13, 21
    Germany compared, 123
    internal divisions in, 136
    inter-war violence in, 151
    nationalism in, 123
    pro-Palestinian demonstrations in, 223
    student movement in, 200
    on unification (1990), 212
Franco-Prussian War, 2, 97, 105–106, 111
Fränkel, David, 18
Frankenthal, Käte, 154–156, 158
Frankfurt
    anti-Jewish riots in, 51, 52
    cultural associations in, 55
    delegation to Congress of Vienna, 34
    growing significance of, 119
    Jewish equality under French occupation, 31
    Revolution of 1848–1849 in, 70
    student movement in, 203–204
    tension with Jews in, 203–204
Franz Ferdinand (Austria), 131
Franz-Joseph (Austria), 73
Free Schools, 86–87
Frei, Norbert, 198
Freikorps, 156
French Enlightenment, 14–15
French Revolution
    Jewish equality under, 21
    as starting point of modern history, 13, 21
Freud, Sigmund, 10, 124, 153
Friedländer, David, 34, 46
Friedländer, Saul, 144, 180–181, 205–208
Friedrich II (Prussia), 14
Friedrich Wilhelm IV (Prussia), 66–67, 78
Fries, Jakob Friedrich, 50, 51, 52

Galicia, German-speaking Jews in, 106–107
Galinksi, Heinz, 209, 218
Gans, Eduard, 55–56, 57, 65, 79

Garde-Kavallerie Schützendivision (GKSD), 150–151
Gay, Peter (Fröhlich), 16, 169–170
Geiger, Abraham, 71–72
gender history, 7
German Confederation, 35
German–Danish War (1864), 94
German Enlightenment, 14
German history
    DDR perspective on Nazi Germany, 209–210
    Enlightenment as starting point for, 13–16
    Nazi Germany, revisionist perspectives on, 205–208
    unification (1871), differing conceptions of, 102–103
    unification (1990), renewed interest in Holocaust following, 213–214
German Jews, 119–121
Gestapo, 153, 154, 160, 167, 172
Gierke, Otto von, 137
Glagau, Otto, 113, 114
Gleim, Johann Wilhelm Ludwig, 18
Globke, Hans, 191
Gobineau, Arthur de, 117
Goebbels, Josef, 173, 175
Goethe, Johann Wolfgang von, 2, 22–23, 24, 125–126, 174, 194
Goldhagen, Daniel, 180, 213–214
Goldman, Nahum, 189, 191
Goldstein, Moritz, 130
Gorbachev, Mikhail, 208–209
Göring, Hermann, 165, 170
Graetz, Heinrich, 17, 21, 73–74, 115
Grass, Günther, 211–212
Grevinus, Georg Gottfried, 14
Grundgesetz (Basic Law, Bundesrepublik), 191
guilds, anti-Jewish sentiment among members, 52
Gumbel, Emil Julius, 150, 151
Gundolf, Friedrich, 132

Haase, Hugo, 144
Haber, Fritz, 166
Habermas, Jürgen, 206–207, 211–212
Haffner, Sebastian, 131, 152, 167
Halle, violence against Jews in, 223
Hamburg
    anti-Jewish riots in, 51
    growing significance of, 119
    Jewish equality under French occupation, 31
    Jews at time of Congress of Vienna in, 41

Hamburg America Line (HAPAG), 135, 140
Hamelin, Glikl von, 88, 153–154
Hanover, reforms in, 67
Harden, Maximilian, 140–141, 143
Hardenberg, Carl August Freiherr von, 32, 39–40
Haskalah (Jewish Enlightenment), 17, 21, 22
Hauptmann, Gerhart, 123–124
Hebraists, 2
Hegel, Georg Friedrich Wilhelm, 65
Heidegger, Martin, 159
Heine, Heinrich
  on antisemitism, 51
  conversion and, 57
  education of, 86
  on emancipation of Jews, 64
  on Germany, 57–59
  on Jews and Germany, 78–79, 80
  poetry of, 57–58
Helfferich, Karl, 140–141
Hep-Hep riots (1819), 51–52
Herbert, Ulrich, 189, 201
Herder, Johann Gottfried, 3
Herz, Henriette, 46, 49
Herz, Leopold Edler von, 35
Herzl, Theodor, 129–130
Hess, Jonathan, 22
Hesse, Hermann, 132
Heydrich, Reinhard, 173
Hilberg, Raul, 179
Hillgruber, Andreas, 181, 206–207
Hindenburg, Paul von, 145, 148, 158, 168
Hirsch, Julius, 135
"historicization," 180–181, 206
Hitler, Adolf
  "Beer-Hall Putsch" and, 150
  as chancellor, 148
  as Führer, 168
  "Jewish Question" and, 175–176
  UK and, 172
  United States and, 172
  war aims of, 175–176
Hobsbawm, Eric, 7
Hofmannsthal, Hugo von, 174
Hohenloe, Prince (Choldwig Karl Viktor), 133
Hölderlin, Friedrich, 174
Holocaust
  antisemitism and, 179–180
  commemoration of victims, 214–217, 221–222
  denial under Allied occupation, 186
  different perspectives on, 178–182
  extermination camps, 178
  functionalist perspective, 181
  "historicization" of, 178–179, 180–181
  ideology and, 179
  intentionalist perspective, 181
  lack of historical attention to, 5
  making political use of, 219
  mass extermination in, 177–178
  moral perspective, 180–181
  pressure to terminate prosecutions of Nazis, 198–199
  reparations to survivors, 188, 189, 190, 191
  survivors of, 183
  T4 euthanasia project, 177, 197
  Wehrmacht, role of in, 214
Holocaust (television mini-series), 205
Holy Roman Empire, 44
homosexuals, Nazi suppression of, 171
Honecker, Erich, 209
Horkheimer, Max, 15, 16, 184
Humboldt, Wilhelm von
  on civil society, 49
  at Congress of Vienna, 36, 37–39
  on conversion, 64–65
  educational reforms of, 33
  on failure of Congress of Vienna to protect Jewish rights, 42
  Jews and, 36, 37–39, 49
  as liberal, 39
  Metternich and, 40
Hungary
  inter-war violence in, 151–152
  Revolution of 1848–1849 in, 67
hyperinflation, 148

identity
  "imagined communities" and, 103–104
  nationalism and, 104–105
  religion as main source of, 1–2
  scientific narrative of, 4
"imagined communities," 103–104
Independent Social Democratic Party (USPD), 143, 144
industrialization, 82–83
infant mortality, 80
Institute for Social Research, 214
International Military Court (Nuremberg Tribunal), 186
intolerance
  in Enlightenment, 25–27
  within Jewish community, 25–26
  Mendelssohn on, 23–24, 25, 26
Iraq War, 219
Iro, Karl, 135

Index

Israel
  Bundesrepublik, relations with, 188–190, 192
  DDR, relations with, 209, 210
  Eichmann case and, 193, 196
  Gaza terror attack and response to, 223–224, 226
  Mossad, 193, 196
  occupation policy, criticism of, 224
  Palestinians and, 223, 224
  Six-Day War (1967), 201
  unification (1990) and, 212
  Yom Kippur War (1973), 201
Israel, Jonathan, 22, 30
Italy
  emigration to Germany from, 203
  inter-war violence in, 151
  unification of, 2, 94

Jäckel, Eberhard, 179
Jacoby, Johann, 70
Jagow, Gottlieb von, 140–141
Janz, Oliver, 132–133
Jaspers, Karl, 158, 184–185
Jaurès, Jean, 131
Jenninger, Philipp, 204–205
Jersch-Wenzel, Stefi, 66
Jewish history
  Bundesrepublik and, 188, 190, 201–202
  contemporary Germany, Jews and, 218, 220, 222
  DDR and, 187–188, 209–210
  Enlightenment as starting point for, 16–17, 21–22
  German Jews, 119–121
  Kaiserreich, Jews as coherent minority in, 119
  unification (1871), impact of, 94–95
  unification (1990), renewed interest in Holocaust following, 213–214
  uniqueness of Jewish perspective, 9–10
  Weimar Republic and, 147, 161–162
"Jewish Renaissance," 159
Jochmann, Werner, 143
Joffe, Adolf, 144
Jonas, Hans, 185
Jones, Mark, 149
Joseph II (Habsburg Monarchy), 29
Jost, Isaac Markus, 73
Judaism
  Enlightenment, compatibility with, 26
  German nationalism and, 71–72
  Marx and, 65–66, 79
  Mendelssohn and, 23–24, 26
  modernity and, 98

Neo-Orthodox Judaism, 119
rabbis, 104, 107
Reform Judaism, 119
synagogues, 119, 222
Verein für Cultur und Wissenschaft des Judentums (Association for Culture and Science of Judaism), 55–57
Zunz and, 56–57

Kaiser Wilhelm Institute, 166
Kant, Immanuel, 18, 19–21, 58, 125–126
Kapp Putsch (1920), 149–150, 151
Katz, Jacob, 6, 17, 22, 74, 104
Kaznelson, Siegmund, 153
Kerr, Alfred, 166
Klemperer, Otto, 166
Knobloch, Charlotte, 214–215
Kohl, Helmut, 204, 205–206, 210
Königsberg, anti-Jewish riots in, 51
Konitz, anti-Jewish riots in, 123
Kortner, Fritz, 166, 185
Kosovo, involvement of Bundeswehr in, 219
Kotzebue, August von, 52
Kriegsrohstoffabteilung (Department of Raw Materials in War 1914–1915), 134
Kristallnacht, see Reichskristallnacht (November Pogrom)
Krojanker, Gustav, 153
Kulturbund, 174–175
Kulturkampf, 112
Kuznets, Simon, 83

Lafontaine, Oskar, 211
Lämel, Simon von, 36
Lamey, August, 96
Landauer, Gustav, 145, 160
Langbehn, Julius, 125–126
Lasker, Eduard (Yitzhak)
  Bismarck versus, 101–103, 112–113
  on capital punishment, 102
  life of, 100–101
  in politics, 101
Lassalle, Ferdinand, 112
Lavater, Johann Caspar, 23, 24, 25, 27
Law for the Protection of German Blood and Honor (Nazi Germany), 169, 170
Leibniz, Gottfried Wilhelm, 18
Leipzig, protests against DDR in, 208, 209
Leo Baeck Institute Yearbook, 4
Lepsius, Rainer Mario, 199, 209
Lessing, Gotthold Ephraim, 18, 23, 25, 27, 125–126, 194
Levi, Hermann, 96

Levin, Shmarya, 122
liberalism
  antisemitism and, 51, 113, 118
  Congress of Vienna and, 39–40
  constitutionalism, crushed hopes for, 47–48
  emancipation of Jews and, 66
  Humboldt as liberal, 39
  Jews and, 75–76, 98
  nationalism versus, 66, 71, 72–73, 96
  "otherness" and, 63
  Prussia, lack of in, 42
  Revolution of 1848–1849 and, 67, 71–73
  unification (1871) and, 95, 98
  Zionism and, 174
Lichtheim, Richard, 143–144
Liebermann, Benjamin Joachim, 84, 85
Liebermann, Josef, 84, 85
Liebermann, Louis, 85
Liebermann, Max, 85
Liebermann, Pincus (Philipp), 84
Liebermann, Therese (Tiebchen), 85
Liebermann family, 84–85, 91
Liebeskind, Daniel, 222
Liebknecht, Karl, 144, 150, 151
Lissauer, Ernst, 133–134
Locke, John, 18, 26
Louis XIV (France), 26
Lübeck
  delegation to Congress of Vienna, 34
  Jewish equality under French occupation, 31
  Jews at time of Congress of Vienna in, 41
Ludendorff, Erich, 142, 145
Lueger, Karl, 125
Lusitania, 141
Lutheran Reformation, 14
Luxemburg, Rosa, 144, 150, 151, 160

Mahler, Gustav, 124
Maier, Charles, 151
Mainz, synagogues in, 222
Mann, Thomas, 123–124, 174, 184
Marcuse, Herbert, 184–185
marginalization of Jews, 10
Mark, Franz, 132
Marr, Wilhelm, 113, 114
marriage prohibitions, 168–169
Marwitz, Friedrich August Ludwig von der, 39, 78
Marx, Julius, 139
Marx, Karl, 7, 65–66, 79
Marxism, 7, 90, 200
Mayer, Hans, 185, 201
McCloy, John, 187, 189–190

Mecklenburg-Schwerin, Jewish equality under French occupation, 33
Meinecke, Friedrich, 135–136, 137
Melchior, Carl, 135
Mendelssohn, Moses
  antisemitism and, 23–24, 25
  assimilation and, 21–22
  on compatibility of Judaism and Enlightenment, 26
  Enlightenment and, 19–21, 26, 45–46
  Goethe and, 22–23, 24
  Haskalah and, 22
  on intolerance, 23–24, 25, 26
  Judaism and, 23–24, 26
  Kant versus, 19–21
  life of, 18
  Prussian Academy of Science and, 55
Mengele, Josef, 195–196
merchants, anti-Jewish sentiment among, 52
Merkel, Angela, 224
Mestern, Adolf, 85
Metternich, Klemens von
  confronting needs of reforms, 44
  at Congress of Vienna, 34, 35, 38, 40–41
  constitutionalism and, 47
  Humboldt and, 40
  Jews and, 34, 35, 38, 40–41
  Revolution of 1848–1849 and, 71
Metz, declining significance of, 119
Meyer, Michael A., 98
Michaelis, Johann David, 3, 23, 25, 49
migration
  Bundesrepublik, immigration to, 201–202, 203, 222–223
  Kaiserreich, migration of Jews in, 99–100
  rural areas, migration of Jews out of, 171
  violence against immigrants, 219
Mitterrand, François, 212
Mittwochsgesellschaft, 20
modernity
  differences in, 90–91, 92
  economic growth, role of Jews in, 83–84
  education and, 86
  industrialization, 82–83
  Jews and, 78–82, 89–92
  Judaism and, 98
  Marxism and, 90
  occupational structure of Jews, 81
  textile industry, 84–85
  urbanization, 79
Mommsen, Theodor, 120, 123–124, 216
Moravia, Revolution of 1848–1849 in, 67
Mosse, George, 125–126
Mühsam, Erich, 145

Index

Müller, Adam, 78
Munich, synagogues in, 222
Munich Olympic Games (1972), 200–201
music, Jews in, 54
Muslims, 219, 223

Napoleon (France)
  Jews in territories conquered by, 30–32
  modern history, as starting point for, 13
Napoleon III (France), 94
nationalism
  ambivalence of Jews towards, 106
  antisemitism and, 117–118, 123
  First World War and, 136–137
  identity and, 104–105
  Jews and, 98, 103, 106
  Judaism and, 71–72
  liberalism versus, 66, 71, 72–73, 96
  Revolution of 1848–1849 and, 71–73
  unification (1871) and, 95, 98
  Zionism and, 103
nationality, slow development of in Germany, 2
National-Liberal Party, 96, 101, 111–112, 142
National Socialist Party (Nazis, NSDAP)
  antisemitism and, 159
  Sturmabteilung (SA), 157, 161, 172
Nationalverein, 95–96, 98
Navy-League, 127
neoliberalism, 206
neo-Nazis, 214, 216
Neo-Orthodox Judaism, 119
Neumann, Franz, 179
Neustettin, anti-Jewish riots in, 123
Nicolai, Friedrich, 18
Nietzsche, Friedrich, 106, 123–124, 125–126
"Night of the Long Knives," 167–168
Nipperdey, Thomas, 13, 74–75
Nolte, Ernst, 206
North America, Jewish historiography in, 5–6
North Atlantic Treaty Organization (NATO), 191–192
North German Bund, 95, 97, 105–106
Nuremberg, attacks on Jews in, 161
Nuremberg Laws, 154, 169, 170, 172
Nuremberg Tribunal, 186

occupational structure of Jews, 81
Office for Coal Provision, 135
Oldenburg, attacks on Jews in, 161
Orientalists, 2
Ostpolitik, 200

"otherness," 63, 64
Owens, Jesse, 170

Palestinians, Israel and, 223, 224
Pan-German League, 127, 128–129, 142, 145, 160–161
Papen, Franz von, 148
Pappenheim, Bertha, 153–154, 158
Paris Commune (1871), 106
Peace of Westphalia (1648), 14
Peres, Shimon, 212
pogroms, *see also* antisemitism
  Hep-Hep riots (1819), 51–52
  in Kaiserreich, 123
  Reichskristallnacht (November Pogrom), 170, 172, 173, 216
  in Revolution of 1848–1849, 69–70, 74–75
  in Russia, 122
Poincaré, Raymond, 131
Poland
  condition of Jews in, 176–177
  Holocaust in, 177
  post-war violence against Jews, 183
Portugal, emigration to Germany from, 203
Posen
  migration of Jews from, 100
  Revolution of 1848–1849 in, 67, 72–73
Posner, Julius, 185
post-modernity, 6–7, 16
Prague
  declining significance of, 119
  German-speaking Jews in, 107
Preuß, Hugo, 147
Price Controlling Agency, 135
"productivization," 70, 81
professions
  entry of Jews into, 86, 156–157
  Nazi Germany, exclusion of Jews in, 167
propaganda, 172
prosecutions of Nazis, pressure to terminate, 198–199
Protestants
  Catholics versus, 90, 91–92, 136
  Jews compared, 119–120
  Lutheran Reformation, 14
  secularization and, 98–99
protests
  against DDR, 208, 209
  against First World War, 132–133
"Protocols of the Elders of Zion," 145, 160–161
Prussia
  antisemitism in, 28
  Austria and, 77, 94

Prussia (cont.)
  barriers to emancipation of Jews in, 66–67
  categorization of Jews in, 28–29
  citizenship of Jews in, 32–33
  Constitutional Conflict, 97, 101–102
  conversion in, 65
  delegation to Congress of Vienna, 36–37
  emancipation of Jews in, 95
  Kaiserreich and, 111, 135–136
  liberalism, lack of, 42
  migration of Jews from, 99
  reforms in, 29, 44–45
  Revised General Code of 1750, 28
  Revolution of 1848/1849 in, 73
  "Third Germany" and, 77
  uneven development of reforms in, 45
Prussian Academy of Science, 55
Prussian Progressive Party, 96

rabbis, 104, 107
race, antisemitism and, 117–118, 128–129
racism in contemporary Germany, 223
Ranke, Leopold von, 1
Rathenau, Emil, 85
Rathenau, Moritz, 85
Rathenau, Walther
  antisemitism and, 121, 122
  assassination of, 151, 156, 160
  on colonialism, 127–128
  First World War and, 131, 134–135, 140, 142
  as head of Kriegsrohstoffabteilung, 134
Reagan, Ronald, 204
Red Army Fraction (RAF), 200
Red Front Fighters' Association, 157
Reform Judaism, 119
reforms
  Jewish reaction to, 30
  in post-Congress of Vienna period, 53
  in Prussia, 29, 44–45
  uneven development of, 45, 47, 76, 116
refugees
  in contemporary Germany, 223
  Jewish refugees, 183–184, 185
Regensburg
  anti-Jewish riots in, 51
  synagogue in, 222
Reich Citizenship Act (Nazi Germany), 169
Reichsbanner Schwarz–Rot–Gold, 157, 194
Reichshammerbund, 138
Reichskristallnacht (November Pogrom), 170, 172, 173, 216
Reichstag fire, 165

Reichsvertretung der Juden in Deutschland, 169
Reinhardt, Max, 166
Reitlinger, Gerald, 179
religion
  conversion (*see* conversion)
  Enlightenment, compatibility of Judaism with, 26
  Judaism (*see* Judaism)
  as main source of identity, 1–2
  Neo-Orthodox Judaism, 119
  receding significance of, 99
  Reform Judaism, 119
  secularization of Jews, 98–99
Remer, Otto Ernst, 195
reparations to Holocaust survivors, 188, 189, 190, 191
Revolution of 1848–1849
  anti-Jewish riots in, 69–70, 74–75
  antisemitism in, 67–68
  in Austria, 73
  in Bavaria, 67, 71
  historiography of, 73–75
  Jewish participation in, 70
  Jewish rights and, 70–73
  liberalism and, 67, 71–73
  Metternich and, 71
  minority rights and, 71–73
  nationalism and, 71–73
  rural uprising, origins as, 67–68
  turning point in Jewish history, viewed as, 73–74
Richarz, Monika, 80, 83–84, 171
Riesser, Gabriel, 70, 72, 95–96
Rilke, Rainer Maria, 123–124, 132
riots, *see* pogroms; violence
Roma and Sinti, Nazi suppression of, 171, 225
Rostock, violence against immigrants in, 219
Rotstein, Sigmund, 209
Rotteck, Karl, 64
Rousseau, Jean-Jacques, 18, 24
Ruderman, David, 22
Rühs, Friedrich Christian, 50, 51, 52, 56
rural areas, Jews in, 79–80, 171
Rürup, Reinhard, 63, 64, 75
Russia, *see also* Soviet Union
  antisemitism in, 122
  Bolshevik revolution, 144
  First World War and, 134
  pogroms in, 122
Russo-Japanese War, 125

Sabrow, Martin, 156
Salonnières, 46, 89, 160

Index

Saxony
  antisemitism in, 116
  emancipation of Jews in, 95
  Jewish equality under French occupation, 33
Scheidemann, Philipp, 150, 156
Schiller, Friedrich, 2, 174, 194
Schily, Otto, 214
Schleicher, Kurt von, 148
Schleiermacher, Friedrich, 46–47
Schmelz, Uriel, 99
Schmerling, Anton Ritter von, 97
Schnitzler, Arthur, 124, 130
Scholem, Erich, 159
Scholem, Gerhard (Gershom), 121–122, 152, 159
Scholem, Reinhold, 159
Scholem, Werner, 159
Schörnerer, Georg Ritter von, 125, 135
Schüler-Springorum, Stephanie, 6
Schutzstaffel (SS), 172, 178
Schwaner, Wilhelm, 140
Schwarzenberg, Felix Prince zu, 73
sciences
  Nazi Germany, scientists fleeing, 166
  in Weimar Republic, 153
scientific narrative of identity, 4
secularization of Jews, 98–99, 119
Shaftesbury, Lord, 18
Shin'ar, Felix, 196
Siemann, Wolfram, 74–75, 76, 96
Silesia
  industrialization in, 82, 85
  Revolution of 1848–1849 in, 67
Simmel, Georg, 132
Simon, Ernst, 139–140
Six-Day War (1967), 201
Social Democratic Party (SPD)
  Bismarck and, 112
  coalitions and, 148, 200
  colonialism and, 126
  First World War and, 142
  Jews and, 125–126, 143
  Nazi suppression of, 165, 171
  Reichsbanner Schwarz–Rot–Gold, 157, 194
  reparations and, 189–190
  split within left and, 149
  suppression of, 106
  Weimar Republic and, 148
  working class and, 136
social history, 6, 7
social market economy, 192
solidarity among Jews, 174
Sombart, Werner, 83
Sonnenberg, Max Liebermann von, 114
Sorkin, David, 22
South West Africa
  atrocities in, 126–128
  German colonialism in, 126–128
Soviet Union, *see also* Russia
  antisemitism in, 187
  Bolshevik revolution, 144
  DDR and, 191, 208–209
  deportation of Jews from, 184
  emigration of Jews from, 210, 222–223
  on unification (1990), 212
Sozialistische Arbeiterpartei Deutschlands (SAP), 155
Sozialistische Einheitspartei Deutschlands (SED), 208–209, 210
Spain, emigration to Germany from, 203
Spartacists, 143, 149, 150, 151, 152
"stab in the back" legend, 145
Stahlhelm, 157, 158
Stein, Karl Freiherr von, 32, 39
Stein, Leopold, 72
Sterling, Eleonore, 50, 51
Stern, Frank, 212–213
Stern, Fritz, 214
Stern, Günther (Anders), 160
Stöcker, Adolf, 113–114, 116–117
Strauss, Franz Josef, 192, 198
Strauss, Richard, 123–124
Strousberg, Bethel Henry, 83
student movement, 199–200, 203–204
Sturmabteilung (SA), 157, 161, 172
Suez Canal, war (1956), 192
Swabia, migration of Jews from, 100
Sybel, Heinrich von, 105
synagogues, 119, 222
Syria, refugees from, 223

Tal, Uriel, 50
Tänzer, Arnold, 133
textile industry, 84–85
Thatcher, Margaret, 212
theater, entry of Jews into, 54
"Third Germany," 45, 77, 94
Thomson, David, 5, 178–179
Tivoli program, 117
Toller, Ernst, 132
"topography of terror," 221
Toury, Jacob, 54, 75, 93, 143
Treaty of Versailles (1919), 148–149
Treitschke, Heinrich von
  antisemitism and, 114, 115, 117, 122
  opposition to, 115–116
  on starting point of modern history, 14
  unification (1871) and, 105

Trotha, Lothar von, 126
Turkey
  emigration to Germany from, 201–202, 203, 219
  Young Turks, 125

U-boats, 141
unification of Germany (1871)
  Austria and, 96–97
  Bismarck and, 94, 95, 105, 106–107, 111, 136
  Catholics, impact on, 105
  differing conceptions of, 102–103
  Jewish history, impact on, 94–95
  liberalism and, 95, 98
  nationalism and, 95, 98
  Treitschke and, 105
unification of Germany (1990)
  international reaction to, 212
  Israel and, 212
  opposition to, 211–212
  renewed interest in Holocaust following, 213–214
Union Générale, 123
United Kingdom
  colonialism and, 127
  German Jews and, 172
  internal divisions in, 136
  pro-Palestinian demonstrations in, 223
  student movement in, 200
  on unification (1990), 212
  Zionists and, 184
United States
  American Revolution, 13
  First World War and, 141
  German Jews and, 172, 193
  pro-Palestinian demonstrations in, 223
  student movement in, 200
  on unification (1990), 212
  Zionists and, 184
"Universalization," 209
universities, entry of Jews into, 54, 56
urbanization, 79, 88

Valentin, Veit, 74
Van Dam, Hendrik George, 191
Varnhagen, Rahel (Levin), 46, 47, 49, 52, 64–65, 160
Varnhagen von Ense, Karl August, 52, 64–65
Veblen, Thorstein, 10
Veit, Moritz, 95–96
Verein für Cultur und Wissenschaft des Judentums (Association for Culture and Science of Judaism), 55–57

Vienna
  Congress of Vienna, Viennese Jews and, 35
  culture in, 124–125
  declining significance of, 119
  growth of Jewish community in, 107
Vietnam War, 200
violence, *see also* antisemitism
  contemporary Germany, violence against Jews in, 223
  Hep-Hep riots (1819), 51–52
  against immigrants, 219
  inter-war violence, 151–152
  Kaiserreich, anti-Jewish riots in, 123
  post-war violence against Jews, 183
  Reichskristallnacht (November Pogrom), 170, 172, 173, 216
  Revolution of 1848–1849, anti-Jewish riots in, 69–70, 74–75
  Russia, pogroms in, 122
  in Weimar Republic, 149–151, 152, 156, 157–158
Voltaire, 3, 18, 30
voluntary associations, 119

Wagner, Richard, 96, 117–118, 123–124
Walser, Martin, 215–217, 218, 219
Walter, Bruno, 166
Wartburg festival, 51
Wassermann, Jacob, 124
Weber, Max, 83, 123–124
Wehler, Hans-Ulrich, 13–14, 74–75
Wehrmacht, 214
Weil, Kurt, 166
Weizmann, Chaim, 122–123
Weizsäcker, Richard von, 205, 207–208
Wellington, Lord, 35
Wessely, Naphtali Herz, 22
Westphalia
  Jewish equality under French occupation, 30–31
  Revolution of 1848–1849 in, 67
Wilhelm II (Germany)
  Ballin and, 140, 141
  First World War and, 133
  foreign policy and, 133
Wilhelm I (Prussia/Germany), 71, 94
Wirsching, Andreas, 151
Wirtschaftswunder (economic miracle), 191
Wissenschaft des Judentums, 1
Wolff, Christian, 18
Wollstonecraft, Mary, 153–154
women
  Bildung and, 89
  as doctors, 154–155
  education of girls, 88–89

Jewish conservatism regarding, 154
  in Kaiserreich, 136
  right to vote, 147
women's history, 7–8
Württemberg
  delegation to Congress of Vienna, 37
  emancipation of Jews in, 95
  Revolution of 1848–1849 in, 67
Würzburg, anti-Jewish riots in, 51, 52

Xanten, anti-Jewish riots in, 123

Yom Kippur War (1973), 201
Youth Aliyah, 154, 171
Yugoslavia, war in, 219

Zentralrat der Juden in Deutschland, 190, 204, 217
Zimmerman, Arthur, 140–141
Zinn, Georg-August, 195
Zionism
  antisemitism and, 161
  emergence of, 129–130
  First World War and, 134
  Jews as nation and, 103
  liberalism and, 174
  suspicion of Germany and, 184
Zollverein, 97
Zunz, Leopold, 56–57, 69
Zweig, Arnold, 153, 184
Zweig, Stefan, 124–125, 126, 127

For EU product safety concerns, contact us at Calle de José Abascal, 56–1º,
28003 Madrid, Spain or eugpsr@cambridge.org.